# VOICES
# OF
# MESSIANIC JUDAISM

# VOICES OF MESSIANIC JUDAISM

## Confronting Critical Issues Facing a Maturing Movement

Dan Cohn-Sherbok
**General Editor**

**Lederer Books**
a division of
Messianic Jewish Publishers

The following versions of the Bible were used where noted by the authors.

| | |
|---|---|
| CJB | Complete Jewish Bible |
| KJV | King James Version |
| LB | Living Bible |
| NASB | New American Standard Bible |
| NIV | New International Version |
| NKJV | New King James Version |

Printed in the United States of America

05 04 03 02 01        6 5 4 3 2 1
ISBN  1-880226-93-6

Library of Congress Catalog Control Number:  2001090815

Lederer Books
a division of
Messianic Jewish Publishers
6204 Park Heights Ave.
Baltimore, Maryland  21215
(410) 358-6471

Distributed by
Messianic Jewish Resources International
Individual order line: (800) 410-7367
Trade order line: (800) 773-MJRI (6574)
E-mail: lederer@messianicjewish.net
Website: www.messianicjewish.net

# CONTENTS

# FOREWORD

"I am your friend!"

Thus began Dr. Dan Cohn-Sherbok's speech to the annual conference of the Union of Messianic Jewish Congregations in the summer of 2000. With a skeptic's ear, I sat back and listened to this gentle, Reform rabbi explain why he was a friend of Messianic Jews.

In case you don't know this, as a rule, Jewish people who believe in Yeshua the Messiah are usually considered to be outside the Jewish world. Messianic Jews, as they are called, have been labeled as ignoramuses, traitors, self-hating, etc. But, here was a rabbi who claimed to be a friend of the movement.

Actually, I already knew something about Dan Cohn-Sherbok, having read his excellent book, *Messianic Judaism*. In it, he included an illustration of a *menorah*, which represented the seven branches of Judaism. One branch was labeled "Messianic Judaism." He wrote that in a pluralistic model, there is no reason to exclude Messianic Jews. Although for centuries that's exactly what Messianic Jews have been saying, this is the first time a rabbi has been willing to take the position that it might be true.

Being seen as M.O.T.s, ("Members of the Tribe"—Jews) by a respected spiritual leader of our people was a new experience for the thousand attendees and for me. He even predicted that we would be considered an accepted part of the Jewish people in this century—reminding us that every branch of Judaism was at first rejected by the "establishment."

I had been looking forward to talking with this author of over thirty books. We were to meet to discuss the book you're holding in your hands. As he explains in his introduction, he was intrigued by this growing movement and wanted to understand it better. Unlike most "professional" Jews, Rabbi Cohn-Sherbok was willing to give Messianic Judaism a fair hearing. After all, as he quipped, he lives in the rolling hills of Wales, far away from the religious controversy in the U.S. and Israel. He had nothing to lose by telling the truth.

He dedicated many months to researching and writing about what is surely the most misunderstood movement of Judaism. During this time, especially at conferences (Dan and his wife, Lavinia, also attended Messiah '99, the annual conference of the Messianic Jewish Alliance of America, another other major Messianic group), he discovered something.

He saw that the Messianic Jewish brand of Judaism had something other brands lacked. Setting aside the issue of whether Yeshua was the Messiah, he saw joy and celebration, dedication to the Bible and to the traditions of the Jewish people. He saw the fruit of the lives of people who had been transformed. He recognized, as he says in his introduction, "that the

Messianic movement has become a significant force on the Jewish scene." It was fun to watch Dan and his wife, Lavinia, get up and do the *hora* (with only a little coaxing from my wife). They really enjoyed themselves.

When Dr. Cohn-Sherbok and I finally talked, he continued to develop the idea he had for this book. As a friend of Messianic Judaism, he believed that it was important for the movement to grapple with some of its more thorny issues. Compiling a collection of articles by some of its best scholars and thinkers would contribute to the process.

I invited my friend, Dr. John Fischer (also a member of my Board of Advisors) to join us. Before lunch was over, we came up with a list of topics and prospective authors for each issue. When I got back to my office, I asked my editor, Janet Chaiet, to contact each of these writers to see if they'd be willing to write on the subjects "assigned" to them.

Soon, amid her other duties, she got a group of disparate people with different perspectives and backgrounds, to contribute to this book. They conformed to *our* style-guide (pretty much), limited the amount they wrote (even though many wanted to write books on their topics), met deadlines (most of the time), and generated this book.

As you read *Voices of Messianic Judaism*, keep in mind the old saying, "When three Jews get together to discuss a matter, there are at least four opinions." In this book, you will encounter strong opinions on different sides of an issue. You may find yourself agreeing with one side, then find yourself agreeing with the other side after you read it. That's good. It means that each author, expressing his or her own thoughts and opinions, has argued effectively for their position. This kind of discussion and dialogue is a distinctive of Jewish theology called *pilpul*, a way to resolve apparent contradictions.

We selected topics we think are most germane to Messianic Jews at this time, and the authors we believed could do them justice. There are other matters we could have addressed, and other writers who could have contributed to this book. However, we had to make some difficult choices. Perhaps there will be a sequel with a whole new set of discussions and authors. If there's interest, there will be.

We deliberately chose *only* thirteen different topics. Discussion questions are included for twenty-seven chapters. Many congregations prefer materials that can be used over one quarter of a year. It is our hope that you and your group—whether a Messianic congregation or a gathering of Christians who care about the Jewish people and Messianic Judaism—will have your own discussion and dialogue, using these well thought-out articles as a starting point. Doing so will contribute to the maturing of Messianic Judaism.

—Barry Rubin
President, Messianic Jewish Communications

P.S. We've included a glossary in the back of the book to help you with some unfamiliar terms and abbreviations.

# INTRODUCTION

Growing up in the leafy suburbs of Denver, Colorado, it was my intention ever since I was a little boy to become a Reform rabbi. This desire amazed everyone. My father was a successful surgeon. Why, my parent's friends asked, did their son not want to follow in his footsteps? Being a rabbi, they said, was not a job for a nice Jewish boy. Undeterred, I went to Williams College in Williamstown, Massachusetts, and later studied for five years at the Hebrew Union College in Cincinnati, Ohio. During this time, I served as a student rabbi in congregations in Jasper, Alabama; Galesburg, Illinois; Harrisburg, Pennsylvania; and Boulder, Colorado. After ordination, I was a Reform rabbi in Melbourne, Australia before beginning studies at Cambridge University for a doctorate. During my time at Cambridge, I served as a rabbi at the West London Synagogue, and later in Johannesburg, South Africa.

Although I had anticipated that congregants would listen in hushed silence to my sermons and attend study courses, it did not turn out that way. To my astonishment, I discovered that being a rabbi was not at all what I had expected. Services were sparsely attended; hardly anyone came to the courses I offered. In one of my congregations, the parking lot was packed on bingo night at the Temple, but only a few came to synagogue to pray. In another congregation, I was expected to dress up for a fashion show, or play tennis with women members at the Jewish country club. Eventually I decided I could take no more, and I became an academic, first at the University of Kent in Canterbury, England, and now at the University of Wales where I am a Professor of Judaism. During these years, I have written books on a wide variety of Jewish topics, many which deal with modern Jewish life.

Several years ago, my wife and I were writing a book, *The American Jew*, a study of the nature of American Judaism based on a single Jewish community. In the process of our research, we heard about the Messianic movement. One of those who spoke to us was an opponent of Messianic Judaism. At length, he recounted what he perceived as the iniquities of the movement. "Messianic Jews," he declared, "are deceptive and deliberately attempt to hide their true intentions. Although they claim to be Jewish in their approach, in fact they are nothing more than Christians in disguise."

Intrigued, my wife and I contacted a local Messianic Jewish rabbi. His congregation was located in an industrial warehouse on the outskirts of the city. The sanctuary had an Ark, which contained a *Torah* scroll, and there was a purple curtain with an embroidered Star of David hanging in front of the Ark. The bookcases in the rabbi's office were full of Hebrew Texts, and a large photograph of the Walling Wall hung over his desk. The rabbi wore a skullcap, and was anxious to explain about the history and nature of Messianic Judaism.

"In the 19th century," he said, "a small group of Jews proclaimed their faith in Jesus." Referred to as Hebrew Christians, they saw themselves as fulfilling their Jewish heritage by embracing the Messiah in their lives. Throughout the 20th century, Hebrew Christianity grew in strength, but it was only in the l960s that notice was taken of these Jewish Christians. In recent decades, a new form of messianic faith has emerged out of these earlier subgroups within the Jewish community.

"Messianic Judaism," he went on, "is a movement of Jews who, like the Hebrew Christians, believe that Jesus, whom we call Yeshua, is the promised Messiah." In the view of Messianic Jews, Messianic Judaism differs from all other branches of Judaism in relying solely on the Hebrew Scriptures. Their faith is biblical Judaism; centered around the Messiah and the worldwide salvation he brings. Messianic Jews are convinced that they have access to God because of the atoning work of Messiah Yeshua, who has fulfilled them as Jews.

Showing us around his synagogue, he explained that Messianic Jews are one in spirit with Gentile followers of Jesus. Yet, Messianic Jews have their own expression of faith in the Messiah. Messianic Judaism asserts that it is Jewish to believe in Yeshua—this, they contend, is a return to the Jewish roots of the faith. As a result, Messianic Jews observe the biblical feasts and holidays while maintaining that the only route to salvation is through the atoning work of Yeshua.

Adherents of this new movement insist they are not Christians. "In our view," he continued, "the term Christian originally meant 'follower of Christ.'" Yet, over time, the connotations of the term have changed. Unlike Gentile believers in Christ, Messianic Jews do not wish to separate themselves from their Jewish roots. They believe that they have found the Jewish Messiah and are now completed Jews in that Yeshua is the fulfillment of biblical Judaism. Yeshua never intended to start a new religion. Rather, he came to correctly explain the law and the prophets.

After introducing us to several members of the congregation who were wearing skullcaps as well as *tzitziyot*, he continued his description of the movement. "From an institutional perspective," he stated, "Messianic synagogues constitute the heart of the movement: they serve as the place where those who believe in Yeshua as the Messiah can live a Jewish life, raise their children as Jews and worship the God of Israel in a Jewish fashion." Like other Jews, Messianic believers celebrate all the biblical festivals—*Rosh HaShanah, Yom Kippur, Sukkot, Hanukkah, Purim*, and Passover—in a Messianic fashion believing that Yeshua is the fulfillment of all these holy days. The pattern frequently followed involves Davidic worship and praise using musical instruments, singing, Hebraic music, psalms, lifting up of hands, chanting, clapping, and processions. In addition, Messianic Jews incorporate dance into the worship.

Although Messianic Jews are guided in their practice by Scripture, he noted, there is a degree of ambivalence about *Torah*. As Messianic Jews, they believe that it is not possible to be "saved" through religious observance. Yet, while the law does not provide salvation, it is not dead. The moral precepts of the Ten Commandments, for example, are part of the New Covenant. The festivals are for all time. Hence, in varying degrees Messianic Jews seek to uphold the precepts found in Scripture, and often the details of observing the *Torah*.

Because of the centrality of Israel in God's plan for all nations, he pointed out, Messianic Jews are ardent Zionists. They support Israel because the Jewish State is viewed as a direct fulfillment of biblical prophecy. Although Israel is far from perfect, Messianic Jews believe that God is active in the history of the nation and that the Jews will never be driven out of their land again. While God loves the Arabs, he gave the Holy Land to his chosen people.

Concerning the distinction between Messianic Jews and Gentile believers, Messianic Jews maintain that the rabbinic definition of who is a Jew is not correct. According to Scripture, they point out, Jews are preeminently a nation and a people. To be considered Jewish, one must be a physical descendant of Abraham, Isaac, and Jacob. Further, biblical lineage is patriarchal, not matriarchal. Moreover, the Scriptures indicate that if either parent is Jewish, or if a grandparent is Jewish, one can identify himself or herself as Jewish. Therefore, some Messianic Jews have rejected the traditional doctrine that one is Jewish only if born of a Jewish mother. Instead, some maintain that a person is Jewish if he or she has at least one Jewish grandparent.

Returning to his office after a tour of the synagogue, we listened as he discussed his congregation. According to Messianic Judaism, he related, Jewish and Gentile believers are all one in Messiah Yeshua. Spiritually there are no barriers between Jews and Gentiles; they are all one in him. Gentile believers have entered the Jewish faith and have become spiritually circumcised and spiritually Jewish as they have accepted Yeshua into their lives. While Gentile believers cannot become physically Jewish, they are one with their Jewish brothers and sisters because the Spirit of God is within both Jewish and Gentile believers.

In this light, Gentile believers are permitted to be members of Messianic synagogues. It is often the case, he indicated, that there are more Gentile members than Jews. Intermarriage is permitted, and parents are encouraged to live a Jewish lifestyle and raise their children as Jews. Having accepted Yeshua into their lives, Messianic Jews are to grow spiritually. The primary way whereby Jewish believers can continue to live their lives as Jews is by guarding against assimilation. They should become members of Messianic synagogues. Through participating in the life of the community they can continue to worship the Lord in a Jewish way, celebrate the Jewish festivals, raise children as Jews, and be a testimony to faith in Yeshua.

This new movement fascinated both my wife and me, and on return to the United Kingdom, we attended the national conference of Messianic Jews. On our arrival, we were greeted by smiling, friendly people who directed us to the bookshop and market stalls. Hebrew folk music played in the background as we looked at stalls loaded with various ritual objects including *shofar*s, *siddur*s, prayer shawls, pictures of the Wailing Wall, *mezuzah*s, and *menorah*s. On other tables, there were stacks of books dealing with Messianic Judaism, as well as various aspects of Jewish belief and practice. Milling around were attendees to the conference—many women wore Jewish stars around their necks and some of the men wore skullcaps and fringes.

After lunch, we attended a series of lectures dealing with various aspects of Messianic Judaism including Jewish music, theology, and liturgy. Later in the day, my wife and I attended the afternoon service. In the evening all the attendees gathered in a large hall. In the front, a band played loud music as members of the audience flooded to the stage. Joining hands, they sang and danced, praising the Lord. Others stood lifting their hands in thanksgiving. At the end of the service, members of the congregation lined up at the front to receive a blessing from the rabbis. Praying fervently, the rabbis prayed over the faithful, many of whom were overcome with emotion.

Anxious to learn more about the movement, my wife and I traveled to Harrisburg, Pennsylvania for the annual conference of the MJAA, which takes place at Messiah College every year. On the first day of the conference, we went to a session dealing with Messianic identity. The speaker was a bespectacled Messianic rabbi wearing a skullcap who told us that although he believes in Yeshua, he is emphatically not a Christian. Instead, he declared, he is a fulfilled Jew. At another session, one of the Messianic rabbis discussed the enemies of the movement. His message was filled with quotations from Scripture. The audience responded "Amen" and "Praise the Lord."

In the evening, we attended a large service for the entire conference. In the front, there was a splendid band; behind them was a replica of the Wailing Wall in Jerusalem. When the music began, the entire congregation stood; raising their hands in praise, they sang uproariously. Then a mass of people came forward to dance. This was interspersed with a variety of speakers whose words were constantly interrupted with shouts of "Praise the Lord" and "Barukh *HaShem*." Again, at the end of the service, the Messianic rabbis lined up in front as people stood in line to receive a blessing.

When we returned after this conference, I was convinced of the need for an objective account of this important development in modern Judaism. Despite the criticisms made of Messianic Judaism by its opponents, I could see that this new movement had captured the hearts and minds of thousands of pious individuals from the Jewish community, as well as Gentiles who have accepted Yeshua as Lord and Savior. The Messianic movement has become a significant force on the Jewish scene.

In the years that followed, I completed a major study of the movement entitled *Messianic Judaism*, which was published by Cassell in 2000. Beginning with a discussion of the development of Messianic Judaism from ancient times to its transformation after World War II, I focus on the nature of Messianic Judaism, today. The volume then continues with a detailed examination of Messianic practices, including the celebration of the Sabbath, Passover, *Shavu'ot* and *Sukkot*, festivals of joy, and life-cycle events. The book then goes on to consider the place of Messianic Judaism within the contemporary Jewish community. Messianic Jews, I point out, contend that they are fulfilled as Jews and that Messianic Judaism is a legitimate interpretation of the Jewish faith. Its critics, however, argue that Messianic Jews are dangerous and deceptive.

In the final section of the book—which is the most controversial—I confront this contentious issue and outline three alternative models for understanding the relationship between Messianic Judaism and the modern Jewish world. The first model—Orthodox exclusivism—contends that there is only one legitimate form of Judaism: Orthodoxy. Thus, according to Orthodoxy, Messianic Judaism is viewed as totally unacceptable. Despite the claims of Jewish believers that by accepting Yeshua they have become fulfilled as Jews, Orthodox Judaism categorically rejects any form of Jewish Christianity as part of the Jewish tradition. From a theological point of view, Messianic Judaism is viewed as fundamentally distinct from traditional Judaism because of the centrality of Jesus. Furthermore, Orthodox Jews regard Messianic Judaism's conviction that the New Testament is part of God's revelation as a fundamental deviation from the Jewish faith.

The second model—non-Orthodox Judaism—categorically denies legitimacy to Messianic Judaism. Yet, the non-Orthodox rejection of Messianic Jews is more difficult to comprehend given the multidimensional character of contemporary Jewish life. Concerning belief and practice, there are fundamental divisions between the various non-Orthodox movements: modern non-Orthodox movements embrace a wide range of theological and ideological perspectives. There is simply no consensus among non-Orthodox Jews concerning the central tenets of the faith, nor is there any agreement about Jewish observance. Instead, the various branches of non-Orthodox Judaism embrace a totally heterogeneous range of viewpoints. Nonetheless, these disparate branches of modern Judaism are united in their rejection of Messianic Judaism as an authentic expression of the Jewish tradition. Even though the adherents of these branches of the tradition differ over the most fundamental features of the Jewish religion, they have joined together in excluding Messianic Judaism from the range of legitimate interpretations of the faith.

The final model—Pluralism—is a very different approach. According to Jewish pluralists, the non-Orthodox exclusion of Messianic Judaism from the circle of legitimate interpretations of the Jewish faith is baffling. Given the multi-dimensional character of modern Jewish life, pluralists contend that Messianic Judaism should be viewed as simply one among many interpretations of the Jewish heritage. The central difficulty with the non-Orthodox exclusion of Messianic Jews, they point out, is that the various non-Orthodox movements are themselves deeply divided over the central tenets of the faith. Belief and practice no longer unite Jewry; instead, the various branches of the modern Jewish establishment have radically separated themselves from the past. In the light of such an abandonment of the tradition, pluralists maintain that the exclusion of Messianic Judaism from the circle of legitimate expressions of the Jewish heritage is totally inconsistent.

Jewish pluralists understand why there is a visceral rejection of Messianic Judaism within the community. Despite modern ecumenical efforts, Christianity in its various manifestations is still seen to symbolize centuries of oppression, persecution, and murder. Nonetheless, Jewish pluralists insist that given the multi-dimensional character of contemporary Jewish life, the rejection of Messianic Judaism from *K'lal Yisra'el* makes little sense. If non-theistic and non-halakhically observant forms of Judaism are acceptable, why, they ask, should Messianic Jews, who are observant believers, be denied recognition within the Jewish community?

After my book was published, I was invited to be the guest speaker at the annual conference of the UMJC. After discussing the contents of my book, I stressed that in my view Messianic Judaism constitutes an innovative, exciting, and extremely interesting development on the Jewish scene. Messianic Judaism was a new movement, wrestling with the big issues of modern Jewish life. In the articles I had read in the theological journal *Kesher*, Messianic leaders were struggling with fundamental questions: Who is a Jew? What is the authority of *halakhah*? Should conversion be permitted? This quest to make sense of the tradition is fascinating and important. Today many Orthodox, Conservative, Reform, Reconstructionist, and Humanistic Jews are preoccupied with other issues. But from reading about the movement and meeting its members, I could see that Messianic Jews were constantly engaged with central religious issues.

During the UMJC conference, I met with Barry Rubin, the president of Lederer/Messianic Jewish Publishers to discuss a book project exploring the issues now facing Messianic Judaism. After having studied Messianic Judaism for several years, I came to the view that there is a pressing need for Messianic thinkers to address the nature of the movement for the future. This volume, which includes twenty-seven chapters written by leading figures within the movement, seeks to examine a wide range of key topics.

Beginning with a discussion of liturgy, Stuart Dauermann, rabbi of Ahavat Zion Messianic Synagogue, maintains that Messianic Judaism must embrace traditional Jewish music if it is to remain authentically Jewish. Such an infusion of tradition should infuse congregational life, as well as the home. Increased contextualization of Messianic services, he observes, is directly proportional to the increased use of the Hebrew liturgy. Hence, Messianic Judaism must institute ongoing programs designed to nurture liturgical literacy. The greatest obstacles to liturgical renewal are ignorance, fear, and prejudice.

Adopting a different stance, Joel Chernoff, president of the IMJA, argues that the Messianic movement was vitally revived in the 1970s by the inclusion of Jewish liturgical music, including new instrumentation for Messianic Jews. This music was a fresh expression, a hybrid of modern pop and traditional minor key Jewish music. The objective was to express the joy that believers had found in knowing the Messiah. Although appreciative of traditional Jewish liturgy, he argues that Messianic Jewish music must be spiritually moving.

Regarding Scripture, Dan Juster, the director of Tikkun International, contends that the Hebrew Bible and the New Covenant are the primary authorities within the Messsianic community. This view of Scripture is rooted in the biblical material, but theologians have developed it for centuries. For Juster, the Bible is infallible, a view enshrined in the statements of both the UMJC and the IAMCS. Infallibility, he argues, means that the Bible is true in all that the writer claims to teach as true. Because it is the highest and final authority, subsequent teaching cannot supersede Scripture. Yet, it is crucial that Messianic Jews recognize that hermeneutics are of vital importance in understanding the meaning of the biblical text.

Mark Kinzer, Executive Director of Messianic Jewish Theological Institute, argues that the Bible requires interpretation. It is not possible, he writes, to adopt a purely biblical perspective. One never reads the biblical text apart from one's own preconceptions. The historical setting in which one finds oneself shapes the questions addressed to the text, as well as the concepts and terms used to respond. The interpretative tradition, he argues, consists of the accumulated insights of a community transmitted from one generation to the next. In a Messianic context, tradition represents the understanding of Scripture preserved through generations among the Jewish and Christian communities. Hence, interpretive tradition is always necessary in seeking to understand the meaning of the biblical text.

In the view of Russell Resnik, General Secretary of the UMJC and leader of Adat Yeshua Messianic Synagogue, rabbinic *halakhah* is vital for the Messianic movement. *Halakhah*, he contends, serves as the bridge over which the *Torah* moves from the written word into living deed. Without the rabbinic tradition, he argues, Messsianic Judaism lacks integrity as an authentic form of Judaism in the modern world. Even though the *halakhic* system cannot simply be imported into the Messianic community, it is vital that Messianic Judaism is informed by the tradition.

As to congregational life, Bruce Cohen, rabbi of New York's Congregation Beth El of Manhattan, argues that Messianic Jews should orient themselves toward synagogues rather than churches. In his view, adherence to Jewish cultural norms and customs is of primary significance. As a result, Messianic Jews must establish their spiritual home within the context of Jewish life. Rather than disengage themselves from Jewish identification, Jewish believers must embrace *Torah* Judaism as well as Jewish national identity.

Presenting an alternate point of view, Jim Sibley, Coordinator of Jewish Ministry for the Southern Baptist North American Mission Board, maintains that Jewish believers should not be reluctant to join Bible-believing churches. In answer to the question, "Can a Jew go to church and still be Jewish?" he asserts that those who feel comfortable in such a setting should have no hesitations. Jewish believers, he notes, should not deny their unity with Gentile believers. Rather, both groups desperately need one another.

Turning to organizational structure, Barney Kasdan, rabbi of Kehilat Ariel Messianic Synagogue in San Diego, California, argues that Messianic congregations should be run on democratic lines. The movement, he maintains, must listen to the collective voice of its members. As the current president of the UMJC, he stresses the ways in which this body seeks to provide all congregational members with a voice in the affairs of the movement. Such a system, he alleges, provides a vital system of checks and balances. In addition, such a structure can serve as a means for issuing directive policies and insuring interdependent participation in Messianic activities.

According to Robert Cohen, rabbi of Beth Jacob Messianic Congregation in Jacksonville, Florida, it is desirable that the Messianic movement be run by a central governing body. In his view, the democratic model can lead to factionalism. A centrally run organization, however, can provide a basis for the outpouring of God's Spirit, as well as a framework for the provision of rabbinic training, worship, and congregational life.

Turning to Jewish education, Michael Rydelnik, Professor of Jewish Studies at the Moody Bible Institute of Chicago, argues that Jewish studies must be integrated with traditional evangelical theological education. In the Messianic movement, he writes, theological education has often been undervalued; what is now required is for Messianic leaders to be trained in traditional Jewish sources including biblical theology, biblical exegesis, Jewish studies, homiletics, leadership, teaching, and pastoral care. In his view, Messianic Jewish leaders should train in academically accredited evangelical schools whose facilities would encourage and support the Messianic movement.

For Paul Saal, spiritual leader of Congregation Shuvah Yisrael, there is now a need for an indigenous and integrative Messianic Jewish education. As he explains, the UMJC has developed a *yeshiva* program consisting of intensive college level courses leading to ordination. In his view, the movement must develop its own educational institutions along these lines to set high standards for credentialing, education, information dissemination, and platforms for theological and halakhic disputation.

Concerning children's education, Eva Rydelnik, an adjunct professor at the Moody Bible Institute, believes it is vital that children should be taught about the Messiah. In her view, the wealth of educational material available to Messianic congregations provided by Christian publishing houses serves as a vital resource. As she notes, these publishers have been producing children's educational material for decades, and Messianic congregations should not overlook these publications.

According to Jeffrey Feinberg, chairman of education at the UMJC and leader of Etz Chaim Congregation, the nature of Messianic Jewish education must be Messiah-centered, and yet distinctly Jewish. It is the task of Messianic Jewish education, he notes, to transmit a Jewish heritage that integrates an understanding of the Hebrew Bible and the New Covenant into the context of a Jewish community. In this context, Messianic Jews should never lose sight of their calling to transmit the Jewish heritage of membership in a priestly community.

In the next chapter dealing with intermarriage, David Rudolph, editor of *Kesher: A Journal of Messianic Judaism*, contends that intermarriage between Jews and non-Jews can make a positive contribution to Messianic Judaism as long as the non-Jewish spouse is a believer in Yeshua. Noting that the vast majority of Messianic Jews in the United States are intermarried, he stresses that often the most committed, hardest-working members of Messianic congregations are non-Jews. These non-Jewish spouses are vital for the growth and development of the movement.

Michael Schiffman, on the other hand, argues that Jewish life is precious, delicate, and fragile; as such, it is vital that marriage between Jews is encouraged. Fearing the dangers of assimilation, he believes that intermarriage threatens future generations. Although he notes that Messianic Judaism should be reaching out to intermarried couples, the movement should recognize the dangers inherent in such a situation. If the rate of intermarriage continues, he writes, Messianic Judaism will become a movement of people with remote or imagined Jewish ancestry.

Regarding Gentiles, Tony Eaton, congregational leader of Simchat Yisrael Messianic Jewish Synagogue, argues that the leaders of Messianic congregations should be Jewish. He stresses that this is of vital concern if Messianic Judaism is to constitute a Jewish movement for Jews. In this context, he argues that there should be a well-defined, rigorous rite of passage for converts. In this way Gentiles could become part of the Jewish people through a process of conversion, and thereby assume positions of leadership within the Messianic community.

According to Patrice Fischer, Gentiles should be treated as equal participants in the Messianic Jewish community. Fears, misconceptions, and unwritten rules have affected the level of acceptance that Gentiles find within the Messianic movement. She advocates the need for an open discussion of the place of "Righteous Gentiles" who are dedicated to a Jewish way of life and worship. The New Covenant provides a pattern to guide the Messianic Jewish movement in establishing the rights and responsibilities of these modern-day Godfearers.

In his chapter on conversion, Michael Wolf, leader of Beth Messiah Messianic Jewish Synagogue, strongly opposes conversion of Gentiles to Messianic Judaism. There is no basis in Scripture for Messianic Jewish institutions to entertain such a notion, he contends. Further, the practice would bring great confusion to the movement as well as accusation from those the movement seeks to reach. He claims that no one in the mainstream Jewish community would regard Messianic Jewish conversions as legitimate. Messianic Jewish converts would never be considered Jewish by any branch of Judaism.

Opposing this position, John Fischer, rabbi of Congregation Ohr Chadash, points out that there is a basis in the *Torah* for conversion. In his view, Gentiles should be offered the option of converting. The issue should not be whether the Messianic movement should promote conversions—rather, it is whether they should allow individuals to make the choice to convert. Some members of the movement, he notes, have been deeply drawn to Jewish traditions and observances. In many cases, they have evidenced a higher level of Jewish commitment and observance than many of the Jewish people in Messianic synagogues. For such individuals who have demonstrated their commitment—there should be a way for them to identify as Jews.

Concerning the question of whether women should occupy senior roles within Messianic Judaism, Ruth Fleischer, rabbi of the London Messianic Congregation and Executive Director of Yeshua Ministries and Conferences, contends that no sex should be elevated over another; rather both men and women should serve together in a program that utilizes the gifts and calling of each to advance the Kingdom of God. Although the Messianic movement has not officially ordained women rabbis, she argues that the movement should embrace those women who feel called to lead their communities.

Sam Nadler, president of Word of Messiah Ministries and leader of Hope and Israel Congregation, emphasizes that women have served with Yeshua and his apostles; they have judged, prophesized, preached, and prayed as effectively as men. Nonetheless, there are a number of reasons why women should not serve as leaders of the Messianic movement: there were no biblical models of women as senior congregational leaders; there is no biblical authorization given to women to be senior congregational leaders; all instruction assumes men as overseers; in the home the husband was always the leader.

Advocating traditional missions, Mitch Glaser, president of Chosen People Ministries, argues that the Messianic movement needs an organizational structure to communicate with the Jewish people. Traditional Jewish missions, he notes, are a continuation of the apostolic tradition. Today this process should continue and be attuned to contemporary Jewish culture. More than any other organizational structures, missions to the Jews are well equipped to bring the message of Yeshua to the Jewish people.

According to Kay Silberling, who has taught at West Coast colleges and universities, the Messianic movement suffers from its negative image in the Jewish world. Traditional Judaism, she writes, characterizes Messianic Jews as Christians. Hence, the Jewish community is unwilling to grant legitimacy to Jewish believers. Given this position, it is incumbent for Messianic believers to employ new methods of communication and outreach. What is now required is a form of dialogue that opens avenues of communication between Messianic Jews and others.

Concerning Israel, Murray Silberling, Southwest Regional Director for the IAMCS, maintains that for Messianic Jews, Israel is crucial. He stresses the fact that although Messianic Jews tend to view the Diaspora as secondary in the struggle for Jewish survival, it is an essential and effective weapon in the fight against anti-Semitism and assimilation. The Diaspora, he urges, can be a place of innovation regarding Jewish identity and practice.

Adopting a different approach, David Stern, translator of the *Jewish New Testament* and the *Complete Jewish Bible* and author of the *Jewish New Testament Commentary*, argues that Messianic Jews should actively seek to make *aliyah*. Not only would such an act be in accordance with God's will, the land of Israel provides a place where Messianic Jews would be able to live a truly Jewish life. Currently, Messianic Jews frequently excuse themselves from making *aliyah* for various reasons, but they do not actually provide a sufficient basis for refusing to immigrate to the Holy Land.

Discussing the end times, Richard Nichol, rabbi of Congregation Ruach Israel, stresses that it is difficult to predict the coming of the kingdom. Further, he notes that an over-preoccupation with the end times tends to dull our awareness of the importance of creation and the human role in bringing about a better world. Yet, Messianic Jews must continue to anticipate the coming of Yeshua, and the fulfillment of God's plan for the world.

In the opinion of Arnold Fruchtenbaum, founder and director of Ariel Minstries, the promises made in the Jewish covenants apply to Messianic Jews. Jewish believers, he continues, will be caught up and taken to heaven at the Rapture; there, they—along with Gentile believers—will be evaluated on how they served the Lord.

The book concludes with two chapters from outsiders. The first, by Shoshanah Feher, the author of *Passing Over Easter*, outlines three challenges to Messianic Judaism. In her view, Messianic Jews will need to determine the status of Messianic Gentiles, an issue dealt with in other sections within this volume. The movement will also need to consider why some Messianic Jews eventually discarded Messianic Judaism and became members of non-Messianic synagogues. Finally, she notes, Messianic Judaism will need to determine how faith in Yeshua can be passed on from one generation to the next.

Arthur Glasser, former Faculty Coordinator of Judaic Studies and Dean Emeritus of Fuller Theological Seminary School of World Mission, traces the development of Jewish awareness of Yeshua within the Messianic movement. Highlighting the need for the creation of authentically Jewish Messianic congregations, he points out that Messianic synagogues need to reflect the traditional role of serving as faithful custodians of Jewish communal and religious tradition. As the movement developed, he notes, various types of congregations emerged with their own distinctive features—such diversity is an indication of strength as congregations seek to express their faith in Yeshua.

This volume thus focuses on a wide range of issues currently facing the Messianic Jewish community. The various voices within the movement reflect a wide range of attitudes and opinions. This is not a weakness, but rather a reflection of the vitality of Messianic Jewish conviction. The Jewish religious establishment would do well to reflect on the seriousness of this quest to revitalize Jewish life in a post-Holocaust age.

CHAPTER 1

# THE IMPORTANCE OF JEWISH LITURGY

—Stuart Dauermann

This was Mrs. Jacobs' first visit to a Messianic congregation. A middle class Jewish woman with a husband in the aerospace industry and grown children, she had come to Los Angeles to participate in the Elderhostel Program sponsored by the University of Judaism. Her son Daniel, a Messianic Jew, brought her to my congregation for her first-ever exposure to a Messianic Jewish service. Seated between him and his Gentile wife Donna, midway through the service she turned to her and asked a telling question: "So tell me, don't you feel out of place in the synagogue?" Her question revealed that Mrs. Jacobs felt perfectly at home: she was concerned that our congregation did not feel like foreign territory to Donna, her daughter-in-law.

What was it that made our congregation feel like "Jewish space" to Mrs. Jacobs? In large part, it was our extensive use of traditional Jewish liturgy, something our congregation has been known for since its founding in the early 1970s.

## Messianic Jewish Liturgical Renewal—Why?

If the Messianic Jewish movement is to build communities that not only "feel like home" but actually are home to Jews and intermarried couples and their families, we simply must warmly and flexibly embrace the Jewish liturgical heritage. *Ma tov chelkenu umanayim goralenu*—How good is our portion and how pleasant our lot! Our liturgy is just one part of that portion worth handling constantly and lovingly, like a gold watch that shines brighter and brighter the more its contours are caressed.

This "Jewish space" must exist not only in our congregations but also in our individual and family lives. James Kugel, in his masterful book, *On*

*Being a Jew*, invites us to take on such disciplines as a means of constructing a *mishkan*—a tabernacle—where we might encounter and honor the presence of the God of our ancestors. One is reminded of the motion picture *Field of Dreams*, which popularized the phrase, "If you build it they will come." Similarly, for us, it is as we build this *mishkan*—this holy prayer structure—that we will experience in a new way what it means for the God of our ancestors to come to dwell with us.

Some cannot be bothered with believing that such an encounter will occur. They see only the effort involved in constructing the building. Others suggest that since God is everywhere, all this building is a needless bother. They confuse God's omnipresence with his relational and manifest presence. Just because he is everywhere present, that does not mean that he is everywhere known and experienced. Building such a holy structure increases the likelihood that we will know the presence of the omnipresent One in our lives and in continuity with his engagement with the House of Israel throughout time.

Happily, some find it within themselves to believe the promise that such a humble structure is just the kind of place God delights to dwell in. Such a summons comes to each of us individually, and each must respond personally. As with the little child Samuel, so for us—we must personally say to the Holy One, "Speak Lord; your servant is listening."

For Messianic Jews, who draw near to *HaShem* (God) through Yeshua our Great High Priest, and in the *Ruach HaKodesh*, such a *mishkan*—such a Jewish structure of liturgical practice—is imperative. Although Emily Dickinson declared that every bush is ablaze with God, Moses did not find it so—and neither shall we. We must seek the Holy One in the structures he is wont to inhabit—and our liturgy is just such a place, if we, like Moses our Teacher, will but turn aside to look.

What guidelines then might Messianic Jews follow in implementing and developing our own liturgical practice, in building our *mishkan*? I recommend the following principles as a good place to start.

## The *Mah Zot* Principle

There should be markers in our lives which memorialize our involvement in the Jewish people's experience with God and which provide occasions to proclaim and renew awareness of His saving acts.

This principle is repeatedly illustrated in our Scriptures. Our ancestors in Egypt were admonished to put blood on their doorposts as a yearly reminder of the redemption from Egypt (Exod. 11:21–27). First-born sons and animals had to receive special treatment as a reminder of the slaying of the first-born in Egypt (Exod. 13:1, 11–15). Jews were admonished to wear *t'fillin* so as not to forget these saving events (Exod. 13:9–10, 16). *Matzah* (unleavened bread) was to be eaten during Passover as a memorial of the Exodus (Exod. 13:2–6). Twelve stones were to be removed from the midst of the Jordan to serve as a reminder of how God cut off the flow of the river that Israel might pass through (Josh 4:1–9). In each case, the custom or artifact served as a memorial of the saving acts of God and as an occasion for inquiry into the meaning of the form. Someone would ask "*mah zot?*" which means "What is this?" thus presenting an opportunity to recall and to tell the next generation of the mighty acts of God.

We Messianic Jews ought to incorporate such traditional markers into our personal and communal lives. We must never forget that we are participants in a common history with other Jews. The Book of Exodus expresses this clearly and the *haggadah* (Passover liturgy) repeats it for us as each year each father is told to explain to his inquiring son, "It is because of what the LORD did *for me when I came out of Egypt*" (Exod. 13:8). Each father, though born after the events, is nevertheless to see himself as implicated in those events. It is for this reason that the *haggadah* bids us all consider the Passover events as if we ourselves had come out of Egypt, for indeed we did.

We must not miss the crucial implications of this principle. Failure to preserve and honor our Jewish particularity means the neglect of our very own history and identity. More tellingly, such neglect means to egregiously disassociate from other Jews and to display a cavalier forgetfulness concerning God's benefits (Psalm 103:2).

This also means that the communal and personal lives of Messianic Jews ought to be different from those of the wider Body of Messiah *because our history is different and because we share a corporate solidarity with other Jews, which must not be overlooked.*

We need to remember the sacred calendar. The Jewish holy days, both great and small are like family anniversaries and birthdays circled on the calendar hanging in the kitchen of our people. If we consider ourselves members of the family, if we are grateful for what those "circled dates" signify, then we will not treat these occasions just like any other day. We will mark special occasions in special ways, in ways customary among our people. One way those occasions are marked is in the rhythms of our liturgical tradition.

## The First Law of Liturgical Mathematics

*Increased contextualization of Messianic services is directly proportional to increased use of traditional Hebrew liturgy.*

Jews expect Hebrew liturgy in Jewish religious services. Anything less and anything else is apt to be perceived as un-Jewish and inauthentic. In my experience, nothing is more likely to add a sense of authenticity to Messianic services than the use of traditional liturgy—in Hebrew, with translation as appropriate.

Some will object to this idea protesting that since very few American Jews understand Hebrew it is time to get rid of it. This suggests yet another principle, *the law of liturgical tolerance, which states that Diaspora Jews will tolerate more liturgy than they understand so long as they perceive the service to be otherwise meaningful.*

In fact, most of our people do not expect to understand the Hebrew liturgy. We come to synagogue and find it meaningful for a variety of reasons, including the opportunity to associate with other Jews, a time to worship God, an occasion to be enriched in Jewish knowledge, to hear an inspiring sermon, or to reinforce our own identity in the midst of the wider world. Because Diaspora Jews are so tolerant of traditional Hebrew liturgy, we need not be fearful of alienating our people by including liturgy in our services, provided other needs are properly addressed.

## The Dodge Van Principle

The way things stand today—there are those of our people who treat us with suspicion or even hostility. If communications are ever to improve, we must maintain every possible shred of commonality with the wider Jewish community. I call this the Dodge Van Principle.

There is a donut shop not far from where I live, where I used to stop daily as a matter of habit. At that time, I was driving a Dodge van. On one of these occasions, as I exited the shop, coffee and donut in hand, I noticed that in the interim, another motorist had parked his vehicle in front of mine. He was also driving a Dodge van. As I prepared to enter my vehicle, he called out and asked me how I liked my vehicle. What followed was a brief conversation, a conversation which never would have taken place had I been driving a different kind of vehicle. Thus, our communicational context was directly proportional to what we had in common, in this case, the fact that we were driving the same vehicle.

I submit the same must be true of our religious services and other communal expressions. In our congregations we must endeavor to be "driving the same kind of car" as our fellow Jews, otherwise there is no context for communication. Without such communication, there will be no commonality and little prospect of a healing of the breach between us and the rest of *K'lal Yisra'el* (the community of Israel). There will also be little opportunity to explain to other Jews the ways that we are Jews like them with a certain wonderful added extra.

I submit then, that our Messianic liturgical practice should be the same "kind of car" as is "driven" by our fellow Jews everywhere. Unfortunately, too few of our Messianic Jews know how to navigate through the liturgy. That brings us to what I term "the prime directive."

## Messianic Jewish Liturgical Renewal—How?

The prime directive says that *the better people understand the liturgy, the better they will like it. Therefore, we must institute ongoing programs designed to nurture liturgical literacy and competence, beginning with our congregational leaders and opinion leaders.*

Such programs should include instruction in Hebrew, in the history and function of the liturgical units, and practice in all aspects of participation in a traditional-style service, from dress, to bodily postures, to liturgical participation. With user-friendly resources like *The Synagogue Survival Kit* by Jordan Lee Wagner, there is no need or excuse to remain ignorant or inept in our tradition.

Our liturgical education programs must be ongoing because it is not enough to learn simply how to "operate" the liturgy. One must learn by experience how enriching liturgical practice can be, for individuals, and for the group as a whole. James Kugel rightly points out that Americans want to know what they will get out of something before they commit to it. Our tradition tells us we can only know by the tasting: "Taste and see that the LORD is good" (Ps. 34:8). Consequently, those who insist on a description of the taste before they will take a bite will remain forever empty and hungry.

The reason we must begin with congregational leaders and opinion leaders is expressed in another closely related principle, the law of obstructive leadership.

## The Law of Obstructive Leadership

The greatest obstacles to liturgical renewal are the ignorance, fear, pride, prejudice, and negative experiences of opinion-leaders and decision-makers. The next greatest obstacle is a lack of motivation.

Too many American Jews have a low regard for liturgy. For some this is due to negative experiences from their own childhood or the negativity they picked up from someone in their family. Some, with little or no liturgical experience, come from contexts where liturgy is categorically dismissed, being equated with spiritual deadness and "vain repetition." There is a psychological inhibition operating here as well—it is rare to find a leader willing to introduce some practice into his congregation for which he feels himself unprepared or unskilled. Far better to dismiss the practice as unnecessary, rather than admit to ignorance or bias.

For these and similar reasons, congregational leaders and opinion leaders should be the first to receive training in liturgical literacy. Opinion leaders, those people in the congregation who may not hold any kind of office but whose opinion is sought out by others who want to "check things out," must also be trained and won to this approach. Opinion-leaders are the ideological gatekeepers in a congregation. If they say something is O.K., then chances are the rest of the congregation will go along. Therefore, winning the allegiance of opinion leaders is crucial, so that others in the congregation will be convinced of the rightness of liturgical renewal in congregational life.

## Mirroring the Wider Jewish Community

Some fear liturgy— frightened by a boogey-man image of liturgy as a one-size-fits-all straight jacket that is sure to squeeze the life and vitality out of them and their congregations. However, our New Covenant Scriptures clearly demonstrates that the rule in the earliest Yeshua believing congregations was more "different strokes for different folks" than it was "once size fits all." To be convinced that this is true, just compare the portraits provided of congregational life in Jerusalem, Antioch, and Corinth! Now, as then, different communities will evolve different local customs and approaches.

Sidney Schwarz, author of the justly praised book, *Finding a Spiritual Home: How a New Generation of Jews Can Transform the American Synagogue*, reminds us that if we are to attract and hold today's Jewish people, we must introduce variety and creativity into our services—yet within the context of Jewish norms. He suggests that this is precisely what successful synagogues are doing in our day. Following his sage advice, we too must learn to vary and adapt our use of Jewish prayer materials.

My expectation has long been that when the Messianic Jewish movement reaches maturity, it will mirror the wider Jewish community in developing expressions analogous to Orthodox, Conservative, Reform and Reconstructionist Judaism—divergent communities that at the same time demonstrate a rootedness in a common identity and a fidelity to common patterns of worship, but who will interpret a common tradition in different but reverent ways.

In the area of liturgy, our services should mirror the structure of Jewish services. We should include the basic units such as the *Pesukei D'zimra* (Passages of Praise), the *Barkhu* (Call to Worship), *Sh'ma*, *Amidah* (Standing Prayer), and *Torah* section. Many of the *piyyutim* (sacred poems) and hymns like *Adon Olam, En Keloheynu*, and much more—should also be incorporated into the liturgy. Just as the Reform movement adapted this structure, eliminating repetitions of material and streamlining according to halakhic precedent while maintaining an underlying adherence to the tradition, so shall it be for us.

Of course, this latitude must not be interpreted as a license for each person or congregation to simply do what seems right in their own eyes.

That was a bad idea for our ancestors, and it remains so for us. What is called for is a certain liberty expressed in a dialectic with a received tradition and framework. Jewish life calls these factors *"keva"* (the received order of "how things are done") and *"kavvanah"* (personal investment and directedness). We will take the *keva* of the Jewish liturgical tradition, and within the *kavvanah of* our own personalized utilization of it very much make it our own in accord with our communal needs and character. Different varieties of approach are sure to evolve in different localities. For change to be organic and not destructive, innovations will need to be undertaken soberly, with reverent awareness and knowledge of time-honored principles and precedents of liturgical adaptation, and within the context of broad community consensus.

## Messianic Jewish Liturgical Renewal— Reflecting our Uniqueness

Because of the nature of our Messianic Jewish community, some principles of liturgical adaptation are unique to us. Because we as a community accord a unique place to the Messiah and the *Ruach HaKodesh*, Messianic services should supplement traditional Jewish materials by using songs, hymns, *piyyutim*, quotations from the New Covenant Scriptures and related liturgical units which reflect our particular emphases and beliefs. Care should be taken that such additions not be stylistically intrusive. With care, such compensatory measures can be effectively implemented in ways compatible with the Jewish liturgical tradition.

We ought also to remember that *Messianic services should draw people to Yeshua*. Our services are no mere showpieces designed to demonstrate how authentically Jewish we can be. No, the key distinguishing characteristic of Messianic Jews is the centrality we accord to Yeshua, our Messiah. Our services should reflect that centrality and should draw people to honor him as we do.

## Messianic Jewish Liturgical Renewal—A Final Caveat

I teach a principle called "The Second Law of Liturgical Mathematics" which states this: *All other things being equal, increased traditional Hebrew liturgy without increased liturgical literacy yields decreased understanding, enthusiasm and attendance.*

People who are becoming increasingly confused are likely to become less involved. Therefore, members of our congregations will need to be "brought up to speed" as liturgy is introduced, or they may well become disaffected. Therefore, again, the "Prime Directive" needs to be kept in mind: *The better people understand the liturgy, the better they will like it. Therefore, we must institute ongoing programs designed to nurture liturgical literacy and competence, beginning with our congregational leaders and opinion leaders.* And as did Hillel, we too must ask ourselves the question, "If not now, when?"

We have received a precious portion and lot. It will take little effort to lose it and concerted effort to lay hold of it and keep it—but we dare not neglect this heritage. We dare not lose it. The time is now for each of us to make the effort to build this *mishkan*, this liturgical structure, where the God of our ancestors meets with us as through the self-offering of Yeshua, our Great High Priest. So, let us lay hold of the work that lies before us. Let us begin in new ways to address the holy responsibility of so employing and so supplementing this heritage. In this way, all who come after will know us to be people who follow the example of the first Messianic Jews, who said "We've found the one that Moshe wrote about in the *Torah*, also the Prophets—it's Yeshua Ben Yosef from Natzeret!" (Yochanan/John 1:45 CJB).

## Questions for Discussion

- Have your religious practices brought you nearer or taken you farther away from other Jews?
- Describe any negative stereotypes you have encountered concerning liturgy, and whether they are untrue, sometimes true, usually true, or always true—and why.
- In what ways is your congregation "home" to Jewish visitors? In what ways is it strange and foreign? What steps might be undertaken to make your congregation more "user friendly" to Jewish visitors?
- Do you agree that Jewish people will tolerate Jewish liturgy that they do not understand provided they find services otherwise meaningful? What experiences can you point to which contribute to your opinion?

## Bibliography

Kugel, James. *On Being a Jew.* Baltimore: Johns Hopkins Univ., 1998.

Schwarz, Sidney. *Finding a Spiritual Home: How a New generation of Jews Can Transform the American Synagogue.* New York: Jossey-Bass, 2000.

Wagner, Jordan Lee. *The Synagogue Survival Kit.* Northvale: Jason Aaronson, 1997.

Stuart Dauermann has been involved in communicating New Covenant faith in a Jewish context since the 1960s. Since 1991, he has served as rabbi of Ahavat Zion Messianic Synagogue in Beverly Hills. Mr. Dauermann is President of Hashivenu, Inc., an organization that seeks to assist the Messianic Jewish movement "toward a mature Messianic Judaism." His doctoral work involves examining the ways in which synagogue leadership roles are related to those performed by priests and Levites in the Older Testament.

# MESSIANIC JEWISH REVIVAL AND LITURGY

—Joel Chernoff

The modern day Messianic Jewish revival was born by a sovereign act of God's will and propagated by the continuous exercise of his supernatural power. All care and attention must be made to make sure that the paths we commit to in developing and organizing this revival not hinder the marvelous and supernatural flow from which the Messianic Jewish revival emanated. This concern holds the key to understanding my view of the place of liturgy in the modern Messianic Jewish synagogue.

I share the following perspective as the son of two pioneers in Messianic Judaism, Rabbi Martin and Yohanna Chernoff. This perspective on the expression and place of liturgy in Messianic Judaism was shaped by the lessons learned from experience in their Messianic synagogue in Cincinnati, Ohio in the early days of the rebirth of Messianic Judaism. Consequently, I believe that a brief discussion of that history will be helpful in giving a context to my conclusions.

## Historical Context

In 1967, the spiritual revival of the Jewish people and the restoration of Messianic Judaism began in earnest. As Jerusalem was restored to Jewish control during the 1967 Six Day War between Israel and the Arab nations of the Middle East, a powerful and reviving measure of God's *Ruach HaKodesh* was released upon our Jewish people. At first, it was not easily perceived, for this release occurred in the context of a greater spiritual outpouring or revival in the U.S., popularly called the "Jesus People Movement." Although there have been many outpourings of God's Spirit on various people groups since the first century—this was the first revival that included the Jewish people in significant numbers.

By the early 1970s, this new Jewish revival began to attract attention in the press. Most notably, *Time* magazine ran an article describing the Messianic Jewish phenomenon, putting the number of Jewish believers in Jesus (Messianic Jews) at over fifty thousand. Before 1967, there were only a few thousand Messianic Jews at best in the United States and zero Messianic synagogues. No one person or institution could take credit for this spontaneous and unlikely revival among our Jewish people. I say unlikely because of the many persecutions of Jewish people in the name of Jesus, mainly at the hands of people who identified themselves as Christians. These numerous persecutions understandably resulted in a deeply felt Jewish national aversion to even considering the biblical question as to whether Yeshua was actually the promised Messiah. Nevertheless, and despite these accrued hurts the Messianic Jewish revival was reborn in 1967 and has increasingly flourished even to this day.

## The Messianic Vision

Within that initial group of over fifty thousand new Messianic Jews were a very small number of individuals within whom God implanted and began to develop a new vision. This vision was twofold: (1) to proclaim the messiahship of Yeshua within its biblical Jewish context, and (2) to restore an authentic Messianic Jewish lifestyle and worship expression for those who had come to believe that Yeshua is the Messiah. This vision became known as Messianic Judaism and its proponents as Messianic Jews.

A necessary step in reinvigorating a Messianic Jewish lifestyle and worship expression was the establishment of Messianic congregations or synagogues. In the traditional Jewish world, the synagogue has been the center of Jewish expression and communal life. The synagogue is an institution that has enabled our Jewish people to express and develop themselves both culturally and spiritually. In 1970, the Messianic Jewish revival witnessed the establishing of the first independent and self-supporting Messianic synagogue in Cincinnati, Ohio, Beth Messiah. It was founded by Martin and Yohanna Chernoff, my parents, and continues to this day.

In the early 1970s, several other Messianic synagogues were quickly established in various cities around the U.S. and today the number of Messianic synagogues has grown to over 400 worldwide. In fact, I believe that it can be confidently asserted that since 1967, Messianic Judaism is the fastest growing stream of Jewish religious expression in the world today.

# Early Challenges

One of the great challenges facing this new Messianic Jewish congregational movement was how to reconstitute a worship expression within our own synagogues. After all, Messianic Judaism in the twentieth century must balance the place of Jewish tradition and cultural expression (which is by no means uniform) with the fresh, new and reviving movement of God's spirit.

In the first century, Messianic Jewish worship was expressed naturally within the context of the Temple and synagogue life of that time. There was no question as to whether a person could believe in Yeshua and be Jewish. Messianic Jews of the first century were not considered "traitors" to their people because of their faith in Yeshua, as we are often assumed to be today. Christian persecution of Jewish people had not yet become a historical reality.

In order to restore an authentic, new Jewish worship expression and congregational lifestyle, a healthy dose of prayer, creativity, and trial and error was employed. In 1970, there were no examples to follow. For my parents and others, this was a true pioneer endeavor. It was an exiting journey of discovery, which was both dynamic and challenging. There was no shortage of critics to discourage them along the way.

So how did my parents handle these challenges and how did they balance the world of traditional Jewish religious expression with the fresh new wind of revival God was breathing upon our Jewish people? It is their journey of discovery and their simple but powerful conclusions (which I believe and espouse to this day)—that I want to describe as a way of approaching the question of the place of traditional liturgy in Messianic Jewish services.

# Not an Endeavor for the Timid

The one thing I can say about both of my parents is that they were visionaries. They were not afraid to swim against the current of popular worship service expression in both the church and traditional Jewish worlds. When they initially formed the congregation in Cincinnati, they took a tremendous amount of criticism from both groups. Neither of these worlds understood the prophetic objective that they were seeking— to restore a place of worship that would accurately express their faith in Yeshua within a Jewish context even as it was described in the pages of the New Covenant.

In the second chapter of Joel the prophet foretells that in the prophetic period described in the Scriptures as "latter days" God will pour out his Spirit upon all flesh and that your young men will dream dreams and your old men will see visions. My father experienced a literal fulfillment of this passage. In the middle 1960s, my father shared the vision the Lord had given him with his entire family. In that vision, he saw a great banner stretched across the sky with two words inscribed on it: Messianic Judaism. A huge multitude of predominantly young Jewish people were streaming under the banner towards a glorious light that he knew to be the light of Messiah Yeshua and the Kingdom of God. This was a few years before the Messianic Jewish revival suddenly appeared in 1967. Messianic Judaism, as a phrase, was not commonly used. God planted this vision of Jewish revival or Messianic Judaism in my father's heart and by osmosis into my heart.

Soon after this vision, when God began to pour out his Spirit in a great way upon our Jewish people in 1967, my parents recognized this new revival as the one described in my father's vision about Messianic Judaism. They had already begun to have a sense that if Messianic Judaism were to flourish again, Messianic Jews needed to live and worship in a Jewish context rather than be assimilated into the culture of the church. This realization led them to form Beth Messiah of Cincinnati. In the context of this newly formed Messianic congregation they began to more extensively explore what Messianic Judaism was supposed to look like and how it should be expressed.

What was of paramount concern to them right from the start was to avoid what they had observed historically and believed was a potential problem for this revival. In their view, the dynamic vitality of past revivals was deadened by the almost immediate effort of trying to organize and structure the revival too quickly. The result was a dampening of the very move of God's Spirit that spawned the prophetic revival. They recognized that the great numbers of new Messianic Jews were a direct result of the sovereign moving of God's *Ruach*. This concern was the number one priority in deciding what direction their synagogue would take as well as how the synagogue service was to be conducted.

## Early Days at Beth Messiah, Cincinnati

As a young college age man in the early 1970s, I recall the sudden emergence and great enthusiasm for all things Jewish that accompanied the new Messianic Jewish revival. This phenomena was not just resident in me but in all of the youth and many of the adult members of our young Messianic congregation. Not only did God set us on fire spiritually but he also stirred up a tremendous love of all things Jewish. At that time most of us sported long hair, mustaches and beards, which was not only the "look" of the day but also reflected a time when new and free ideas were being explored.

We took great pleasure in wearing our *kippot*, *tallitot*, and ten-pound Stars of David at our services. We were militantly pro-Israel and Zionist.

This was only natural given the fact that we were "on fire" for the God of Israel and saw the restoration of physical Israel as the completion of prophecies that were to be fulfilled right before Messiah returns. Any newly discovered Jewish expression was embraced and explored.

## New Music is Born

Along with the new enthusiasm for Jewish identity and Jewish expression, a critical innovation soon developed that had a great impact on both the liturgy and content of Messianic congregational worship—the birth of messianic music. Messianic Judaism was born in the days of 1960s and 1970s rock and roll music. Since many of the new Messianic Jews were high school and college age "baby boomers," it was only natural that we express our love for God in a style of music that we were comfortable with. Our services embraced the new instrumentation of guitars, bass and drums, which at that time was considered radical for religious service.

I was privileged to have a significant part in popularizing and defining this music through the group known as *Lamb*. This music was truly a fresh new expression. It could be described as a hybrid of modern pop and traditional minor key Jewish music. The objective was to express the tremendous joy we had found in knowing the Messiah Yeshua personally. This new music became the centerpiece of our worship services in Cincinnati. It also spread around the country to the other Messianic congregations and has become increasingly popular in the church.

## Liturgical Trial and Error

In the midst of these innovations in worship, my father and mother along with my brother David and I, began to feel the need to add elements of traditional Jewish liturgy to our services. We slowly began to add elements such as the *Sh'ma*, Sabbath prayers over the candles and many other Jewish liturgical readings. Most of these readings were actually extra-biblical prayers recited from the Jewish prayer books.

The experience was new and initially felt good. However, as we increasingly added the liturgy, we noticed that while the liturgy was aesthetically pleasing, it was also inadvertently restricting the joyful nature and free flow of the Spirit we had been experiencing in the early revival and come to know and love. More and more of the service was confined to the rote recitation of extra-biblical prayers. Simply put, there was less time and room for the Spirit of God to move. An adjustment was needed.

We eliminated much of the traditional liturgy we were currently using. We started over again, this time adding liturgy slowly, but evaluating each new liturgical addition as to whether the addition had a dampening effect on the flow of the Spirit in our *Shabbat* service. In other words, if the liturgical addition would take nothing away from the moving of God's Spirit in the service then it was retained. Otherwise, it was eliminated.

A good example of this process was in the area of traditional prayer book usage. Most prayers in the prayer book, though beautiful, lack the power and authority of the Scriptures. In our experience, too many of such prayers had a deadening effect on our service. One of the ways that we eventually handled this problem was to substitute appropriate Scripture readings for traditional prayers. We did this on *Shabbat* and used the same principle for festival services such as Passover, *Sukkot*, and *Shavu'ot*. This took some time to work out and we, even to this day, continue to experiment with this method.

Once we made this adjustment, the result of increased power in the service was unmistakable. After all, we know that the Scripture says that the word of God is "sharper than a two-edged sword" and "will not return void" (Heb. 4:12). The word of God has the authority and power from God to bring life to the hearer. Although the rote recitation of traditional extra-biblical prayers from the *siddur* is beautiful, it does not have the life changing power of Scripture. In retrospect, this might seem to be a "no brainer," but it took us some time to arrive at the conclusion that it was both acceptable and necessary to make this change.

Very early on, we came to a simple but important conclusion. The traditional Jewish prayer book liturgy was necessary and an important connection to our people. However, traditional Jewish liturgy should be applied to the service in such a way that there is no hindrance to the moving of God's Spirit in the hearts of his people and the consequent release of his power.

Of course, we were conscious of the fact that this principle could be applied in various ways in Messianic synagogues. However, for Martin and Yohanna Chernoff, coming to this conclusion was critical to gaining a sense of balance in the midst of the challenge of creating a Messianic Jewish service that was full of the life changing power of God's Spirit. It was their belief, as well as mine today, that as our Jewish people experience the touch of God's Holy Spirit in our services that lives will be changed forever.

In conclusion, traditional Jewish liturgical expressions are an important component of the modern day Messianic Jewish synagogue service. However, the powerful moving and release of God's spirit is even more important. If we as a spiritually revived Jewish community continue approaching the issue of worship service liturgy creatively, keeping in mind that our primary goal is to see a release of God's "breath" or Spirit on the "dry bones" of our Jewish people as depicted in Ezekiel 37—our services will remain fresh and alive. They will continue to meet not only our own need to be refreshed by God's Spirit—but those visiting us will have the great joy and privilege of experiencing the redeeming power of the God of Israel in a way they didn't know was possible. Surely, the time has come for the "dry bones" of our people to feel the breath of God and live!

## Questions for Discussion

- What was the role and function of the Holy Spirit in both the *Tanakh* and *B'rit Hadashah*?
- What liturgical forms were employed in the Temple?
- Do the Scriptures indicate that there will be a Jewish revival or restoration in the prophetic period called the "latter days?"
- If so, what role will the Holy Spirit and/or the supernatural play in that revival (if any)?

Joel Chernoff is one the pioneers of Messianic music. For over twenty years, he has been lead singer and songwriter for the music group *Lamb*. Besides continuing his musical career, Joel is serving as President of the International Messianic Jewish Alliance and as General Secretary of the Messianic Jewish Alliance of America.

# BIBLICAL AUTHORITY

—Daniel Juster

The Messianic Jewish Community maintains a high view of the Bible, both the Hebrew Scriptures and the New Covenant Scriptures, as our primary authority. This view of the Bible is rooted in the biblical material itself, but has been developed by the reflection of theologians over many centuries. In the Messianic Jewish Community the understanding of biblical teaching settles matters of doctrine and practice.

## An Infallible Bible

The Messianic Jewish community shares with Orthodox Judaism and conservative evangelical Christianity, the view that the Bible is infallible. This is, for example, enshrined in the statements of belief of both the UMJC and the IAMCS, the two largest associations of Messianic Jewish Congregations in the world. Many are familiar with the extent to which this extends in classical Orthodox Judaism (though perhaps not modern Orthodoxy). Indeed, infallibility is said to extend to every word and letter of the Hebrew text, the word order, and the grammatical markings. For educated Messianic Jews, infallibility is not used to support such a minute view. For example, most would hold that by textual criticism, we now have constructed reliable texts in the original languages, but not an infallible text. Only the original autographs were infallible, not their preservation in copies. Textual criticism (which compares copies to reconstruct the original) brings us close to what the original text was; even close enough to trust our present critical texts in Hebrew and Greek (see Metzger and Harris).

Messianic Jewish leadership generally holds the view that both the Hebrew Scriptures and the twenty-seven writings of the Greek New Testament are part of this infallible Bible. Therefore, all teaching and insight in rabbinic texts, commentaries, legal applications, and interpretations, must all be in accord with what the Bible teaches. In addition, all Christian writings, commentaries, and applications must be judged by their agreement with the teaching of the Bible. However, finding out just what the Bible teaches sometimes requires significant effort. Finding out what the Bible teaches is the work of a science (also an art) called hermeneutics. In addition, it is important to give reason for why we accept just those books of the Bible we do as the infallible parts of the Bible. This does not mean that there are no important new insights or regulations that are not found within the Bible but are perceived as wise applications.

## The Meaning of Infallibility

The doctrine of infallibility is based upon the doctrine of inspiration. This doctrine is taught in scripture itself:

> All Scripture is given by inspiration of God (God breathed) and is profitable for doctrine, correction, and instruction in righteousness. (2 Tim. 3:16)

This is also the understanding in the teaching of Yeshua who said that not a "jot or a title of the *Torah* would pass away" until heaven and earth would pass away (Matt. 5:19). He said, "The Scriptures can not be broken" (John 10:35). Indeed, the teaching of Yeshua makes it clear that whatever the Hebrew Bible says is the Word and will of God. The classical compendium of articles by Benjamin B. Warfield, *The Inspiration and Authority of the Bible*, shows in article after article that "It says," "Scripture says," "It is written," and "God says" are equivalents in the teaching of Yeshua. This understanding of the Bible is repeated in updated form in the modern classic by R. Laird Harris cited above. There are too many statements affirming the same view of the Hebrew Scriptures in the New Testament to quote here. Even atheist New Testament scholar H. J. Cadbury affirmed that the teaching of Yeshua was clearly an affirmation of the commonly held view of an infallible Bible held by the religious leaders of his day, especially the Pharisees. That the New Testament teaches such a view is not at issue in scholarship.

The question arises, however, concerning the process and the result of inspiration. Did God simply dictate the Bible to the writer who acted as secretaries? Sometimes statements in both ancient Jewish sources and in Christian sources would seem to indicate this. There are cases where God is quoted as saying something like, "Write these words." Yet, we generally know that the biblical books reflect the personalities of the writers. Indeed, Paul can bemoan his situation of abandonment in jail while he awaits execution. He can be very firm concerning his superior role as an apostle compared to others who have visited the congregations he planted (2 Corinthians 10). He can appeal to Philemon to release his slave and to Mark to bring his cloak. These books seem so obviously human. Proponents of infallibility do not hold that inspiration is dictation. Rather they believe that God so oversaw the biblical writers that the product of their pen was both the Word of God and the word and personality of the writer. The very personality of the writer was used to produce what God wanted to say. God's Word and the writers will and word thus came together in a harmony producing works that are fully human and fully divine. This is known as *confluence*. The will of God and the will of the writer flow together. Therefore, what God says is what Jeremiah says. What Peter says is what God says.

With the doctrine of infallibility, we are dealing with the major questions concerning what we are to believe and how we are to live (*Torah*). Usually it is held that what we are to believe and do is according to what the biblical writer is claiming to teach. *Infallibility means that the Bible is true in all that the biblical writer claims to teach as true.* Perhaps the greatest teacher of this view in recent years has been Dr. Kenneth Kantzer of Trinity Evangelical Divinity School. Unfortunately, he has not published much of his work in books. His fortunate students have his written notes. The view that Kantzer puts forth is the most refined and objective statement of the doctrine of infallibility to date and is reflected in this article. It is also summarized in my book *The Biblical World View, An Apologetic*. This view holds that the intent of the human author is the intent of God. Therefore, we must find the intent of the author in communicating to his original audience. This is the issue of interpretation or hermeneutics.

Infallibility does not mean that there are no errors in the Bible. The Bible may quote sources or common beliefs that include errors. It is only the point that the author is seeking to make (and information that is necessary to that point) that is infallible. The mustard seed does not have to be (literally) the smallest of all seeds. That is not the point. Nor do we have to decide between the Masoretic tradition and the Septuagint tradition concerning whether seventy or seventy-five people came down to Egypt with Jacob. Acts quotes the Septuagint tradition (seventy-five). What the biblical writer seeks to teach is known by the science and art of interpretation or hermeneutics. However, before we deal with this important issue, we must deal with another crucial issue we have only mentioned, that is the issue of canonicity.

## The Issue of Canonicity

The word *canon* has to do with what is lawfully binding. Therefore, we want to determine which books of the Bible are lawfully binding. We begin with the teaching of Yeshua and the Apostles. It is clear from their statements that they accepted the writings that first century Jewry commonly accepted as the Hebrew Bible. This is understood to be the twenty-two scrolls mentioned by Josephus as those the Jewish community revered as the Word of God. These twenty-two books are equivalent to the thirty-nine books accepted by Protestants. Some of the thirty-nine books of the Protestant Bible were combined as one scroll in the Hebrew Canon. For example, the twelve Minor Prophets were combined in one scroll called simply *The Twelve*. While there are other valued ancient Jewish books, such as the Apocrypha, the Jewish community did not give the same weight to them as the books mentioned by Josephus. Indeed, the prophetic gift of inspiration necessary to write canonical biblical scrolls was stated to be absent during this time (2 Maccabees). We note that within many of these books (but not by any means all, such as Esther, Ruth etc.) there is a claim to be speaking and writing from the prophetic unction of the Holy Spirit. This includes the legislative parts of the *Torah* and the great writing prophets such as Isaiah and Jeremiah.

That Yeshua is our primary authority as teacher because he proved his authority by rising from the dead, is a key to the doctrine of both infallibility and canonicity. He taught the full authority of the twenty-two scrolls. That settles the issue of the Hebrew Canon for us.

In addition, he chose twelve apostles and gave them authority as the witnesses and teachers of the New Covenant revelation. They are authoritative teachers and prophets. It is reasonable to expect that they would leave writings that had the same authority as the Hebrew Canon. It also appears that the twelve expanded their circle to a few others including Matthias (Acts 1), Paul (according to his claim in Galatians and Acts that the Apostles recognized his equal authority as the chief apostle to the nations), and James and Jude, the brothers of Yeshua after the flesh. In the case of James, the book of Acts shows his equal authority. When the question of canonicity is therefore asked, two criteria are usually invoked for the New Testament books. The first is, does it give evidence (within or by external testimony) that its author was one of the authoritative apostles? I call this the circle of fifteen. We do have such evidence. Matthew was acknowledged by early sources in the second century as the author of this book. Its Jewish character testifies to its ancient origins. Mark was held by early tradition to be the preaching of Peter (according to Papias). John, Revelation, 1 John, 2 John, and 3 John were ascribed to the Apostle John, as is claimed within the texts themselves. The gospel of John refers to the one that Yeshua loved (clearly John) as the writer of the book. Luke and Acts were considered written under the apostolic authority of Paul, as are the Pauline epistles. 1 and 2 Peter are claimed internally as coming from Peter and were so affirmed in early history. This leaves only Hebrews with no apostolic ascription. Some think the author is Paul because its theology is so consistent with his. However, the language and style, according to some, seems more like John's.

The second criterion is the witness of the Holy Spirit in the hearts of disciples who read the books. Only the twenty-seven books have been widely affirmed by all those who follow Yeshua. This is from the earliest times. Early canonical lists make this clear. A reading of the extra-biblical books (e.g., New Testament pseudepigrapha) have been perceived to have a lower quality.

Since the same God inspires all of these books (in both the Hebrew and Greek Scriptures), they should be consistent and coherent in their teaching. This does not mean that there is no apparent paradox. However, when rightly interpreted, and when the paradoxes are carefully interpreted, these books are fully in accord. *The work of harmonizing biblical teaching is valid as long as this is not done simplistically. There should be good effort at looking for various possibilities of harmonization.*

## No Equal to the Authority of the Bible

The Bible is our highest and final authority. This does not mean that we must reject lesser authorities. However, all other authorities are subject to an evaluation by compatibility with the Bible. For Messianic Jews, only biblical teaching is fully binding, whereas other authorities might be followed because we perceive wise application or respect community practices.

This would also apply to our approach to the Jewish doctrine of the authority of the Oral *Torah*. Orthodox Judaism teaches that the Oral *Torah* is equal in authority to the Written Word. There is a profound problem of defining canon in Orthodoxy. Is the Oral *Torah* the first part of the Talmud, the *Mishnah*? Is it a part of the *Mishnah* that is considered more ancient? Was the Oral *Torah* preserved whole and passed down from Moses? Was it, in part, lost and rediscovered by the conclusions of the Great Assembly down to the conclusions of the rabbinic schools? I recommend Lawrence Schiffman's, *From Text to Tradition*, for a good presentation of the issues here. His point is that the Oral *Torah* myth was created to establish the authority of the rabbis over the Jewish community. In reality, the Oral Law exceeds the Written *Torah* in authority since it authoritatively tells us what the written *Torah* means. Oral Law ends up being the ancient rabbinic consensus. On the other hand, Messianic Jews follow the Oral Law according to the criteria explained above.

## Hermeneutics, the Great Issue for Messianic Jews

An understanding of the basic thrusts of much biblical teaching is available to the average reader who is seeking the truth with the help of the Holy Spirit. This is called *the doctrine of the perspicuity of Scripture*. However, it is not always easy to know what the biblical author is teaching. Many tools have to be applied to obtain an accurate understanding. The science of interpretation (hermeneutics) involves the use of such tools. The rules of hermeneutics are the same for all past literature.

First, hermeneutics takes into account the original languages according to definition, usage, grammar, and idiom. This is done by a broad comparison of available contemporary literature. Interpretation is more than defining words. Words are defined in the larger context of usage in sentences, paragraphs, and even in the context of the writing as a whole. This is well pointed out in the classic *Semantics of Biblical Language* by James Barr (see 21–45). Context also includes cultural backgrounds for understanding biblical ideas, illustrations, life patterns, and common beliefs. The importance of understanding cultural background is gaining greater popular acceptance. The publishing of books like Craig Keener's *Bible Background Commentary: New Testament* is greatly increasing popular understanding.

In addition, the understanding gained from a conservative approach to form and redaction criticism brings gain to the Messianic Jewish community. *Form criticism* gives us cultural background for understanding the different biblical forms of poetry, narrative, short story, miracle story, and parable. This aids us in discovering the intent of author of the text. In addition, much of the Gospel material first circulated in oral form and in different arrangements. *Redaction criticism* seeks to understand the distinct purpose and intent of the final author-compiler of the biblical material. A comparison of the Synoptic Gospels provides us with patterns of variation whereby the intention of the author can be more readily perceived. Messianic Jews believe that the final redactor was an Apostle and that God inspires the redaction purpose and intent of teaching. For example, Christian interpreters used to say that we are not to build theology from descriptive material, but only from explicitly theological material. This is now understood by many scholars to be false. There is much theology in 1 Kings. There is much theology in the book of Acts. Indeed, since the work of Hans Conzelman and I. Howard Marshall, we now clearly recognize that theology is prominent in the book of Acts. The theology and purpose of Luke is very important for Messianic Jews, since one of Luke's purposes is to show the right relationship of Jew and Gentile in one movement. Indeed, the calling of Jews in Yeshua to keep *Torah* is very clear, as is the freedom from Jewish calling for the Gentiles. Another purpose of Luke is to show that followers of Yeshua are good subjects of the Roman Empire

The dangers in hermeneutics today come from contemporary theories that partake of post modernist ideas of historiography. These ideas cast doubt on whether objective historical knowledge can be ascertained. All history is reduced to the power politics of the one who is writing. Such contemporary skepticism and deconstruction is contrary to Messianic Judaism. We claim that the use of good scholarship in hermeneutics brings us closer to an accurate understanding of the Bible. We do not claim perfect understanding, but adequate and growing understanding. Accurate theology is practical for it aids us to walk on the path of *Torah* as it is rightly applied in the New Covenant order.

One significant issue in hermeneutics concerns whether a text is capable of multiple meanings or is to be understood as having one meaning. Two biblical theologians who support Messianic Judaism have different approaches to this question. Richard Longenecker, in his *Biblical Exegesis in the Apostolic Period*, argues that the New Testament writer finds meaning in the Hebrew text that cannot (by any means) be understood as intended by the human author (see 218–219). The New Testament writer really claims that this new meaning is part of the real meaning of the text. In other words, *peshar* and midrashic interpretation do discover real meaning. For Longenecker, because the biblical writers were inspired, their interpretation is valid, but we can not reproduce such exegesis. For Walter Kaiser, there is but one author intended meaning in a text unless there is evidence of an author intended double *entendre* as in some of the passages of the gospel of John (17–23). One meaning is capable of multiple applications, but never as a replacement of the original meaning of the author.

I hold to a more charismatic and prophetic approach whereby the Holy Spirit gives new applications and jumping off points, but never in a replacement of the original author's intended meaning. For example, I do not claim (like Longenecker) that Matthew 2:15 finds a new meaning in the verse "Out of Israel have I called my Son," (that really was not intended by Hosea). I do not claim (like Kaiser) that the meaning of the Messiah really is in Hosea 11:1 because of the technical meaning of the word *Son* and its intended application to the Messiah. Rather, the Holy Spirit reveals new parallels, not intended by original author. Such is the nature of the gift of prophecy.

## New Covenant Application

The New Covenant Scriptures provide a very important key for hermeneutics. These Scriptures are permeated with the idea that the Messiah has come and, in a significant sense, the expected Kingdom has come. It has not come in the fullness pictured in the most awesome terms by Isaiah and the other prophets where the lion lays down with the lamb, world peace is established, and the knowledge of the Lord covers the earth as the waters cover the seas (cf. Isaiah 11). Nevertheless, the Kingdom of God in a new and superior order is now available to human beings. The Good News of the Kingdom is really the message that the government of God is now available to human beings (see Ladd 40–51). The realm of the Kingdom is the realm of love, justice, and righteousness. In this realm of righteousness, there is *shalom*. *Shalom* is more than the English word *peace*. It is wholeness and blessing in all human dimensions. Yes, the Kingdom available now is partial. Our argument with classical Judaisms is really over the issue of this partial reality of the Kingdom, for classical Judaisms will not acknowledge the Messiah and His Kingdom for anything less than the fullness of the Kingdom. However, the whole teaching of Yeshua and the New Covenant Scriptures is that just such a real (but partial) coming of the Kingdom is reality.

As part of this Kingdom reality, we are told to teach all that Yeshua has commanded. His teaching is the *halakhah* for our approach to *Torah*. This has great implications for a Messianic Jewish approach to *Torah*. Therefore as the rabbis anticipated, there would be a change in *Torah* in the Messianic Age (see Davies 147–150). All of the commandments in the New Covenant scriptures are *Torah*. We also look to rabbinic sources for insight to help us make this application of *Torah*. The job of *Torah* application is central to a genuine Messianic Judaism.

## Question for Discussion

- What do we mean when we claim that the Bible is infallible?
- What are the two primary tests for determining which books of the Bible may be accepted as part of the Canon?
- What are the primary issues of hermeneutics?
- How do we relate biblical authority to the authority of the Oral Law?

## Bibliography

Barr, James. *Semantics of Biblical Language*. London: Oxford Univ., 1961.

Conzelman, Hans. *The Theology of St. Luke*. London: Farber and Farber, 1960.

Davies, W. D., *Paul and Rabbinic Judaism*. Philadelphia: Fortress, 1980.

Harris, R. Laird. *The Inspiration and Canonicity of the Bible*. Grand Rapids: Baker, 1970.

Juster, Dr. Daniel. *The Biblical World View, An* Apologetic. Bethesda: Christian Scholars International, 1996.

Kaiser, Walter. *Uses of the Old Testament in the New*. Chicago: Moody, 1985.

Keener, Craig S. *The IVP Bible Background Commentary: New Testament*. InterVarsity: Downers Grove, 1994.

Ladd, George. *The Gospel of the Kingdom*, Grand Rapids: Eerdmans, 1959.

Longenecker, Richard. *Biblical Exegesis in the Apostolic Period*. Grand Rapids: Eerdmans, 1999.

Marshall, I. Howard. *Luke, Historian and Theologian*. Grand Rapids: Zondervan, 1978.

Metzger, Bruce. *The Text of the New Testament*. New York: Oxford Univ., 1964.

Schiffman, Lawrence. *From Text to Tradition*. Hoboken: KTAV, 1991.
Warfield, Benjamin B. *The Inspiration and Authority of the Bible*. Philadelphia: Presbyterian and Reformed, 1948.

Daniel Juster is the leader of Tikkun International and has been at the forefront of the Messianic Jewish movement since its inception. The first President of the Union of Messianic Jewish Congregations, he has served as the spiritual leader of Adat HaTikvah in Chicago and Beth Messiah Congregation in Rockville, Maryland. Dr. Juster is author of *Growing to Maturity* and *Jewish Roots*. He holds several earned degrees including a Th.D. from New Covenant International Seminary.

# SCRIPTURE AND TRADITION

—Mark S. Kinzer

Many Messianic Jews consider the message of the Bible as clear and indisputable, a fact independent of external interpretation. The individual who reads the text with faith and an open heart will understand what it says. Why, then, are there such a plethora of divergent interpretations, so many of which strike us as misleading? The answer must lie, we think, in merely human readings of the text that have congealed into hardened traditions, which prevent others from seeing what is so evident to us.

It is ironic that our contempt for tradition derives from tradition. We may think that such a view follows ineluctably from Yeshua's teaching in Mark 7:6–13 or Paul's in Colossians 2:8. However, there are many other passages in the Apostolic Writings that treat "tradition" with great respect (e.g., 1 Cor. 11:2; 2 Thess. 2:15, 3:6), and even more that employ traditional midrashic motifs (e.g., 1 Cor. 10:4; John 1:1). Distrust of all extrabiblical tradition does not derive directly from the Bible itself, but from a particular stream of Protestant interpretive tradition. In our efforts to be purely biblical, we find ourselves, once again, captive to tradition.

All attempts at a "purely biblical" perspective are destined to fail. One never reads the biblical text apart from preconceptions drawn from one's own particular historical setting and from some stream of interpretive tradition. That setting and tradition will shape the questions we address to the text, the concepts and terms we use to answer those questions, and our selection of the portions of the text that speak most directly to our questions, and therefore seem to be of greatest importance. They will likewise influence how we construe the unified message of the document as a whole, and relate that message to our life today. This does not mean that the Bible lacks the power to reshape our questions, or transform our preconceptions. It does mean that the direction of influence is two-way—our existential situation in the flow of history and tradition forming our reading of the text, and the text in turn forming our existential situation.

Interpretive tradition consists of the accumulated insights of a community transmitted from one generation to the next. In a Messianic Jewish context, tradition represents the understanding of Scripture preserved through the generations among the communities—Jewish and Christian—within which Scripture itself has been preserved. If we are connected to these communities, then we are also heirs of their traditions. The text itself is the core of these traditions. In the words of Paul van Buren, the Bible is always a "carried book."

> But historical scholarship can only *help* us to understand these books, for we shall not have reached the understanding we seek until we have found a way to receive light upon our present path for the steps which we are about to take. For such an understanding, we need to know the steps we have already taken and what light our predecessors received—or thought they received—from this book. In short, we have to realize that we have this book in our hands, not directly from its original authors or even from the communities for which and in the context of which they were first written, but from those who immediately preceded us in the Way, and through the whole long line of those who have walked before them. This carried book—the one we actually read and keep bringing into our own conversation—is the one from which we hope to receive light for each step along the Way. (121)

Respecting tradition and learning from it, is a way of recognizing that we have "predecessors," that we are part of a community with a history. It involves the humble recognition that we are not the first ones to encounter the sacred text, and that we must listen to what our parents have said about it before we speak in turn.

## Scripture Always Accompanied By Tradition

The distinction between Scripture and tradition is problematic. In part, this is because Scripture is itself, the core of tradition. However, the distinction is also problematic for another reason: unless we are scholars dealing with ancient manuscripts, we never encounter Scripture unaccompanied by tradition. We are usually unaware of its presence, but it is as much a part of our reading of the text as the air we breathe is part of our daily physical activity. How is this the case? First and foremost, tradition is reflected in the canonical selection and arrangement of the books of the Bible. In the case of *Tanakh*, the basic outline of this selection and arrangement were determined before the first century C.E., but the definitive listing of books did not come till after the destruction of the Second Temple. In the case of the Apostolic Writings, the basic outline was clear by the end of the second century C.E., but the final listing of books was not complete until the fourth century. One can engage in theological disputes about whether the Jewish and Christian communities established the canon or merely recognized it. However, the essential historical fact remains: the decision as to which books are in the Bible and how they are arranged was not made through a prophetic pronouncement or an apostolic decree, but through a protracted process of communal discernment. The canon is delivered to us as a product of Jewish and Christian tradition.

Second, tradition accompanies the text through the massive edifice of scribal clarification. In the case of *Tanakh*, the original manuscripts would have contained an unpunctuated, unparagraphed consonantal text. The Masoretic scribes developed a complex system of vocalization (vowel pointing) and punctuation, and added it to the text in a way that reflected traditional readings of that text. They also added paragraph divisions, and even indicated through their novel system of vocalization where the consonantal text needed to be corrected. Whenever we read the Hebrew text of *Tanakh* in a printed Bible, we encounter not only the work of the original author or authors, but also the interpretive framework supplied by the Masoretes. In the case of the Apostolic Writings, the original manuscripts have no word divisions, paragraph divisions, chapter divisions, or punctuation. Even those of us who are able to read a printed Greek New Testament do not encounter the text in its original form. We benefit from generations of scribes and scholars who supplied reading aids that the original manuscripts lacked.

Third, interpretive tradition accompanies the text whenever it is read in translation. Translation is the most elementary form of interpretation. It always involves restating *in other words* what is understood to be the meaning of the original text. The interpretive power of translation should be especially evident to us as Messianic Jews, since we must deal with anti-Jewish and anti-*Torah* biases every time we pick up a leading Christian version of the New Testament. This is why David Stern's labors have been of such great importance to the Messianic Jewish movement. The *Jewish New Testament*, like every New Testament translation, presents an interpretation of the text; but in this case, the interpretation reflects the convictions and culture of Messianic Judaism. Awareness of the interpretive power of Bible translation is reflected in the emergence of diverse translations in the second half of the twentieth century. As D. G. Hart notes in a review of Peter J. Thuesen's *In Discordance with the Scriptures: American Protestant Battles over Translating the Bible*:

In the twentieth century, the debates about the Bible escalated as Protestants recognized that even such simple matters as translation were bound up with interpretation. Consequently, evangelicals suspected the Revised Standard Version as a liberal Bible, and eventually countered with the New International Version, a translation produced by conservative scholars. Along the way, Protestants demonstrated what Catholics already knew—namely, that the Bible never stands alone but, even in its translation, is situated in a web of relationships that involve the authority of church leaders and questions about who has responsibility for determining orthodoxy. (Hart 65)

Similar controversies over translation have occurred within the Jewish world. The Orthodox refused to participate in the production of the New Jewish Publication Society (NJPS) translation of *Tanakh*. Use of the Stone *Tanakh* or the NJPS *Tanakh* identifies one's brand of Judaism as much as use of the KJV, NASB, NIV, RSV, or NAV (a Catholic translation) marks one's Christian loyalties. Diverse translations embody diverse interpretations found in diverse communities that are heirs of diverse traditions.

Fourth, interpretive tradition accompanies Scripture whenever we read the text in a reference edition. Study Bibles often include, along with a particular translation of the text, introductions and outlines for each book, commentary for each unit, and cross-references for each verse. Such study aids might appear to be neutral guides through the text, but they contain and conceal just as many interpretive decisions as do translations. Even cross-references entail such decisions, for they inevitably involve a selection among potential correspondences, thus inviting the reader to connect certain verses and ignore other possible relationships. Just as one's choice of Bible translation displays the interpretive tradition with which one identifies, so with study Bibles. In fact, one particular study Bible—the Scofield Bible—served as the single most powerful vehicle for the promotion of dispensationalist theology in America in the early twentieth century. Now, each community of interpretation has its own study Bible, or is in the process of producing one.

It should be clear by now, that we never deal with the biblical text apart from interpretation and tradition. The question is not whether we will draw upon an interpretive tradition. Instead, the question is *which* tradition (or traditions) we will draw upon, and whether we will do so consciously or unconsciously.

## Entering the Conversation

This question poses a special challenge for Messianic Jews, for we have no continuous interpretive tradition of our own. The early community of Jewish followers of Yeshua became extinct in the first half of the first millenium B.C.E. Yet, we do share in the heritage of two communities—Jewish and Christian—each of which possesses a rich and continuous tradition of biblical interpretation and lived faith. Unfortunately, throughout much of their history, these two communities, though both rooted in the soil of Second Temple Judaism, have been locked in conflict and have defined themselves over against one another. Thus, our parents divorced with great acrimony, and though they are beginning to talk to one another again, their new identities seem to preclude genuine reconciliation.

This challenge is also an opportunity. At the heart of our vision as Messianic Jews are two convictions, one treasured by the Jewish people and denied by the Church, the other guarded by the Church and denied by the Jewish people: (1) The eternal and irrevocable election of Israel (i.e., the Jewish people) as an ethno-covenantal community, with a central role to play in the Divine plan for history, and with a particular God-given way of life rooted in the *Torah*; and (2) The Messiahship and Divine Sonship of Yeshua, light to the nations and glory of Israel, who died as an atoning sacrifice and rose from the dead as the first-fruits of the eschaton. Therefore, we see both the Jewish and Christian traditions as bearing imperishable truth in what they affirm as their core message, and as lacking something important because of what they deny in the affirmation of the other. Our parents may find it difficult to listen to one another, but each is incomplete on its own. Our vocation is to bring our parents together again, not just as friends but as partners.

As members of the one elect ethno-covenantal community of Israel, Messianic Jews receive the text of the *Torah* as it has been "carried" by the Jewish people throughout their history, and are obliged to enter into that conversation about its meaning and application that has been central to Jewish life as long as Judaism has existed. In fact, the summit of Jewish piety—*talmud Torah* (study of the *Torah*)—consists of just such cross-generational conversation. Jewish study of the sacred text is never conceived of as a purely individual task, but as a communal obligation, which binds Jews across space and time. Like every Jewish conversation, this one involves argument and disagreement. Giving tradition its due in the Jewish reading of Scripture does not mean bowing before an unquestioned authority, but entering into the discussion as a serious listener and disputant.

The nature of Jewish study of *Torah* is revealed most vividly in the classic rabbinic study Bible, *Mikraot Gedolot*. Edward L. Greenstein describes this text as follows:

> The traditional Jewish edition of the Bible, *Mikra'ot Gedolot*, "Great Readings," or "Big Scriptures" . . . is essentially a medieval product. It presents the standard Hebrew text of the Bible, an ancient rab-

binic translation into Aramaic—the *targum*—and a number of medieval commentaries in Hebrew. . . . Although most extant works of
the major commentaries are available in separate editions and can be
read in isolation from the others, the arrangement in *Mikra'ot
Gedolot* encourages dialectic among the distinguished voices on the
page, confirming the well-known witticism that where there are two
Jews, there are three opinions. (214–15)

In his novel, *In the Beginning*, Chaim Potok describes how young
David Lurie first learns from his teacher, Mr. Bader, how to read *Mikraot
Gedolot.*

I opened my *Mikraot Gedolot* and reread the Rashi commentary on
the first word of the Hebrew Bible, *bereshit*, "in the beginning."
Then I reread the Ramban, another commentary. "Listen to how
they talk to one another, David," Mr. Bader had said to me the
week before in his study. "Look at how the different parts of the
page are arranged and you'll understand how Jews have been talking to each other for two thousand years about the Bible. . . . You'll
learn to listen to their voices, David. You'll listen to the way they
talk to each other on the page. You'll hear them agreeing and dis-
agreeing with each other. Sometimes the Ramban gets very nasty
when he disagrees with Ibn Ezra. At times he disagrees strongly
with Rashi." (249-50)

David immerses himself in *Mikraot Gedolot*, and he experiences the
biblical text in a new way.

I shuttled back and forth between ancient Palestine and medieval
France, Spain, Portugal, and Italy. I listened to them talking to one
another about the words of the Torah. . . . Through their voices,
the text of the Torah took on a luminous quality. (256)

Yet, David eventually finds that he must enter into the discussion himself and offer his own answers. He does not become a scholar of rabbinic
commentary on the Bible, but a true biblical scholar. Still, he never leaves
the conversation—that would be to leave Judaism.

Thus, *Mikraot Gedolot* functioned for centuries as the authorized Jewish study Bible, presenting traditional Jewish interpretation and defining
the issues that were important in the text. However, unlike most modern
study Bibles, it did not present one view of the text, but several divergent
views. The reader was summoned to make choices among possible interpretations. In this way, the reader learned that the text was not simple and self-

evident in its meaning. Also, the way was implicitly left open for new read-ings of the text. This approach to the study of Scripture is of crucial impor-tance for us as Messianic Jews. If Messianic Judaism is truly Judaism, we must imitate David Lurie: we must offer our own explanations for the diffi-culties posed by the text, explanations that reflect our distinctive Messianic perspective, yet always as our contribution to an ongoing cross-genera-tional conversation.

At the same time, Messianic Jews also share in the heritage of that multi-ethnic people who have been joined to Israel in Messiah. Just as Israel was entrusted with the *Torah* and has carried it through the centuries, so the Messianic community was entrusted with the Apostolic Writings and car-ried it faithfully. We have received these writings through the Messianic community, and are obliged to enter into its conversation about the mean-ing of the person and work of Yeshua for Israel and the Nations. We are not free to ignore or reject with contempt, those fundamental decisions reached in the fourth and fifth centuries regarding Yeshua's identity and its implica-tions for our understanding of the Divinity. We may have concerns with some aspects of the conclusions reached or the language used to express them, but they embody the unified insights and intuitions of the commu-nity which transmitted the Apostolic Writings and the Apostolic Faith to us, and must be treated respectfully, and engaged with seriously.

## The Primacy of Scripture

If the distinction between Scripture and tradition is problematic, it is none-theless necessary. An appreciation for tradition and a serious engagement with it in our reading of Scripture need not imply an obliteration of the line separating biblical tradition from post-biblical tradition or an elevating of the latter above the former. Michael Wyshogrod asserts this point from an Orthodox Jewish perspective:

> The rabbis instituted the reading of the Pentateuch in the syna-gogue and not the reading of a rabbinic interpretation. However important the rabbinic interpretation of scripture is—and it is very important—it is scripture without further interpretation that is read . . . Sometimes we are so eager to validate the divine origin of the oral Torah that we refuse to recognize any difference between the two Torahs. But that is profoundly unrabbinic . . . Many Or-thodox Jews have lost the ability to read a biblical text as it stands, without rabbinic commentary . . . We must be careful not to be-come so anti-Karaitic that we lose direct contact with the text of scripture. (xxii, xxiv)

Just as Scripture shapes our lives at the same time as our life-setting shapes our reading of Scripture, so direct engagement with the biblical text informs our understanding of tradition at the same time as our participation in the tradition informs our reading of the text.

Messianic Jews have an important role to play in the ongoing Jewish and Christian conversations about Scripture. Our sharing in the Jewish conversation affects our reading of the Apostolic Writings in a way that will surprise and enlighten the Christian community. Our commitment to direct and sustained contact with the biblical text can stimulate a move in the wider Jewish community in the direction that Wyshogrod recommends. Our inclusion of the Apostolic Writings within the framework of the sacred writings will make our part in the Jewish conversation a unique one, but it need not remove us from the discussion. Our voice, though long silent, needs to be heard again. It is only by listening to all the voices speaking from the margins of the page that one hears clearly that One Voice at the center of the page, and encounters him anew in the sacred text.

## Questions for Discussion

- What major differences in biblical interpretation have you encountered in religious groups you have been part of? How did participation in the group affect your way of reading the text?
- How has the translation or study Bible you use influenced your understanding of Scripture?
- Have you ever been absolutely convinced that a certain biblical text had a particular meaning, only to change your mind at a later date? If so—what caused you to change your mind? Did the experience of this change alert you to the difficulty in interpreting Scripture, and the potential for diverse interpretations inherent in the text itself?
- How does Jewish tradition resemble a cross-generational conversation? Is it possible for Messianic Jews to enter into that conversation? Is it desirable? If so, what contribution can this movement make to enrich the overall conversation?

## Bibliography

Greenstein, Edward L. "Medieval Bible Commentaries." *Back to the Sources*, Ed. Barry W. Holtz. New York: Touchstone, 1984.

Hart, D.G. "Scriptura without Solace," *First Things* 106 (October 2000): 65.

Potok, Chaim. *In the Beginning*. New York: Knopf, 1985.

Thuesen, Peter J. *In Discordance with the Scriptures: American Protestant Battles over Translating the Bible.* Oxford: Oxford Univ., 1999.

Van Buren, Paul. *A Theology of the Jewish-Christian Reality, Part 1: Discerning the Way.* San Francisco: Harper & Row, 1980.

Wyshogrod, Michael. *The Body of Faith.* Northvale: Jason Aronson, 1996.

✡ ✡ ✡

Mark S. Kinzer, Ph.D., University of Michigan, is Executive Director of Messianic Jewish Theological Institute, a graduate-level training center for Messianic Jewish leaders. He has taught at both the University of Michigan and Michigan State University, and is an adjunct assistant professor of Jewish Studies at Fuller Theological Seminary. He is also the spiritual leader of Congregation Zera Avraham in Ann Arbor, Michigan.

# HALAKHIC RESPONSIBILITY

—Russell Resnik

Josh grew up in an established Messianic synagogue on the east coast where he remained committed through high school. When it was time to go to college, he chose a school near another well-known Messianic synagogue in a neighboring state. Josh's first *Shabbat* at Beth Lo-Shem brought some surprises. Instead of opening with *Ma Tovu*, as was the custom back home, this service began with a greeting and prayer from the rabbi, who ended by asking the congregation to "stand up and praise the Lord." This phrase launched a drum roll and a series of lively tunes. Josh enjoyed the songs, but he was taken aback when the congregation replaced the recitation of the *Sh'ma* with a musical version, complete with drums and dancing, and none of the ceremony to which he was accustomed. Josh's misgivings only increased when the *Torah* was taken out of the ark without the usual blessings and carried among the congregation as the song service continued. At one point the *Torah* was caught in a traffic jam as two lines of dancers converged in front of it. There was plenty of joy at Beth Lo-Shem—but not much *Yiddishkeit* (Jewishness). Josh was determined to remain connected to Messianic Judaism, but he felt edgy and disconnected in this new synagogue. He hoped he would become more relaxed as he tried to accept these new ways of worship.

### The Need for *Halakhah*

Josh's experience highlights one of the prime purposes of *halakhah*—to build and stabilize community. *Halakhah* is the body of rulings derived from the classic rabbinic writings, especially the Talmud. These rulings form not just a shared liturgical tradition, but an entire way of life. As Eliezer Berkovits writes: "Halakha is the bridge over which the Torah moves from the written word into the living deed. Normally, there is a confrontation with the text, which is set, and life, which is forever in motion. . . . Halakha is the application of the Torah to life" (1).

Judaism has always been conveyed through shared traditions shaped by *halakhah*. Without it, we do not have religious community, but as in today's Messianic Judaism, a loose confederation of more-or-less related congregations. If Messianic Judaism is to have integrity as a form of Judaism, it must first take responsibility for developing a halakhic process.

Lisa Schiffman expresses this essential Jewish distinctive in her popular book, *Generation J*:

> If Christianity's message was *Follow your heart*, Judaism's was *Follow the directions*. Jews, however, never follow directions without asking why. They analyze words with the intensity of scientists. They find loopholes in the law, stretch the meaning of a sentence, and spend hours turning over a single Hebraic syllable. They know that Judaism is itself a language. And, like any language, it evolves, fits itself to different pockets of people, and is held up, always, by an undeniable structure. (8–9)

If Judaism is a language, as Schiffman claims, *halakhah* is the evolution by which it "fits itself to different pockets of people." *Halakhah* is essential, not only to build community, but also to any genuine claim to be a Jewish faith expression.

Likewise, the concrete spirituality implied by *halakhah* is essential to Judaism. The *Tanakh* portrays the Almighty as Creator of this world, the God of history who acts within the mundane realm, and calls his followers to do likewise. Thus, Rabbi Joseph B. Soloveitchik writes, "When halakhic man pines for God, he does not venture to rise up to Him, but rather strives to bring down His divine presence into the midst of our concrete world" (45). Far from shrinking from such a spirituality, Messianic Judaism may be its ultimate expression, embracing a Messiah in whom Deity took on our humanity and endured the essence of "our concrete world."

## Limitations of Rabbinic *Halakhah*

Despite the value of *halakhah*, we cannot simply import into Messianic Judaism traditional halakhic content as a whole. Mark Kinzer argues that the ritual provisions of the Mosaic Law "now have a modified purpose, obligatory force, and sanction," and are subordinate to the "weightier matters of *Torah*" (96–97). Furthermore, New Covenant principles "differ substantially from those held within the rabbinic tradition. Therefore, a Messianic Jew who holds them will not be able to offer unqualified submission to rabbinic halacha."

Indeed, "unqualified submission to rabbinic halacha" would violate the very *purpose* of *halakhah*, which is to apply Scripture to a living community in all its specificity and uniqueness. Traditional *halakhah* is flexible, but it cannot accommodate such New Covenant realities as the entry of Gentiles *as* Gentiles into the worshiping community, the universal outpouring of the spirit, or atonement through the blood of Messiah.

Further, rabbinic *halakhah* rests upon an "Oral *Torah*" supposedly given by God on Sinai and interpreted by an unbroken chain of divinely ordained authorities. Thus, the familiar opening of *Pirke Avot* traces the transmission of *Torah* from Moses to the "Men of the Great Assembly" to successive pairs of teachers down to the Mishnaic era in which *Pirke Avot* was written (see Kravitz and Olitzky 1–11). Few Messianic Jews would accept the direct divine inspiration of Oral *Torah* in this sense.

A famous talmudic story found in *Bava Metzia* 59b captures both the strength of traditional *halakhah* and its limitations. Rabbi Eliezer disagrees with the majority of his colleagues on a certain matter, and produces miracles to prove that his opinion is correct. His colleagues are unimpressed. Finally, a voice from heaven declares that whenever Rabbi Eliezer expresses an opinion, the *halakhah* is according to him. Upon hearing the voice, Rabbi Y'hoshua stands up and calls out: "It is not in the heavens." The Talmud interprets these words as meaning: "The Torah has already been given us from Sinai. We are not to listen to a heavenly voice [i.e., in matters of halakhic decision]. For Thou hast already written for us at Sinai to make decisions in accordance with the opinion of the majority" (see Berkovits 47–48).

This corporate responsibility for applying *Torah* to life would help build a healthy Messianic Judaism. The day of each man doing "what is right in his own eyes," even if allegedly under the prompting of the Holy Spirit, must give way to deference and communal decision making. We must no longer avoid tough decisions by reference to "waiting on the Lord" or "letting the Spirit lead." We cannot build community if we are unwilling to shoulder the shared responsibility for the guidance of community.

"It is not in the heavens," however, goes too far for Messianic Judaism. We can imagine cases in which one leader would be justified on the authority of Scripture in standing against the majority. This is obviously a prophetic act. For Messianic Judaism, the prophetic does not supersede *halakhah*, but it must inform it. Thus, in a Messianic Jewish version of the story above, the heavenly voice would be welcomed, not necessarily to override the entire discussion, but certainly to reopen it on a new basis. Messianic Judaism must take responsibility not only for forming *halakhah*, but also for forming a *halakhah* that is faithful to the genius of the New Covenant.

## A Model for Messianic Jewish *Halakhah*

Messianic Judaism could posit a pre-halakhic Judaism as its model—which may be what those among us who speak of "biblical Judaism" have in mind. However, such a model would disregard both the living continuity of the Jewish people in the post-biblical era when *halakhah* became a dominant force, and the power of *halakhah* for building genuine community today. Acceptance of *halakhah* in some form is essential for our transformation from a religious movement to an enduring religious community. In rabbinic thinking, *halakhah* implies not only specific content, but also the process of developing that content. Thus, Avi Shafran writes, " . . . for those who accept Judaism's millennia-old conviction that the Torah and the key to its understanding, the Oral Law, are of divine origin, there are clear rules (part of the Oral Law itself) for applying halachic principles to new situations" (54). Our challenge is to create a halakhic process that respectfully departs from the traditional rabbinic foundation as necessary to accommodate the realities of the New Covenant.

The Apostolic Writings provide a model for such a process. We will briefly consider Yeshua's discussion of marriage in Matthew 19:3–8 and *Sha'ul*'s development of it in 1 Corinthians 7 as an example.

> Some *P'rushim* [Pharisees] came and tried to trap him by asking, "Is it permitted for a man to divorce his wife on any ground whatever?" He replied, "Haven't you read that at the beginning the Creator made them male and female, and that he said, 'For this reason a man should leave his father and mother and be united with his wife, and the two are to become one flesh?' Thus they are no longer two, but one. So then, no one should split apart what God has joined together." They said to him, "Then why did Moshe give the commandment that a man should hand his wife a *get* and divorce her?" He answered, "Moshe allowed you to divorce your wives because your hearts are so hardened. But this is not how it was at the beginning." (CJB)

Yeshua bases his ruling, which is radical for his time, on the specific wording of a passage of *Torah*. This is typical halakhic discourse—to discover evidence within the text itself to substantiate a ruling, even one that might appear unconventional. In typical halakhic fashion, Yeshua rules to protect the weaker party, the wives. Later, other rabbis also sought within the text of *Torah*, or at least in constant reference to it, for ways to protect women within the institution of marriage.

A superficial reading of *Torah* appears to grant the husband an unrestricted right of divorce, provided only that he "give a certificate a divorce." Yeshua's more holistic reading provides protection for the wife. He does not set aside the Mosaic ordinance, as some interpreters claim, but takes the responsibility implied in "It is not in the heavens" to apply *Torah* humanely to real-life conditions. As Berkovits explains, " . . . in case of a conflict between a specific law and another supervening concern of the Torah, one does the will of God by eliminating the specific law in the case at hand" (78). In other words, Yeshua "eliminates"—or rather, limits—the law of Deuteronomy 24 to support the "supervening concern of the Torah" for the inviolability of marriage.

Berkovits goes on, however, to provide a contrast with Yeshua. "However, interpreting and deciding in all these matters has been entrusted to the *Rabbanan*, the sages of Israel." We might well argue that Yeshua is the greatest of the "sages of Israel," but he is not recognized as such by most of Israel, and he does not always function in concert with the recognized sages. Indeed, Jacob Neusner points out that Yeshua deliberately teaches on his own authority, not on the authority of the unbroken chain of halakhic discussion that preceded him (18–36). He claims, "at many points in this protracted account of Jesus' specific teachings, we now recognize that at issue is the figure of Jesus, not the teachings at all" (31). No matter how many similarities we may trace between Yeshua and traditional *halakhah*, there will always be this contrast over the issue of authority. Yeshua places himself as the final authority. Nevertheless, he handles Scripture with the same creative flexibility as the best traditional *halakhah*, a flexibility intended to preserve the deeper principles of Scripture.

*Sha'ul* continues the discussion of divorce in 1 Corinthians 7:12–15.

> To the rest I say—I, not the Lord: if any brother has a wife who is not a believer, and she is satisfied to go on living with him, he should not leave her. Also, if any woman has an unbelieving husband who is satisfied to go on living with her, she is not to leave him. For the unbelieving husband has been set aside for God by the wife, and the unbelieving wife has been set aside for God by the brother—otherwise your children would be "unclean," but as it is, they are set aside for God. But if the unbelieving spouse separates himself, let him be separated. In circumstances like these, the brother or sister is not enslaved—God has called you to a life of peace. (CJB)

*Sha'ul*'s bold statement in verse 12, "to the rest I say—I, not the Lord . . . " is a clear application of "It is not in the heavens." He takes responsibility for dealing with the difficult ramifications of Yeshua's teaching. In typical halakhic fashion, he rules to uphold *shalom bayit*, the peace of the household. Verse 14 is also typical in its use of a broad *Torah* principle (children are a fulfillment of God's holy purpose) to address the more specific question of the holiness of a marriage with an unbeliever. Finally, in verse 15, *Sha'ul* protects the more vulnerable party, the abandoned believing partner, who is "called . . . to a life of peace." The implications of this "peace" remain controversial, but the point is that *halakhah* works to preserve peace, even within difficult and complex situations.

On the other hand, in contrast with traditional *halakhah*, *Sha'ul*, like Yeshua, invokes his own authority rather than the authority of a pre-existing majority opinion. This distinction underscores a unique feature of Messianic Judaism—its recognition of the abundant presence of the Holy Spirit in this age and the ability of spirit-empowered individuals to speak directly for God. Some would argue that such ability rested solely with Messiah and the original apostles, but the contrast with more traditional forms of Judaism remains.

## Conditions for *Halakhah*

These examples help us to identify conditions that are needed for the development of a halakhic process within Messianic Judaism:

1. *Build Messianic Judaism as a Jewish movement for Yeshua rather than a church movement for Jewish roots.*

Such a movement will naturally remain deeply connected with Jewish tradition and perspectives, but it will be firmly centered on Yeshua as Messiah. John Fischer portrays this balance well:

> The focus of Messianic Judaism *must* remain squarely on Yeshua, but this does not mean setting aside the traditions. Further, the traditions are *not* authoritative, *only* the Bible is. Nor are we under "the authority" of the Rabbis; we are under Yeshua's authority! However, the prayers and teachings of the Rabbis are valid and helpful as they reflect and do not contradict Scripture. In fact, rather than obstacles, the halachic traditions serve as rich and meaningful pointers to, and reinforcers of, Yeshua! (79)

2. *Couple a high view of Scripture with a realistic sense of the needs of contemporary life.*

Yeshua and *Sha'ul* demonstrate this essential balance. *Halakhah* requires leaders who take responsibility to guide the life of the community in all its concreteness and complexity according to the principles of Scripture. *Halakhah* differs from fundamentalism in avoiding a simplistic reading of the text that would preserve dogma at the expense of the weightier matters of *Torah* or the peace of the community.

3. *Provide structures for halakhic discussion.*

Rob Berkowitz, in his article "A Model for Messianic Jewish Halacha," develops "one possible scenario for the process of elaborating *halakhah* within the Union of Messianic Jewish Congregations" (46). This worthwhile scenario involves a *halakhah* committee that interacts with discussion groups within individual congregations. The process properly focuses on discussion and consensus building rather than codification. Berkowitz concludes his article, "If we set our goal for a codified halacha far into the future, and focus for now on the benefits we can garner from the process itself, we may well become a better educated movement with more consistent practices."

Another structure would be informal discussion among like-minded leaders seeking to resolve real problems within their congregations. Again, the goal would be discussion and consensus rather than codification.

4. *Ask the right questions.*

Halakhic process will be strongest as it responds to real questions that arise within Messianic congregations. Therefore, Messianic Jews need to begin asking the sort of questions that lead to *halakhah*. This questioning in turn requires a greater earnestness to apply *Torah* to the specifics of life. Structures for halakhic discussion already exist, such *as Kesher: A Journal of Messianic Judaism*, which devoted an entire issue to *halakhah*, or the UMJC leaders' e-mail listserve, which has been a forum for extended halakhic discussions. The UMJC Judicial Board is authorized to issue advisory opinions, which could provide a precedent and basis for further halakhic discussion. These structures have not reached their potential, however, because they are generally not responding to specific, real-life questions. This element is essential.

5. *Be willing to defer for the sake of common practice between congregations.*

Perhaps, if Messianic leaders take responsibility for building a more consistent multi-congregational community, members will take responsibility to live according to the values of this larger community. Then the right questions *will* arise and the halakhic process will go forward.

## To the Future

May the leaders of Josh's two synagogues agree on the need to create a multi-congregational community for Josh and others like him. May these leaders have the wisdom to address their differences in a halakhic process.

And may they practice the deference required to make *halakhah* a living reality.

## Questions for Discsussion

- What is *halakhah*? Provide a brief definition of one or two sentences.
- What features of the New Covenant point beyond traditional rabbinic *halakhah*?
- What is the significance of the phrase "It is not in the heavens!" to our discussion of *halakhah*, especially the title "Halakhic Responsibility"?
- What are some ways in which the rulings of Yeshua and *Sha'ul* typify halakhic process? How do they differ from more traditional *halakhah*?

## Bibliography

Berkovits, Eliezer. *Not In Heaven: The Nature and Function of Halakha.* New York: Ktav, 1983.

Berkowitz, Rob. "A Model for Messianic Jewish Halacha." *Kesher: A Journal of Messianic Judaism* 5 (Summer 1997): 42–29.

Fischer, John. "Would Yeshua Support Halacha?" *Kesher: A Journal of Messianic Judaism* 5 (Summer 1997): 51–80.

Kinzer, Mark Kinzer. "Forum: Authority Old and New" *Kesher: A Journal of Messianic Judaism* 5 (Summer 1997): 96–116.

Kravitz, Leonard and Kerry M. Olitzky, eds. and trans. *Pirke Avot: A Modern Commentary on Jewish Ethics.* New York: UAHC, 1993.

Neusner, Jacob. *A Rabbi Talks with Jesus: An Intermillennial, Interfaith Exchange.* New York: Doubleday, 1993.

Schiffman, Lisa. *Generation J.* San Francisco: Harper, 1999.

Shafran, Avi. "The Conservative Lie." *Moment* (February 2001): 52–54.

Soloveitchik, Rabbi Joseph B. *Halakhic Man.* New York: Jewish Publication Society, 1991.

✡ ✡ ✡

Russell Resnik serves as General Secretary of the Union of Messianic Jewish Congregations and leader of Adat Yeshua Messianic Synagogue in Albuquerque, New Mexico. Ordained through the UMJC, he also maintains credentials as a clinical mental health counselor. Russ is a frequent contributor to Messianic Jewish periodicals and the author of *The Root and the Branches: Jewish Identity in Messiah*, and *Gateways to Torah: Joining the Ancient Conversation on the Weekly Portion.*

# MESSIANIC JEWS SHOULD ATTEND MESSIANIC JEWISH SYNAGOGUES

—Bruce L. Cohen

> They have been told of you that you teach all the Jews who are among the nations to *forsake Moses*, saying that they ought not to *circumcise* their children, nor to walk after the *customs* . . . do therefore what we say . . . then all will know that these rumors about you are nothing, but that you yourself still walk in order, observing the *Torah*. (Acts 21:21, 24, author's translation, emphasis added)

This essay advocates that Messianic Jews should attend Messianic Jewish synagogues rather than churches. We shall primarily be exploring, in Scripture, the premise that New Testament faith neither models nor advocates Messianic Jews abandoning *circumcision* of sons, the *Torah of Moses*, or the *customs* of our Forefathers. Such Scriptures form the best possible foundation for choosing where Messianic Jews should worship, because the life of practices they describe can most successfully be lived in a synagogue context.

Our twenty-century *Galut* (Dispersion) among the nations complicates developing an answer to this question, because an authoritative response must be faithful to Scripture (Isa. 8:20), and Scripture does not view the question as we presently might. The Jewish world today is very different from that of Yeshua's *sh'lichim* in the first century. Our long exile from our Homeland has bereaved many of our people of a national or racial sense of self. It is possible for a Jew in today's world to be without any personal history of Jewish identity or experience of life in Jewish context; however, neither testament of Scripture looks at a Jewish person as culturally or religiously neutral.

The question posed by Scripture (Matt. 5:17–19; Acts 15:1–19; 21:18-25) is not whether a Jew should *take on* Jewish practices like circumcision, the *Torah* and Jewish custom. Scripture assumes those practices already exist in the life of any Jew, and addresses whether Messianic Judaism teaches that a Jew who becomes a follower of Yeshua should *abandon* (*apostasia*) the three-fold inventory or practices mentioned above. Retention of Jewish identity and practice is seen by Scripture as a given, and that understanding is vital to addressing the issue of where Messianic Jews should attend worship.

Let us further remember the false rumor addressed in Acts 21 was that faith in Yeshua of Nazareth as Messiah *teaches Jews to forsake* the three-fold inventory of Jewish practices described above. That false rumor is still so rampant in the Jewish world that even the Israeli Supreme Court repeats it as if it is true. Justice Menachem Elon wrote in 1989, "It was rejection of all authority to the *Torah* . . . which placed [New Testament faith] outside the bounds of Judaism. Here was the fork in the road" (Stern 21). Yet, Yeshua's *sh'lichim* promptly labeled this rumor *false* the moment it surfaced, and called it "*nothing.*"

We should treat it way! My view of where Messianic Jews should make their primary spiritual communities embarks from the idea that the scripturally *normal* condition of a Jewish believer is a life containing circumcision of sons, the *Torah* of Moses and the customs of the Jewish people (Acts 21:24).

Note that the above applies as an incumbent responsibility to *Jewish* believers only. Moreover, it is not a *salvation* necessity (Matt. 5:19). Jews and non-Jews all come to salvation—the rescue of our spirit from eternal death—the exact same way (Gal. 3:28). Yet, all that are saved do not *walk* exactly the same way *after receiving* salvation. There are differing New Testament instructions to all the Galatians 3:28 groups: men and women (Eph. 5:22–28), masters and servants (Col. 3:22–4:1), Jews and non-Jews (Acts 21:24–25).

Reinforcing this reality, after Scripture tells us what "walking in order" is for a Jewish believer (Acts 21:21–24), the very next verse (21:25) goes on to state:

> "But concerning the Gentiles (non-Jews) who believe, we have written and decided that they should observe *no such thing*, except that they should keep themselves from things offered to idols, from blood, from things strangled, and from sexual immorality." (Acts 21:25 NKJV, emphasis added)

"No such thing?" What *thing* is Scripture saying is not incumbent upon non-Jews? Adherence to circumcision, *Torah* and Jewish custom, as is incumbent upon Messianic *Jews*. Non-Jewish believers have been free to develop worship within the context of their own national cultures, and they have done so (Romans 14:5). This freedom has given rise to what we now see as the multi-cultural "church." The other nation-groups coming to faith in the one True God and His Messiah have chosen their own days for worship (predominantly the first day of the week), and they have developed their own particular holidays, customs and rites for worship. Scripture accorded them these rights, and firmly removed Jewish practice as a necessity for non-Jews.

However, such churches are not culturally *neutral*. They only *seem* that way to their inhabitants for the same reason cool, dry air feels "normal" to someone from Russia, and warm, humid air feels normal to someone from the Caribbean. An American church is not a neutral assembly of the "one new man" (Eph. 2:15)—it is an American assembly. A French church is French. A Korean church is Korean. Churches are reflective of the customs and cultures they inhabit. What are Jewish spiritual assemblies by custom and culture?

They are synagogues. The Greek word *sunagogi* is used abundantly throughout the New Testament as the word referring to a Jewish house of worship. By the New Testament era, it is well-established historically that Jewish people gathered together in local *synagogues* for several socio-religious purposes, including the public reading of the *Torah* and study of the commandments (see Levine 54–55). Of Yeshua himself, the New Testament tells us, "And as His *custom* was, He went into the *synagogue* on the *Sabbath* day, and stood up to read" (Luke 4:16 NKJV, emphasis added).

Hebrews 10:25 commands Messianic Jews to a life "not forsaking the synagoguing *(episunagogeen)* of yourselves together, as is the habit of some" (author's translation). There are several other Greek words for assembling, collecting, and gathering, but it seems the writer of Hebrews was deliberate about his vocabulary concerning what Jewish believers should not forsake. The tone of the words "as is the habit of some" makes it clear that the writer disapproves of Jewish believers drifting away from the "synagoguing" of ourselves. It is incumbent upon us (Messianic Jews) to worship in a *synagoguing of ourselves*, when possible.

Why do I say "when possible?" During the last eighteen centuries, for Messianic Jews, a church was usually the only faith community available. As famed screenwriter William Goldman put it in *The Lion in Winter*, "There's no point questioning the air when it's all there is to breathe." While there are still regions in which it is difficult to find suitable Messianic synagogues, the earlier restricted zone of choices is no longer so dominant. The landscape of history has changed, and with it, our imperatives have changed as well. Yet, it must be recognized that we are presently in a transitional season of history, and transitions deserve respect. Many of the Messianic pioneers of the last century started their journeys from within church theologies. They had an entrenched view of Jewish culture as *antithetical to New Testament grace*. The fact that Messianic Jews in meaningful numbers were able to retrieve any substantial reconnection to our Jewish cultural and faith roots at all, from 1880 to the present, is a miracle of upstream swimming. It should be acknowledged as such—even as we labor in order that the vision the modern pioneers began may mature.

Jewish people in our present era become churchgoers either because (1) they *want* to disengage themselves from Jewish identification for some personal reason, or (2) they have been *taught that they should* on some theological basis.

The former experiential reason is readily understandable concerning abuse survivors in this post-Holocaust, post-pogrom era. The roots of the latter theological reason go back nearly eighteen centuries into the era that led fourth century Christendom to make a deliberate separation of Two-Testament faith from its Jewish source. A fourth century Jew believing in Yeshua was required to make the following oath:

> "I renounce all customs, rites . . . and all other feasts of the Hebrews . . . all Sabbaths . . . hymns and chants and observances and synagogues, and the food and drink of the Hebrews; in one word, I renounce absolutely everything Jewish, every law, rite and custom" (Cohn-Sherbok 6).

Later seasons of church history were equally anti-Jewish. Such was the case when Luther advocated the eradication of all evidence of Jewish national existence (Nicholls 270-271). The wake of this scripturally unfounded de-Judaization has rippled out into the present day. This idea would have horrified Yeshua of Nazareth and Rabbi Saul of Tarshish.

I am not alone in this view. Influential historian William Nicholls recently wrote, "Historical scholarship now permits us to affirm with confidence that Jesus of Nazareth was a faithful and observant Jew, who lived by the Torah, and taught nothing against his own people and their faith" (xxvi). Among scholars of "the historical Jesus," we find similar views of first-century Messianism's message, ". . . to Israel precisely as prophets working *within* and for Israel. This prophetic critique of *Israeli-within-Israel* will take on an entirely different meaning when the early church uses it in its *debates with Israel* as a justification for *separation from Israel*" (Meier 29, emphasis added). The contra-Judaic diatribes of early "church fathers" like John Chrysostom right through to later authorities, advocated that Jewish believers in Yeshua should abandon every iota Jewish life (Nicholls 221). Such an idea would have been *unrecognizable* to the same Yeshua and Paul the church fathers claimed to be representing.

Yeshua commanded us not even to *think* his coming meant diminishment of the *Torah* of Israel, and he never envisioned the creation of a new religion (Matt. 5:17–19, 23:2–3). *Rav Sha'ul* and the rest of the *sh'lichim* merely sought the establishment of an inclusive faith context for non-Jews that did not deprive them of their individual non-Jewish national uniqueness (Acts 15:19, 21:25, Eph. 3:14–15). The idea of a Jew singing the Doxology rather than the *Sh'ma* was not their plan. *Rav Sha'ul* stated bluntly, "I am indeed a Jew" (Acts 22:3 NKJV). Please notice that Paul did not say, "I *was* a Jew." He said further, "I have done nothing against our [the Jewish] people or the customs of our fathers" (Acts 28:17 NKJV). This is a far different theology than that of the fourth century enforced oath of departure demanded of Jewish "converts" to Christianity, as quoted earlier.

Also crucial to the decision Messianic Jews make about where to make their spiritual home are the Scriptures stating that Jewish national identity will either cease or be irrelevant *only* when the physical laws of universal gravitation cease.

> Thus says the LORD, Who gives the sun for a light by day, The ordinances of the moon and the stars for a light by night, Who disturbs the sea, And its waves roar (The LORD of Hosts is His Name): "If those ordinances depart from before Me," says the LORD, "Then the seed of Israel also shall cease from being a nation before me forever." Thus says the LORD: "If heaven above can be measured, and the foundations of the earth searched out beneath, I will also cast off all the seed of Israel for all that they have done," says the LORD. (Jer. 31:35–37 NKJV)

As to whether God would ever cast Israel aside for our sins and replace us with another more favored group called "The Church" (the bedrock position of "Replacement Theology"), the above passage of Scripture states that this could only occur if mankind could measure the universe exactly on the macro-scale (above) or the micro-scale (beneath). Since physicist Werner Heisenberg's "Uncertainty Principle" has fairly well established we will *never* be able to measure the sub-atomic realm accurately; and since the universe itself is of such magnitude that to inventory its *exact* dimensions and *total* contents seems eternally unachievable; it seems any "replacement" theology lacks biblical basis.

Unfathomably, however, a supersessionist view of "The Church over Israel" forms a major part of the justification for some Yeshua-believing Jews to choose church going. Strong voices such as John Chrysostom's directly contrast Jewishness against New Testament faith. Chrysostom is hailed into the modern era as one of the best voices of Christian doctrine, and yet he said, "Don't you realize, if Jewish rites are holy and venerable, our way of life must be false?" (Nicholls 271). Chrysostom advocates *departure from Jewish customary practice*. By so doing, he contradicts the direct prescription of Scripture for Jewish believers.

Examination of customary faith practices is how the need for Messianic Jews to attend Messianic synagogues becomes most apparent. Yeshua of Nazareth spoke of Jewish practice of *Torah* as follows:

> Do not think that I have come to destroy the *Torah*, or the Prophets. I have not come to destroy, but to fulfill. For truly I say to you, *until heaven and earth* pass, *not one yod or one stroke shall in any manner pass from the Torah,* until all is fulfilled. Whoever therefore *breaks one of the least of these commandments, and teaches other men so,* he shall be called the least in the kingdom of heaven; but *whoever does and teaches them,* he shall be called great in the kingdom of heaven. (Matt. 5:17–19 NKJV, with modifications and emphasis)

This passage is about *practice* and the *teaching of practice*. Is it not fascinating that Yeshua cited Jeremiah's same *physical* timepieces when explaining the relevance of the *Torah* for Jewish believers in light of his redemptive mission? Upon the above basis, in light of Jeremiah 31:35–37, the idea that God is somehow either pleased by (or indifferent to) abandonment of Jewish identity or *Torah* observance seems biblically untenable.

Yet, this is exactly where synagogue life shines. Synagogues convene for worship on the day of *Shabbat* because the *Torah commands Israel* to have a holy convocation on that day, (Lev. 23:3). Thus, a synagogue attending Messianic Jew dwells in and broadcasts Jewish perpetuity by his worship attendance habits. Church going has the opposite effect. Jews, by custom, study the Scriptures in our holy convocations in the context of the *Torah* and *Haftarah* ceremonies, with the traditional blessings of the *Torah* forming the setting in which the jewel of the *Torah* rests. Church services do not practice these customs, nor must they (Acts 15:19; 21:25). We have not even included life-cycle events such as circumcisions, *b'nai mitzvah* ceremonies, and marriages.

Scripture benignly assumes the presence and availability of synagogue practice for whoever wants it (Acts 15:21). It is not condemned or tagged for avoidance. For Jews, there are synagogues. For Messianic Jews, there is the "synagoguing of yourselves together" (Heb. 10:25). These places of assembly are now known as Messianic synagogues.

God speaks of the season of spiritual return in which we are living: "And I will put My Spirit within you, and cause you to walk in My statutes (*hukai*), and you will keep My judgments (*mishpatai*), and do *them* (Ezek. 36:27 KJV)." The *hukim* and the *mishpatim* are the Hebrew words for the ceremonial, and national incumbencies upon Israel such as Passover (Exod.

12:14), *Yom Kippur* (Lev. 16:31), the social laws of Leviticus 18, and the entire body of Law conveyed at Sinai (Lev. 26:46). The passage does not merely use the generic Hebrew word *Torah* (instruction) that has been held forth by some supersessionist theologians as "The Law of Messiah"—a *Torah*/Law supposedly different from and superseding the Law of Moses (see Fruchtenbaum 649-657).

We will not just be *generically Messianic* (Acts 21:25). We will be Messianic *Jews* (Acts 21:24).

This is not to say that we Messianic believers swallow all historic Jewish precepts or talmudic culture wholesale. I believe Messianism has as much to teach by what it rejects as by what it affirms. The practical core of talmudic Judaism is the *S'yag l'Torah* (fence around the *Torah*) philosophy, by which the "fence" of man-made commandments has been erected to keep us distant enough from the biblical commandments to prevent their breakage (*Avoth* 1:1; 6–7). This and many other arenas of Jewish faith will be undergoing *takkanah* (doctrinal revision) among all segments of Jewry as the Messianic movement makes more inroads into Jewish conversation across time. Yeshua modeled this kind of healthy reevaluation for us (Mark 7:1–25). So long as the standard we hold is faithful to the letter and spirit of Scripture (Deut. 18:21–22, Isa. 8:20), we shall do well.

May the Holy One of Israel do as He sees fit among us, in His own good time.

## Questions for Discussion

- What Scriptures speak directly to the question of Jewish practice being retained by Jewish believers in Yeshua?
- What early church father spoke strongly against Messianic Jewish retention of Jewish customs and rites, and what did he say?
- What customs in the Jewish life cycle would Jewish churchgoers find difficult to practice in a church setting?
- Is there any Scripture indicating that Yeshua or Paul ever broke with a *Torah* commandment, or established Jewish custom? If so, where and under what circumstances?

## Bibliography

Blackman, Philip, ed. *Mishnayot*. New York: Judaica, 1983.
Cohn-Sherbok, Dan. *Messianic Judaism*. London: Cassel, 2000
Fruchtenbaum, Arnold. *Israelology*, Tustin: Ariel, 1992.
*Hebrew Old & New Testaments*, Jerusalem: Bible Society in Israel, 1991.

Kittel, Rudolf, ed. *Biblia Hebraica Stuttgartensia,* Stuttgart: Deutsche Bibelgesellschaft, 1977.

Levine, Lee I. *The Ancient Synagogue,* New Haven: Yale, 2000.

Meier, John P. *A Marginal Jew: Rethinking the Historical Jesus.* New York: Anchor, 1994. Nestle, Erwin, Eberhard Nestle, Kurt Aland, and Barbara Aland, eds. *Greek-English New Testament,* Stuttgart: Deutsche Bibelgesellschaft, 1981.

Nicholls, William *Christian Antisemitism: A History of Hate,* Northvale: Jason Aronson, 1993.

Stern, David H. *The Beresford Case Judgment: Unofficial Translation,* Jerusalem, 1990.

*The Lion in Winter.* Dir. Anthony Harvey. Acvo Embassy, 1968.

Bruce L. Cohen is founding rabbi of Congregation Beth El of Manhattan. In Messianic ministry since the 1970s, he has served as principal and teacher in a Messianic day school, and director and teacher of synagogue *yeshiva* and *b'nai mitzvah* programs. Rabbi Cohen has also been the Development Chairman for the Messianic Jewish Alliance of America and a composer/producer for the *Kol Simcha* musical ensemble. He and his wife, Debra, have two sons.

# MESSIANIC JEWS MAY JOIN BIBLE-BELIEVING CHURCHES

—Jim Sibley

The pastor of a new Baptist congregation in a northern city called my office with a request for assistance. A Messianic congregation in the area had split over significant doctrinal error. A substantial segment had left the congregation and for weeks had been meeting in homes for Bible study and prayer. None, however, felt qualified or gifted for leadership, and thus they were exploring their options. Finally, they had decided to join this young church. The pastor told me that this decision had awakened his church to the needs of the substantial Jewish population in the area. He also realized his own lack of preparation to minister effectively to his new, Messianic Jewish members.

In the weeks that followed, I had the opportunity both to encourage the Jewish believers and to offer training to the pastor and his congregation. This body of believers eventually decided that they should launch a Messianic fellowship within the church. The Gentile believers were instructed about the Jewish roots of their faith, and the fellowship afforded an opportunity for the Jewish believers to maintain and to deepen their own Jewish identity and heritage. They also received solid Bible teaching and demonstrated the unity of Jewish and Gentile believers in Messiah.

The rise of the Messianic congregational movement in the last half of the twentieth century has afforded Jewish believers an unprecedented choice. In many cases, Messianic congregations are a viable alternative to membership in denominational churches. In the future, these congregations will doubtless multiply and mature. At present, however, the decision can be agonizing for some. The fact of the matter is that the vast majority of Jews who believe in Yeshua are members of culturally Gentile churches. I recently heard that there were more Jewish believers at Willow Creek Community Church, alone, than the combined Jewish membership of all the

Messianic congregations in the Chicago area. Whether this is actually the case or not, the larger point is hardly to be argued.

In the first century, the question was, "Can a Gentile believe in Yeshua without first becoming Jewish?" More recently, the question is, "Can a Jew believe in Jesus and still be Jewish?" However, in Messianic Jewish circles, the question seems to be, "Can a Jew go to church and still be Jewish?" Who has the right to determine if the choice to join a local church is "acceptable"? Do the leaders of Messianic organizations or Jewish mission executives or church leadership have the right to decide whether any particular Messianic Jew should join a church or a Messianic congregation? Ultimately, the decision rests with the individual or the family as they prayerfully seek the Lord's direction for their lives. Others are entitled to their opinions, but must trust that God is leading in the lives of his children. The only absolute and objective standard of "acceptability" is the Word of God.

I write as one who has both planted and led Messianic congregations in Israel and who enthusiastically affirms the value of biblically sound, culturally Jewish congregations. Yet, too often, one may see the very attitudes of spiritual pride on the part of Messianic Jews that have characterized—and all too often still characterize—the predominantly Gentile Church throughout most of its history. Because Christendom has excluded and persecuted Jewish people throughout most of its history, it is understandable that some Jewish believers would want to move away from the Church and to focus exclusively on the development of Messianic Judaism. Sometimes, predictably, one encounters Church-bashing in Messianic circles. Sometimes there are partisans in Messianic congregations who sneeringly refer to any Jewish member of a church as a "Hebrew Christian," in an effort to disenfranchise such a person of his or her Jewishness. We must remember the words of *Ya'akov*, leader of the first Messianic congregation when he said:

> Do not speak against one another, brethren. He who speaks against a brother, or judges his brother, speaks against the law, and judges the law; but if you judge the law, you are not a doer of the law, but a judge of it. (James 4:11)

This admonition should serve as a reminder that all must take pains to speak and act out of humility and the awareness that we cannot claim any credit either for our ethnicity, which we received through our parents, or our salvation, which has been received as a gift.

## A Biblical Perspective

Ethnically, there are only two categories in the Scriptures: Jew and Gentile. Culturally, all Gentiles, whether French, Chinese, African, or Latin American, share something in common—their cultures are not Jewish. This is not just an ethno-centric inanity, for of all nations, God has chosen Israel alone:

> For you are a holy people to the LORD your God; the LORD your God has chosen you to be a people for His own possession out of all the peoples who are on the face of the earth. (Deut. 7:6)

God has said that through Israel he would bless all nations:

> Now the LORD said to Abram, "Go forth from your father's country, and from your relatives and from your father's house, to the land which I will show you; and I will make you a great nation, and I will bless you, and make your name great; and so you shall be a blessing; and I will bless those who bless you, and the one who curses you I will curse. And in you all the families of the earth shall be blessed." (Gen. 12:1–3)

This blessing would come pre-eminently through Israel's Messiah and the New Covenant that he would initiate with the remnant of Israel. This was prophesied in Jeremiah:

> "Behold, days are coming," declares the LORD, "when I will make a new covenant with the house of Israel and with the house of Judah, not like the covenant which I made with their fathers in the day I took them by the hand to bring them out of the land of Egypt, My covenant which they broke, although I was a husband to them," declares the LORD. (Jer. 31:31–32)

Jeremiah's prophecy was fulfilled symbolically in the Last Supper that Yeshua shared with his disciples (as representatives of the remnant of Israel) and ultimately in the death of Messiah: "And in the same way He took the cup after they had eaten, saying, "This cup which is poured out for you is the new covenant in My blood" (Luke 22:20).

At the first Shavu'ot following the resurrection of Messiah, this New Covenant community would be empowered by the Holy Spirit (Acts 2) and Messiah would begin to build an entirely new entity (Matt. 16:18), a people comprised of both the remnant of Israel together with Gentiles who would place their faith in Messiah for the atonement of sin. This new entity is thus a composite unity comprised of the remnant of Israel, together with Gentile believers, who have joined themselves to the God of Israel, through the death, burial, and resurrection of Messiah.

This is not a unity of uniformity, however, but of diversity. For example, Paul writes, in Eph. 3:4, 6:

And by referring to this, when you read you can understand my insight into the mystery of Messiah, . . . *to be specific*, that the Gentiles are fellow heirs and fellow members of the body, and fellow partakers of the promise in Messiah Yeshua through the gospel. (cf. Rom. 11:17–24; Eph. 2:11–22)

God has promised to preserve the remnant of Israel in this unity. Arnold Fruchtenbaum is correct in highlighting the importance of this doctrine by beginning with it in his essay, "Messianic Jews and Their Congregations" (123–124). Paul was insistent, as well:

I say then, God has not rejected His people, has He? May it never be! For I too am an Israelite, a descendant of Abraham, of the tribe of Benjamin. God has not rejected His people whom He foreknew. Or do you not know what the Scripture says in *the passage about* Elijah, how he pleads with God against Israel? "Lord, they have killed Thy prophets, they have torn down Thine altars, and I alone am left, and they are seeking my life." But what is the divine response to him? "I have kept for Myself seven thousand men who have not bowed the knee to Baal." In the same way then, there has also come to be at the present time a remnant according to God's gracious choice. (Rom. 11:1–5, cf. vv. 16–17, 24)

This new unity is one in which he has ordered that no Gentile should become a Jew and that no Jew should become a Gentile.

Was any man called *already* circumcised? Let him not become uncircumcised. Has anyone been called in uncircumcision? Let him not be circumcised. Circumcision is nothing, and uncircumcision is nothing, but *what matters is* the keeping of the commandments of God. Let each man remain in that condition in which he was called. (1 Cor. 7:18–20)

Yet it is a unity—in order that in Yeshua, "He might make the two into one new man" (Eph. 2:15). Here we find not a separate body for each nation and people, not two brothers (one Jewish and the other Gentile). In fact, the New Covenant is replete with passages that speak of the fact that in Messiah, there is no distinction between Jew and Gentile with reference to salvation or fellowship in the Body. For example, Paul says in Gal. 3:27–29:

For all of you who were baptized into Messiah have clothed yourselves with Messiah. There is neither Jew nor Greek, there is neither slave nor free man, there is neither male nor female; for you are all one in Messiah Yeshua. And if you belong to Messiah, then you are Abraham's offspring, heirs according to promise. (cf. Rom. 10:12; Gal. 6:15; and Col. 3:11)

These passages are not saying that these distinctives are no longer present or relevant. There are still instructions in the New Covenant that are addressed specifically to men *as* men and to women *as* women. Likewise, Paul specifically addresses Gentiles in Rom. 11:13, and we have an epistle in the New Covenant addressed to the "Hebrews." These passages are simply saying that the way of salvation is the same for all, and that our differences should not contradict our unity in Messiah. In fact, the Church of the New Covenant was one composed of both Jew and Gentile.

A variety of local congregations are described in the New Covenant. The congregation in Jerusalem was, apparently, fully Jewish with no mention of Gentile members. The congregations in Samaria, as far as we know, were comprised only of Samaritans. There may have been other congregations that did not have any Jewish members. However, if this is so, I am unaware of them. The vast majority of the congregations mentioned in the New Covenant were of mixed (i.e., both Jewish and Gentile) membership.

## A Congregational Perspective

Gentile believers too often want to deny Jewish believers the right to be distinct, and Jewish believers too often want to deny their unity with Gentile believers. In other words, some of the Gentile members are not very happy about including the Jewish members, and some of the Jewish members are equally unhappy about being lumped in with the *Goyim*. How much evidence is required to demonstrate the obvious: That we desperately need each other?

How can this need be met unless there is a vital connection between Messianic Jews and Gentile Christians? If there are deficiencies and misunderstandings in the predominantly Gentile congregations, how will it help to quarantine them from Messianic Jews? Separatism is not the answer. We must not abandon the Church! If one loves Yeshua, he will love the things Yeshua loves. Paul said:

Husbands, love your wives, just as Messiah also loved the Church and gave Himself up for her; that He might sanctify her, having cleansed her by the washing of water with the Word, that He might present to Himself the Church in all her glory, having no spot or wrinkle or any such thing; but that she should be holy and blameless. (Eph. 5:25–27)

Translations are problematic. If you translate *ekklesia* as "Church," it does not sound as though you are referring to Messianic Jews. If you translate it as "Messianic community," it does not sound as though the reference includes the predominantly Gentile Church. But, let there be no misunderstanding. That for which our Messiah died, and that which he loves, includes both Jewish and Gentile believers, in both Jewish and Gentile culture congregations.

Messianic Jewish leaders and authors have made the same point. Jeffrey S. Wasserman, in his book, *Messianic Jewish Congregations: Who Sold This Business to the Gentiles*, quotes Dan Juster and Stuart Dauermann (see 101–103). In *The Nature of Messianic Judaism*, Mark Kinzer provides a different application (see 34–35). Yet, the way forward is not articulated often. The answer lies not in an "either/or" framework, but in "both/and." We must affirm the validity of both Messianic congregations and of the full participation of Jewish believers in churches; of Jewish congregational planters and evangelists in both Jewish and in Gentile contexts. There is a rich heritage of Jewish believers in pioneer work in many countries of the world. Have not the redeemed of Israel been made a "light of the nations so that [His] salvation may reach to the end of the earth" (Isa. 49:6)? Yes, there are times when even "a Hebrew of Hebrews" (Phil. 3:5) needs to become as "those who are without the law . . . that I might win those who are without law" (1 Cor. 9:21).

Another way to approach this separatism would be to imagine the consequences, should this view really prevail. A case could be made that Messianic congregations would become ingrown and fractious; anti-Semitism would be allowed to regain a foothold in the Church; Replacement Theology would be largely unchecked; and Jewish evangelism would drop precipitously. Wasserman says, "Traditional Protestant Evangelical churches have been far more successful in Jewish evangelism than Messianic congregations." He then points out that in Rom. 11:11, "The apostle Paul saw Gentile salvation as God's primary method for Jewish evangelism" (106).

Actually, the neglect of Jewish evangelism, in particular, by all of the major denominations following the Holocaust had the effect of marginalizing Jewish believers and Messianic ministries. The lack of active support from the major denominations gave credence to the charge that it was indeed impossible to be both Jewish and a follower of Yeshua, and those who objected were written off as either deranged or dishonest. Yet, paradoxically, when the major Protestant and evangelical denominations give their support and encouragement to Jewish ministry and to Messianic Jews, not only does the number of Messianic Jews and Messianic congregations increase, but they are seen as more legitimately Jewish.

## The Challenges for the Future

The primary challenge for the future will be to raise up healthy congregations in both Jewish and Gentile cultures that are biblically sound and spiritually vibrant, and that are following the biblical mandate of proclaiming the Good News of Messiah "to the Jew especially and also to the Gentile" (Rom. 1:16, author's translation). These congregations should enthusiastically affirm differing cultural expressions, yet with a focus on the source of our unity—the person and work of Yeshua HaMashiach. He is the essence of Jewishness. He is the crown jewel of the *Torah*. When a believer wants more than Yeshua, he usually gets less, for he is the *Alef* and the *Tav*, the *Alpha* and the *Omega*.

Within churches, ways need to be developed to assist Jewish believers in maintaining their Jewish identity and heritage. Messianic fellowships are part of the solution, but Sunday school literature that emphasizes the Jewishness of our faith would be a welcome addition. Contexts in which Jewish believers could lead their predominantly Gentile churches in celebrating the feasts of Israel and in instructing them in how better to pray for, and reach out to, the non-believing Jewish community are also desperately needed.

Affirming Messianic Jews who choose to join Bible-believing churches enriches the heritage of all Jewish believers. Instead of identifying only with a movement that began to fade from the scene in the second century, Jewish believers can claim a heritage that stretches back two thousand years ("Christianized" Jews who were motivated more by a desire for revenge than sincere faith, such as Nicholas Donin, notwithstanding). They can praise the God of Israel, not only for the preservation of the Jewish people, but also for the preservation of the remnant of Israel throughout history.

*Note: For all quotations of Scripture, I have used the NASB, with two modifications: I have substituted "Messiah" for "Christ" and "Yeshua" for "Jesus."*

## Questions for Discussion

- What additional steps should churches take to assist Jewish members in enhancing their distinctives as Messianic Jews?
- How can informed and sensitive Gentile believers assist Jewish believers in having a voice in churches?
- What biblical passages suggest that witness will be enhanced through a demonstration of the unity between Jewish and Gentile believers in Yeshua?

- How can one legitimately express ethnicity, yet avoid the dangers of ethno-centrism?

## Bibliography

Fruchtenbaum, Arnold. "Messianic Jews and Their Congregations." *Jewish Identity and Faith in Jesus*, Ed. Kai Kjaer-Hansen. Jerusalem: Caspari Center, 1996. 123–135.

Kinzer, Mark. *The Nature of Messianic Judaism.* West Hartford: Hashivenu Archives, 2000.

Wasserman, Jeffrey S. *Messianic Jewish Congregations: Who Sold This Business to the Gentiles?* Lanham: Univ. Press of America, 2000.

✡ ✡ ✡

Jim Sibley is Coordinator of Jewish Ministry for the Southern Baptist North American Mission Board and is based in Dallas, Texas. An SBC representative in Israel for fourteen years, he helped plant two messianic congregations. Jim served on the editorial board of *Mishkan*, and as a member of the International Coordinating Committee of the Lausanne Consultation on Jewish Evangelism. He has taught courses related to Judaism and Jewish Evangelism at SBC seminaries and colleges.

# A REPRESENTATIVE PRESENCE

—Barney Kasdan

As one reflects on the rebirth of Messianic Judaism in recent decades, many observations become apparent, including its statistical growth as well as its qualitative development. Not surprisingly, such growth has also brought several requisite challenges. One of the vital questions confronting us in the 21st century is how will we structure ourselves in the coming decades? This is not a simple question, especially in light of the diversity and independence reflected within the Jewish community. As the story goes, Golda Meir was once meeting with a foreign dignitary who commiserated that he was having a difficult time as the Prime Minister of a country of ten million citizens. To which Golda asked, "How would you like to be the leader of a country that has three million Prime Ministers?" Despite our independent spirit, there has also been a felt need among most Messianic Jews to come together, as illustrated by the various Jewish missions, conferences, and member organizations. What can we learn from history and what might our movement look like in the coming years? I see three key values that help answer these questions: *Representative Presence, Directive Policies, and Interdependent Participation.*

By the first concept, *Representative Presence*, I mean that our movement must hear the collective voice of our members. Certainly, this has long been a cherished value in the Jewish community. As God spoke in the *Torah* concerning the structure of Israel, we see a representative voice for the various classes of society. Necessary lines of communication were established through the heads of families, clans, and tribes. The establishment of the Levites also served this purpose, as they were to be, in this sense, the voice of the people before God. This structure was not fully democratic in essence. However, it was a representative form of government that gave virtually every Israelite a voice in the community. While post-exilic Judaism saw some significant changes in emphasis, this value of representation remained strong, as illustrated in the times of Ezra with the development of the local synagogue and the Great Assembly.

The *B'rit Hadashah* also reflects this value of a Representative Presence as the early believers in Yeshua sought to effectively organize themselves. In his statement, "I will build my *k'hillah*," we should not assume that Yeshua was foreseeing an entirely different structure than the one which he and his Jewish followers would already be familiar with (Matt. 16:18). The earlier models of the Temple and synagogue would most assuredly be the first ideas that would come to mind. This is why one of the tenets of Messianic Judaism is that we are indeed a Judaism which can and should make use of Jewish models when they are consistent with our faith. The record of the larger first century Messianic community also confirms this. *Ya'akov* wrote to the Messianic Jews of the Diaspora, who were meeting in synagogues (see James 1:1; 2:2 CJB). *Sha'ul* has much to say about the structure of the local believers including the need for *z'keynim* to be a representative voice of the congregations (Titus 1:5). Clearly, there were some excesses in later history, most notably in the hierarchical structures of the episcopal/papal models of the church. This was one of the reasons that Luther's Reformation took hold, as a large group of New Testament believers desired a more representative form of government. Much of the modern Protestant movement and the Jewish community still uphold the importance of the voice of the larger community.

Since this theme of Representative Presence is found throughout both the Scriptures and later historical models, in our day, we would do well to consider the implications. Among Jewish believers today, there are organizations ranging from alliances for individual membership (in many countries including Israel) to the para-congregational Jewish missions that are closely connected to Gentile church structures. However, the centralized voice of Messianic Judaism is being clearly heard through the more recently founded organizations for congregations that are based in the U.S.A. Among them, are the IAMCS, which is affiliated with the MJAA, and the UMJC. As the current President of the UMJC, I can speak to the strengths of the latter. One of the main reasons for the formation of the UMJC in 1979 was, in fact, to encourage the value that I call "Representative Presence." The felt need at the time was to provide a voice for the growing number of Messianic synagogues in America and the rest of the world.

One of the differences between the UMJC and the MJAA was the creation of a system of delegates who would represent every member congregation. The UMJC continues to be a delegate-based organization that consequently, provides every full member congregation with an equal voice. This filters down throughout the structure in that every significant policy must be delegate approved. These representatives also have the right to be appointed to the Steering Committee, which directs the various subcommittees of the organization. Likewise, the delegates nominate and elect the Executive Committee that contains the officers of the Union. While there may be different formats of structure (e.g., hierarchical, autonomous, pure democracy, etc.), I believe that the UMJC structure provides a healthy model that is consistent with the principles of *Tanakh* and the modern Jewish community. At first glance, the democratic (majority rules) model appears as a noble alternative, but it is actually the republic/representative form that insures the equal rights of the minority. This representative form, similar to the government of the United States of America, fosters communication as well as a vital system of checks and balances.

As we think about the future of Messianic Judaism, there is a second need to be addressed—a structure that can formulate *Directive Policies*. We should admit that much of the last few decades of our movement have emanated from a quasi "anti-establishment" and free spirit of the 1960s. Many of the current leaders in Messianic Judaism (myself included) came to our faith in Yeshua during this tumultuous time with a strong assist from the "Jesus movement." No doubt, this foundation brought a certain vitality and zeal to our community. However, just now, we are becoming more fully cognizant of our need for concrete directives. At this point, it is informative to note this structural need within Jewish history and to see how it was addressed. In the *Torah*, this need became apparent as Moses sought direction for the newly redeemed nation. While the Levites served a vital religious need in the community, judicial policies were to be formulated through a series of *z'keynim*, *shoftim* (judges), and later, through kings. No one group was to wield an inordinate amount of power as a system of checks was built in. Proper representation was tempered with accountability through such checks and balances. Post-exilic Judaism also exemplified these deeply held values, albeit within the newly developed forms of the local synagogue, local *beyt din*, and the famous Sanhedrin (Supreme Court). All of these served to give direction—with accountability—to the community of Israel. Those of us who are involved in Messianic Judaism would do well to learn the lessons of these historical entities as we seek to guide our contemporary movement.

It is a healthy indicator that the great majority of our contemporary congregations have a system of checks and balances through a plurality of elders. Interestingly, *Sha'ul* notes that many of the Messianic congregations were affiliated together within the various locales (note the plural term "congregations of Galatia" in Galatians 1:2). Likewise, as theological questions or disputes arose, there was a form of a Messianic "Sanhedrin" to address these issues. The Acts 15 controversy (over the Gentile inclusion into the faith of Yeshua) was addressed within this structure. Hence, we see that although the realities of New Covenant faith bring certain changes in our approach to God, the early Jewish (and Gentile) believers in Yeshua most naturally followed the only form of government with which they were familiar. The fact that they perceived themselves as still grafted into the rich olive tree of Israel is reflected not only theologically and culturally, but also in the structures of the new movement (cf. Rom. 11:17–18).

As the past eras of Israel illustrate, there is also a growing need in Messianic Judaism for a somewhat centralized structure in which to give directives. As with the larger Jewish community, it behooves us to place great emphasis on educational credentials. As with other new movements, Messianic Judaism has sometimes had to combat the belief in some circles that institutional education was somehow "unspiritual." However, as we have matured, many now see the desirability, in fact the need, for qualified clergy. If we are to direct our movement and even establish common policies, we must have more trained leaders who are theologically equipped and culturally astute. The UMJC has been on the forefront of this trend and continues to raise the bar in the Yeshiva program (which now requires seventeen core courses). We have also emphasized the Excellence in Ministry Continuing Education program for ordained UMJC leaders. Other programs are growing as well, including various Messianic Institutes across North America and the world. Like other Jewish denominations, we must pursue a high standard for *s'michah* of our future rabbis—as well as quality training programs for Messianic cantors and even *mohelim* (ritual circumcisers). We are still the "People of the Book" and our educational programs need to strongly reflect this as we face the 21$^{st}$ century. In times past, there were not many strong Messianic Jewish educational institutions. Many, like myself, did graduate work on both the Christian and Jewish sides. Although some may still opt for such a dualistic educational approach in the future, it is the major congregational organizations (e.g., UMJC, IAMCS, etc.), which will be best equipped to provide such structure within a specifically Messianic Jewish context.

Besides the need for a Messianic Jewish *s'michah*, our trained clergy will be called upon to decide issues of *halakhah*. As with the early New Testament believers, the modern Messianic movement will be faced with some crucial issues. How will we answer such questions as the conversion of Gentiles, the ordination of women, intermarriage, and the response to divorce? As the Acts 15 council, in essence, decided some halakhic issues, we will surely be faced with some similar, contemporary issues to be addressed. Likewise, there will certainly be some judicial or disciplinary controversies to be adjudicated. Unlike our earlier ad hoc approach to such things, I believe we will need established bodies to serve as a *beyt din* to resolve such questions. Messianic Judaism of the 20$^{th}$ century was forced to face such issues within each autonomous congregation, or perhaps, by leaning upon existing, non-Jewish structures. The UMJC has made good strides in both areas by offering non-binding, theological papers as well as an in-house Judicial Committee. Surely, one of the looming challenges we face in the coming years is the establishment of respected bodies that will be able to give Directive Policies.

A third element that affects the organizational structure of Messianic Judaism can be summed up in the phrase *Interdependent Participation*. This may be contrasted with the polarities of total *independence* or centralized *dependence*. No doubt, many Messianic Jews tend to be independent thinkers. We have had to think "outside the box" to even come to our faith in Yeshua. Although we have come together in such structures as the UMJC or MJAA, we have thus far, stopped short of developing a centralized denomination. Again, we can learn from the development of synagogue history.

For many centuries, after the destruction of the Second Temple, Judaism retained an almost exclusive homogeneity. The only brand of rabbinic Judaism to be found was what we call Orthodox Judaism. This began to change in the 18th century due to the forces of the *Haskalah* (European Enlightenment). An alternative form of liberal Judaism, Reform Judaism, was birthed in Germany. In the early 20th century, yet another form called Conservative Judaism emerged, taking the middle ground between the two other movements. Today, there are several denominational structures within world Jewry. Some, like Reform Rabbi Dan Cohn-Sherbok, question why Messianic Judaism should not be considered as a valid branch of the *menorah* connected to the larger, pluralistic Jewish community (Cohn-Sherbok 212). It is noteworthy that each of these groups takes it upon themselves to ordain their own clergy, decide judicial issues, and define *halakhah* as they see it. I believe that the 21st century will see Messianic Judaism draw closer towards this model. In fact, it is rather amazing that the Messianic movement (including missions, alliances, and unions) has had such broad consensus and unity in so many areas up until now. In my estimation, it would be ideal to continue in a format like the UMJC; that is, a "big umbrella" organization which can encompass a broad spectrum of Messianic Jewish congregational expressions.

We have seen great benefit by working together even within our present diversity. Differences in Jewish expression (Orthodox to liberal), theology (covenant to dispensational), and spiritual practices (Pentecostal to non-charismatic) have sometimes challenged our flexibility. Yet, they have also added a richness in the unity of the UMJC. It has probably been to our benefit that, as a younger movement, we have not had the luxury or critical mass to split over such non-essential issues. Realistically, as we continue to grow, the day may come where, like the larger Jewish community, there will be a multitude of expressions within mainline Messianic Judaism. Perhaps, we will develop denominational structures for "Orthodox, Conservative, and Reform" expressions of Messianic Judaism. While some may oppose such a concept, I believe this may actually serve as a blessing as our movement expands—if done for legitimate reasons and with the proper spirit. Indeed, if important differences develop in issues of theology or *halakhah*, it could be more problematic to try to stay together under the same organizational umbrella. Unity among believers in Yeshua will always be vital, yet this does not demand uniformity.

In an ideal world, most Messianic synagogues would happily join the existing, local Jewish Federation. Perhaps the future will bring enough understanding and trust that the larger Jewish community, in the spirit of sincere pluralism, will officially welcome Messianic Judaism into their midst. Undoing two thousand years of misunderstandings on both sides will be no easy matter, but God has done even bigger miracles in our history! If it is not to be, there are yet other options. As the Jewish Federation brings together such a wide range of organizations and synagogues, so too the Messianic community may develop to a point of joining together in a similar structure for support on common issues such as Israel, shared resources, and our mutual faith. We should likewise note that even within autonomous Messianic Jewish organizations, it will be vital to continue the spiritual relationship and interaction we have with the Gentile branch of the church. However, instead of assimilating into it, I propose that we can best serve the interests of both the Jewish and Gentile branches as we retain our Jewish "saltiness" in Yeshua (cf. Matt. 5:13).

Whatever form it may take, the desired core value that we must pursue is Interdependent Participation; that is, interacting together while acknowledging our diversity. Since our people are often described as the Jewish "community," it follows that a relevant and successful Messianic Judaism should relate via a similar model of community. Organizations for individual Jewish believers will continue to have an important role (e.g., the IMJA, which connects people globally). The Jewish mission structures can likewise continue to contribute to the Messianic community as they share the message of Yeshua in the public square. The weakness of the mission approach is that there is often a "conversion of communities" as well to the non-Jewish church. While there are some Jews who will opt for this choice, it will continue to not be a viable option for the greater percentage of Jews who desire to stay (at least) culturally Jewish. The future of Messianic Judaism must continue to embrace this central value by relating to our world within the Jewish cultural milieu. If organizational structures relate more within the context of "churches," "missions," and "pastors"—then they face the historic danger of being irrelevant to the bulk of the Jewish community. It seems much more logical, even biblically based in principle, to sincerely relate in the context of "synagogues," "federations," and "rabbis"—as we express the Jewishness of our faith in Yeshua as the Messiah (cf. 1 Cor. 9:19–20).

Nonetheless, even if we differ in structures and methodology, we need to realize our interdependence upon one another in the larger Messianic community. This is illustrated in the *Midrash* that describes Israel "like a company of men on board a ship. One of them took a drill and began to bore a hole under him. The other passengers said to him, 'What are you doing?' He replied, 'what has that to do with you? Am I not making the hole under *my* seat?' They retorted, 'But the water will enter and drown us all!'" (*Lev. Raba* IV.6). The Messianic Jewish community, as diverse as it may be, is seated together in the same boat. God has been faithful to watch over us in the early years of our renewed movement. As we navigate the future, these three values will assist us greatly: *Representative Presence, Directive Policies*, and *Interdependent Participation*. We have the promise that we will indeed fulfill our calling within the organizational structures of the future as we keep our eyes on Yeshua, the Author and Finisher of our faith (Heb. 12:2).

## Questions for Discussion

- Why were the Levites chosen to represent the larger body of Israel?
- Who were the members of the Sanhedrin?
- How were the values of *Representative Presence, Directive Policies* and *Interdependent Participation* demonstrated in the *Tanakh* and *B'rit Hadashah*?
- What are the differences between the episcopal, presbyterian, and congregational models of church structures?

## Bibliography

Cohn-Sherbok, Dan. *Messianic Judaism*. London: Cassell, 2000.

Barney Kasdan is the founding rabbi of Kehilat Ariel Messianic Synagogue in San Diego, California. He has a B.A. degree from Biola University and an M.Div. from Talbot Seminary. He served on the staff of Ariel Ministries for eight years and is ordained through the Union of Messianic Jewish Congregations, where he currently serves as President. Rabbi Kasdan is the author of the popular books, *God's Appointed Times* and *God's Appointed Customs*, both published by Messianic Jewish Publishers.

# A CENTRALLY RUN ORGANIZATION

—Robert Cohen

The question before us is "How should an association of Messianic congregations be structured?" I will argue that such an association should be centrally run, as is the IAMCS—as opposed to democratically run.

The IAMCS is a Steering Committee comprised of nine members, all of whom are rabbis, appointed by a chairman. The President of the MJAA appoints this chairman. The President's appointment of the chairman is made with the approval of the Executive Committee of the MJAA, a body elected from the member-ship at the bi-annual business meeting during the Messiah Conference. Although the IAMCS is appointed as the Steering Committee to oversee the rabbinical organization, the Executive Committee is elected in a democratic manner.

Since the beginning of the IAMCS, the Executive Committee of the Alliance has been composed mostly of rabbis. In effect, we have rabbis appointing rabbis, which produces a consistency of leadership. The reason this structure works best for us is because it evolved out of who we are as an organization. Our vision, history, leadership, and theology have shaped and formed the structure we have.

The seeds for the vision of the modern Messianic Jewish synagogue movement began in the early years of the MJAA. In 1917, Elias Newman addressed the second Messiah Conference of the MJAA with these words:

> Is the Alliance a mere organization or a providential movement? If it is simply an organization, like one of hundreds of others that exist, we can afford to disregard its principles and its progress. . . . But if the Alliance is a great providential movement and not a mere organization, if it is born of God, as we believe it to be, then we must look into God's design and shape our course by the Divine

compass. . . . We believe that the Alliance is more than an organization, greater than an idea and is in fact a spiritual force.

Later he states, "No council of fathers decreed it. No assembly or conference said it must come . . . There was divine life in this Alliance seed and it grew. This is its history in a single sentence . . . Men may start an organization, but God starts a movement." In this quote, the Alliance viewed itself as part of God's Divine plan. Leaders like John Zacher and Mark Levy would also call upon the Alliance to look favorably upon Jewish Believers in Yeshua, keeping their Jewish identity and starting Messianic Jewish Synagogues. In 1923, John Zacher presented a paper entitled "*Untrodden Paths*" at the Seventh Annual Conference of the Hebrew Christian Alliance of America (HCAA), the predecessor of the MJAA, which called upon the Alliance to embrace the idea of establishing Messianic Jewish Synagogues. "We venture to prophesy that the future Jewish missionary effort will accomplish infinitely more through three Hebrew Christian congregations than all the Jewish missions on the American continent combined" (Winer 111). The seeds of the vision were planted. Fifty-two years later the Alliance would look favorably upon the creation of a congregational organization.

In the mid 1970s, the vision and history of the Alliance changed forever. The name was changed from the HCAA to the MJAA; but of more importance, the growth of Messianic synagogues replaced the branches of the Alliance, which were in various cities. By the end of the 1970s, the Messiah Conference of the MJAA saw as its vision, the promoting, assisting and encouraging of the development of Messianic Jewish Synagogues in the U.S. and throughout the world. An intermediate step taken by the formation of a fellowship of leaders, but it was not until 1986 that the IAMCS was formed.

Although the vision of the concept of Messianic synagogues had its early prophetic voices in the Alliance, latter prophetic voices like those of Martin Chernoff and his family and others in the mid 1970s effected the change of the name and the vision to Messianic Judaism and Messianic Jewish Synagogues. Marty's vision of an alliance of independent Messianic Jewish congregations coming together in an affiliation under the umbrella of the MJAA would finally happen. As David Chernoff, Marty's son, and the first chairman of the IAMCS states, "I view the IAMCS as a permanent ministry of the Alliance that God has established. If one thinks of the YMJA [Young Messianic Jewish Alliance] as the right hand of the Alliance, then the IAMCS is the left hand. Together all three form a composite whose strength is greater than any of its separate parts. Our ultimate vision is not just to see the growth of Messianic congregations in the U.S., but to see the movement of Messianic Judaism break forth world-wide" (Winer 65).

Most corporations, both non-profit and for-profit, have what is known as a Mission Statement, a proclamation of its purpose for being. This purpose is the key to an organization's structure. The structure is an outgrowth of the mission statement as evidenced by the following examples. In an interview with Dr. Ruth Fleischer in 1991, Rabbi Daniel Juster, the first General Secretary of the UMJC, said, "The primary purpose of the UMJC is to strengthen and foster Messianic Jewish Congregations" (Fleischer 104). Because of this, the congregation is viewed as the centerpiece. The presbyterian form of government represents it. Congregations send delegates to conferences to vote on various papers and hold elections. The purpose of the individual delegates is to represent their congregation.

The conferences provide educational resources, leadership training, fellowship, and forums for communication between member congregations. Member congregations support the organization by paying a tithe of two percent. Rabbinical ordination, a Yeshiva, fund-raising programs, inspiration to congregations to plant other congregations, and outreach to the Jewish and Christian communities are some of the missions of the conferences.

Conferences are held both nationally and regionally. Recently, a Rabbis' Conference has been instituted as well. Its structure is much more formal and denominational that of the IAMCS.

I perceive some drawbacks with the democratic model. Factions and politics could play a big role where nothing could be done if the delegate composition were split, as the U.S. Senate is today, 50-50. Individuals that do not hold to the same values as the organization could get in. As we all know, splits have developed along theological issues in some major denominations. The culture that this model creates is more formal and corporate than that of one-on-one or of fellowship. This may be due to the fact that since it is a delegate structure, the delegates view themselves as being there to conduct business.

The IAMCS mission statement is found on its brochure: "The Spiritual Vision of the IAMCS is to see the outpouring of God's Spirit upon our Jewish people through Messianic Congregations. The IAMCS is not designed to be a denominational structure, but rather to be an instrument in promoting Messianic revival and to provide for the needs of its members, whatever their affiliations." From reading the mission statements of both organizations, their differences are apparent.

I want to focus on eight major distinctions of the IAMCS mission statement. Because of them, the only way this organization can prosper is to be centrally run.

The first distinction is a spiritual or theological one; to see the outpouring of the *Ruach HaKodesh* upon the Jewish people through Messianic Congregations. This is based theologically on the belief that we are in the last days, evidenced by the return of Israel to the Land and the fact that Jerusalem is back in Jewish hands. These are viewed as key prophetic events which have been fulfilled, along with the revival of Jewish people receiving Yeshua as their Messiah and the outpouring of God's Spirit (Ezek. 36, 37; Joel 2:20–

32; Deut. 30:4–10; 1 Kings 21:24.) This is the *central fact* on which the IAMCS is based. Today we have 125 congregations in our organization.

The second distinction is that the IAMCS views itself as an instrument or vehicle for this move of God's Spirit. Its defining itself as "not designed to be a denominational structure" emphasizes this. Its goal is to promote spiritual revival for its members and the revival of the Jewish people. It views congregations as vehicles, not as destinations. The goal is not the congregation, but what that congregation can do to impact the Jewish people.

The third distinction is found in what it has done since its inception; namely, to hold a Rabbis' Conference yearly. Not only is the IAMCS vision-driven but also leader or rabbi-driven. As someone has said, "Everything rises and falls on leadership." The emphasis of the IAMCS is to build, strengthen, encourage, and train leaders and to provide support through prayer and ministering one to another, as we do during our Rabbis' Conference.

The fourth distinction is that the rabbis are interconnected with each other through the planning of our regional conferences, rabbi forums on the web, and the national Rabbis' Conference, as well as the MJAA national conference. Time is set aside for personal ministry and sharing. Much of the teaching is geared toward the personal and spiritual life of the rabbis, as well as congregational issues. This care flows from the top down. The Steering Committee is diverse and yet its members enjoy and thrive on personally networking with each other. Two of our great values are the unity we have in our common vision and the value of working together as a team. Regional Directors get together with rabbis in their regions to pray for and encourage one another. This is the glue that holds our relationships together. We may come together because of a vision, but we stay together because of the bond of unity and love we have for each other.

The fifth distinction is that we are continually open to more of God's Spirit in our movement. Messianic Davidic praise and worship (Hebraic music and Israeli dancing) within our congregations, as well as at our conferences is a vital part of our identity.

The sixth distinction is that we actively help in the formation and establishment of new congregations. From the very beginning, we viewed the overall Messianic synagogue movement as a pioneering ministry. The result was that we made joining, ordination, and the Yeshiva more accessible. Because we viewed ourselves as a vehicle, we were able to help congregations establish the criteria for joining the IAMCS, not based on whether the congregation had a certain number of Jewish believers, but based on a percentage. We did not require two percent of the member's annual income as a membership fee, but $25.00 (the membership fee in 1986, which has increased over the years). Our goal was to help congregations and encourage them in fellowship with a greater community of congregations. Our Yeshiva courses are designed to help them in practical areas. These classes can be taken by correspondence, at one of our regional or national conferences, or at the rabbis' conferences. We have also given away thousands of dollars to works that have already been started and are in their first couple of years of existence.

The seventh distinction is in our process of ordination. First, the prospective ordinees must already be leading a congregation and a relationship must be established with them through our regional directors. The prospective members must join the MJAA and attend either regional or national conferences. They go through an intern program so they may fulfill the course requirements and develop relationships with those in leadership and with fellow rabbis. This gives the leadership time to know them personally and deal with any issues that may arise. This approach is totally different from that of a seminary or Bible school. We accept that they may have a calling on their life to be a Messianic rabbi, but we will only confirm ordination on them if we are satisfied that they have met the requirements of ordination. However, the process does not automatically result in ordination. The Steering Committee must believe that these persons have a call and have met the requirements; only then will they lay hands on them in ordination. To this date, we have ordained only forty rabbis.

The eighth distinction is what I call the governmental distinction. We operate under the biblical model of appointment to leadership and confirmation by the governing body. The democratic model of voting (much like the process of voting for a congressman or senator) provides for people to select members to represent them in the body, leaving it up to the body to make decisions for their selectors. I believe this is not the biblical model. We see this in a number of Scriptures. In Acts 6, the disciples lay out the requirements; leaders picked other leaders. The apostles then laid hands on them and confirmed them in the duties and privileges of their office. The governing body of the IAMCS, the MJAA Executive Committee, appoints and confirms the leadership of the Steering Committee. Since the vast majority of those who sit on the Executive Committee are rabbis, we have rabbis appointing and confirming rabbis to lead the rabbinical organization of the MJAA, in the same manner as *Rav Sha'ul* directed the appointment of elders over Crete. The commission of *Sha'ul* and Barnabas in Acts 13 provides the example; they were appointed and confirmed with the laying on of hands, and then sent out.

In summary, the organizational structure of the IAMCS, as a centrally run organization, evolved out of the history and vision of the MJAA and its sense of Divine purpose. Though seeds were planted early on, it was not until the 1970s that Marty Chernoff and others began to see the fruition of Messianic synagogues. It was to take another ten years before we saw the formation of the IAMCS. That the IAMCS is a part of the MJAA, not distinct from it, coupled with its mission statement and the eight distinctions, provides evidence that the only workable governing system is one which is centrally run. Most importantly, the appointment and confirmation of members to the Steering Committee conforms to the biblical model of the early Messianic Jewish community. In the next fifty years, we will see which model will prevail.

## Questions for Discussion

• Who votes for the members of the Executive Committee and what are the qualifications for membership in this committee?
• What are the major differences between the mission of the MJAA and the mission of UMJC in theory and in practice?
• Since those seeking ordination must already be leading a congregation, have they already been ordained somewhere? If so, what is unique about ordination by the MJAA?
• Describe the benefits of a centrally run organization of Messianic Jewish congregations?

## Bibliography

Fleischer, Dr. Ruth. "So Great A Cloud of Witnesses." U.K. Unpublished paper, 1996.
Winer, Dr. Robert. *The Calling.* Wynnewood: MJAA, 1990.

✡ ✡ ✡

Robert Cohen was a radical leftist during the hippie movement of the 1970s. After becoming a believer in Yeshua in 1975, he began working in Cincinnati, Ohio for Messianic Ministries under Martin and David Chernoff. In 1987, he and his wife, Roxanne, answered a call to lead Beth Jacob Messianic Congregation in Jacksonville, Florida. Rabbi Cohen has been involved in Alliance leadership for the past twenty years, and presently serves as Chairman of the IAMCS.

# MESSIANIC JEWISH HIGHER EDUCATION: AN INTEGRATIONIST APPROACH

—Michael Rydelnik

Learning has always been a vital element of Jewish life. Even in the *Torah*, the king was more than political figure. He was to make his own copy of the *Torah* and study it all the days of his life (Deut. 17:18–19). Ours was the only nation ever required by God to have its rulers be scholars. However, this was not limited to our leaders. God required all Jews to study the *Torah*, to meditate upon it, and to teach it to our children (Deut. 6:4–9).

In time, the Talmud elevated scholarship to such a degree that it stated that "the scholar takes precedence over the king." Jewish life is centered on study because we are a people of *The* Book (as well as other books). After God gave us the sacred Scriptures, the rabbis developed the *Mishnah*, *Gemara*, and the *Midrash*. Thus, the search for meaning from the sacred text became a central feature of the Jewish spiritual quest.

In the medieval period, particularly while under Islamic rule, our people not only studied Jewish subjects, but also philosophy, law, philology, poetry, mathematics, medicine, and science. We transmitted this learning to the Western world, thereby maintaining the spark of knowledge in the dark ages. At this time, when most Gentiles were illiterate, even among the ruling classes, all Jewish people knew how to read. We had to—because of our commitment to the sacred text.

In modern times, we Jews maintained our commitment to learning. The *Haskalah* (Jewish enlightenment) afforded Jewish people the opportunity to apply Hebrew to secular subjects. Emancipation enabled us to study secular subjects and we responded by becoming physicians, attorneys, and scientists. In the United States, not only were Jewish immigrants allowed to study, they were actually sent to night school to learn the language. The government required Jewish children to go public school with all the other immigrant children. This was remarkable in light of Europe's exclusion or quota systems. To the further amazement of our grandparents and great-grandparents, this was free of charge.

## The Need for Messianic Jewish Theological Education

So why this paean to the history of Jewish learning? Because unfortunately, we in the Messianic movement, have too often undervalued the need for theological education in our congregations. Perhaps, we do this because we want only to be taught "by the Spirit" or maybe we only want Messianic Jewish (and not Gentile) teachers. Whatever the reason, our lack of learning has resulted in some Messianic leaders who know little or no Hebrew, cannot defend sound doctrine, or are weak at understanding and/or teaching the Scriptures. Too often, our preaching is comprised of simplistic homilies with a smattering of Yiddish or Hebrew. If this is the state of the leadership, then what of the people? For the Messianic movement to grow in size, strength, and spiritual vitality, our leaders must be well trained in biblical theology, biblical exegesis and exposition, Jewish studies, leadership, homiletics, teaching, and pastoral care. Education is not a panacea to cure all our ills. However, it will provide for a stronger Messianic movement in the future.

## The Options in Messianic Jewish Theological Education

There are a variety of ways for the Messianic movement to approach theological education. In the past, we have encouraged potential leaders to attend evangelical Bible colleges and seminaries. This option has provided sound biblical/theological/practical training in accredited schools, but it has had some drawbacks. Frequently, these schools taught through a Western Hellenized grid and were occasionally insensitive to the learning needs of Messianic Jews.

A second option has been to study at Jewish schools or in university Jewish studies programs. While very frequently helpful in providing for a Jewish perspective, these programs do not provide for a New Covenant or Messianic perspective. Additionally, some Messianic Jews who have attempted this option have not been welcomed in these schools or programs because of their identification as Messianic Jews.

Recently, a third option has been proposed: to establish graduate level Messianic *yeshivot*. Hopefully, these schools would combine biblical, theological, and Judaic studies with a distinctly Messianic Jewish perspective. While certainly a worthwhile approach, there would be significant difficulties with accreditation, library resources, and the development of a faculty capable of devoting themselves to this kind of work. Since the Messianic movement presently needs—and will continue to need—trained leaders to assure a healthy future, all these approaches seem appropriate and commendable. But which approach is the best for us?

## A Proposal for Messianic Jewish Theological Education

In light of the great need for theologically sound and academically strong Messianic Jewish education, I propose an integrationist approach. By that, I mean that Messianic Jewish leaders train in academically accredited evangelical schools whose faculties support and encourage the Messianic Jewish movement. It would be particularly helpful if these schools would develop Jewish studies programs that could be staffed by Messianic Jewish scholars and supported by an umbrella organization of various Messianic Jewish associations.

My own experience as a student and now a teacher at the Moody Bible Institute (MBI) encourages this perspective. In 1923, the Moody Bible Institute foresaw a need to train workers in Jewish ministry. So with the support of the Hebrew Christian Alliance of America (now the MJAA) it began a Jewish Studies program. Since that time, all the Jewish Studies professors were Jewish followers of Yeshua, from Solomon Birnbaum to Max Reich to Nathan Stone to Louis Goldberg. Shortly after the inception of the Jewish Studies program, Moody committed to funding it without Alliance support. As an institution for theological and ministry training, MBI has fostered in its graduates, sound theology, biblical expertise, practical skill for service, high integrity and spiritual commitment, as well as knowledge of Jewish studies. It is a model for what the Messianic Jewish movement needs and should pursue for its training in the future (see Ariel, 2000).

The integrationist approach to theological education is not limited to the Moody Bible Institute. Other institutions have attempted similar programs, the most recent being Fuller Theological Seminary. Furthermore, Fuller has expressed great interest in adjusting their program to meet the needs of the Messianic Jewish movement. Other colleges and seminaries have expressed interest in doing the same. Some theological schools have begun to offer courses in Jewish studies even if they do not yet offer them as a major course of study. Gordon-Conwell Divinity School belongs to a consortium of schools that enables their students to take Jewish studies courses at neighboring universities such as Harvard Divinity School, as well as at Jewish institutions.

Additionally, students that attend colleges or seminaries that do not offer any Jewish studies can study in local Jewish schools. For example, Trinity Evangelical Divinity School students have taken courses or completed M.A. degree programs at the Spertus Institute of Judaica in Chicago. Students at the Talbot School of Theology have studied at the University of Judaism. Although these courses lack the integration available when the professors are Messianic Jewish scholars, they are still valuable for training leaders for Messianic synagogues.

The benefits of the integrationist approach are manifold. *First, the integrationist approach to theological education provides academic credibility.* By attending schools with recognizable accreditation, a scholarly faculty, sufficient library resources, and educationally effective curricula, graduates will have a better education. Furthermore, they will not be subject to the criticism that they were trained in academically limited and unaccredited schools.

*Second, the integrationist approach provides sound scholarship.* Certainly, the Messianic movement has developed a number of scholars in Bible, theology, Judaic studies, worship, and homiletics. However, at this time, we do not have sufficient numbers of scholars to fully staff a school in all the subjects necessary for a sound education. By joining with established schools, we will share in the benefits of studying with world-renowned scholars in their fields, and provide Messianic Jewish scholars to enrich these schools. Learning from such scholars can only enhance our own biblical exegesis, theological reflection, and practical exposition.

*Third, the integrationist approach provides a broader perspective.* I fear that if we limit ourselves to Messianic Jewish schools we will become narrow and ingrown in our thinking. Rather, we must benefit from exposure to alternative theological perspectives and methodology. The Messianic Jewish movement has not yet reached the summit of our knowledge. We must guard against the arrogance of thinking that we alone have all truth. It will be to our advantage to study in schools taught by others—not merely among ourselves.

*Fourth, the integrationist approach provides for greater interaction.* It is imperative that Messianic Jews not become isolated from the entire body of Messiah. In fact, one of the factors that caused the initial Messianic Jewish movement to dwindle and die was that it became disconnected and ultimately excluded from non-Jewish followers of Messiah Yeshua. By interacting with non-Jewish scholars and teachers, we will benefit from their knowledge and experience.

*Fifth, the integrationist approach provides for greater influence.* If the Messianic movement maintains its participation in evangelical theological institutions, it will prevent us from becoming a marginalized sect. Most groups that refuse interaction with other followers of Messiah, ultimately, are seen as separatist and out of the mainstream. As such, we will lose our influence on non-Jewish followers of Messiah. However, as long as we participate and benefit from broader theological education, we will continue to influence teachers and fellow students alike. They will learn sensitivity to Jewish people and obtain a positive perspective of a Messianic Jewish lifestyle.

## Conclusion

The future leaders of Messianic Judaism must learn to teach well so that their congregants, in turn, will learn well. This includes teaching the entire Jewish Bible, sound doctrine, and holy living. The *Midrash* says, "Anyone who teaches Torah in public and does not make the words as pleasant as honey from the honeycomb for those who are listening, it were better that he not teach the words at all" (*Mid. Rab.* Song 4:11). "A good teacher makes learning a joy" (Prov. 15:2 LB). To secure our future as a movement, Messianic leaders must be both strong learners and sound teachers.

One of the most effective ways to produce fine leaders and teachers is through an integrationist approach to theological education. However, regardless of the preferred approach, the entire Messianic Jewish movement should be in agreement with the need for theological education. In *Living a Jewish Life,* Anita Diamant and Howard Cooper write, "Study may be the only undisputed and shared value upon which all Jews, regardless of affiliation or belief, can agree" (144). We Messianic Jews should excel in holding that "undisputed and shared value."

## Questions for Discussion

- Why has theological education been so important to Jewish people throughout our history?
- How has the Messianic Jewish movement sought to provide theological education and what limitations have we faced in past efforts?
- What is meant by an "integrative approach" to theological education for the Messianic Jewish movement and what are its advantages?
- How can an integrative approach to theological education be successfully implemented in the Messianic Jewish movement?

## Bibliography

Ariel, Yaakov. *Evangelizing the Chosen People*. Chapel Hill: Univ. of North Carolina, 2000.

Cooper, Howard and Anita Diamant. *Living a Jewish Life*. New York: HarperCollins, 1991.

Michael Rydelnik is Professor and Coordinator of Jewish Studies at the Moody Bible Institute of Chicago. Raised in an observant Jewish home, Dr. Rydelnik is the son of Holocaust survivors. After receiving a diploma in Jewish Studies from MBI, he earned three degrees including a D.Miss. from Trinity Evangelical Divinity School. In the past, he has served as the spiritual leader of several Messianic congregations and the Northern Regional Director for Chosen People Ministries.

# MESSIANIC JEWISH INSTITUTIONS OF HIGHER LEARNING

—Paul Saal

Licensed and accredited universities, colleges and institutes of higher education, many of which teach religious studies, proliferate throughout the United States. Included are seminaries, divinity schools and *yeshiva*s from the broad range of Christian and Jewish sects represented by constituencies in this country. So, why should Messianic Judaism, a small and incipient religion, invest the large financial and human resources requisite to launch its own brand of higher education? I believe the following story will help to exemplify the need.

In 1995, I took the opportunity to attend a seminar on *Midrash* offered at a local university, which was taught by a prominent Jewish scholar-in-residence. The seminar was well attended by both Jewish and Christian clergy, many of whom I already knew. It soon became clear that the professor's primary purpose and hope for this class was to promote an understanding of Jewish interpretive practice that would help fund a respectful dialogue between Christian and Jewish religious professionals. The questions asked revealed the intentions of the students. The Christians were largely there to learn about Judaism. The Jewish clergy wished to discover new bridges between the writings of antiquity and the contemporary needs of their congregations. While I also found this aspect important, I was most interested in the potential of discovering cognate methods of interpretation that connected the midrashic writers and their apostolic contemporaries. I suspected this would be of some interest to the other attendees, but I did not ask any questions, fearing I might be stepping over a boundary that would make my teacher uncomfortable. I was uncertain whether he knew who I was, but I sensed that he knew and was uncomfortable with my attendance. I wanted to be careful not to give the impression that I was, in any way, challenging him.

To his credit, while teaching on the *akeydah* (the story of the binding of Isaac), the professor did not avoid the obviously Christological implications of several of the *aggadot* (legends), including a particular story that portrayed Isaac's death and resurrection. He explained them as Jewish reactions to Christian hegemony in the fourth century and Jewish alternatives to "Christian answers." After class, I asked to speak to the professor, to ask whether he thought it plausible that this *aggadah* existed in an inchoate oral tradition during the first century, since it seemed to parallel the writings in the Book of Hebrews (Heb. 11:19). He did not seem at all surprised by the question, and in fact, appeared prepared for it. He replied "of course it's plausible, but if I believe that, then I would have to believe what you believe."

This class proved helpful and informative, but it became increasingly clear that if I was going to find an organic relationship between Judaism and belief in Yeshua, I was going to find it alone. My concern about asking questions was well founded since my interests were well outside the pale of the collective understandings and concerns of the remainder of the class. Both the Christian and the Jewish clergy who took the class, as well as the scholar who taught it, were interested in the symmetrical relationship between the two religions, not in the harmonization of the foundational traditions and history that constituted the formative sea from which both religions emerged. Certainly, I was the only person in the room who was oddly occupied with how to understand Yeshua in and through contemporary Jewish practice.

These experiences were not new to me. While attending a Baptist Seminary, I had already developed internal filters by which to sift the residue of historical anti-Jewish bias from the inductive reasoning of my professors, my classmates, and my textbooks. At first, I was surprised that I appeared to be the only person who noticed that this bias even existed, but after awhile, I realized that it was so deeply acculturated that it could not be separated from the general dogma. And why should it be? For Baptists, the universality of the gospel is understood through particularity of the elect—in other words, those who give intellectual and verbal ascent to the widely held ideology of their denomination. So, despite limited conversation by some about the election of Israel, the relevance of flesh-and-blood Jewish people was of small importance unless they became "Christians." Jewish group identity, then, counted for very little inside the walls of a Baptist Seminary.

The seminary tried to accommodate the special needs and context of my chosen ministerial path, but lacked both the resources and the perspective to do so. I was allowed to complete some of my coursework by contracted independent study, especially in the area of ministerial skills, but I did not receive the appropriate guidance or encouragement. A faculty member who had a background in Jewish studies was assigned to mentor me, but his fascination with Jewish tradition was like a paleontologist's absorption with fossils. If there was anyone at the school who understood my reverence for the rites, customs, traditions, and the writings of my people, they were certainly not letting on. Yet, my polite disinterest with Christian hymns and school chapels was viewed by some as unspiritual and cause for suspicion. Those who could understand that these were cultural distinctions could still only appreciate Jewish religious norms for their inherent missiological value. To contextualize a baptism with Hebrew prayers was admirable, but to officiate over a *bar mitzvah* was potentially legalistic and definitely separatist. The source of my difficulties was not the school, the instructors, or the students. I had merely come to the wrong place to learn how to be a rabbi.

Unfortunately, my story is not unique. Many of Messianic Judaism's religious leaders have spent a great deal of time and effort distilling multiple religious disciplines into a Messianic Jewish education. Clearly, there is a need for an indigenous and integrative Messianic Jewish education. In recognition of this need, the UMJC has developed a Yeshiva program, which consists of a series of intensive college level courses leading to ordination in the Union. I attended my first UMJC Yeshiva class in 1994 and immediately recognized what I had been missing—others who were on the same journey I was, attempting to be religious functionaries in a world that did not—quite yet—exist. While the Yeshiva provides a good supplemental education, it is not an accredited degree program. It still falls short of being a legitimate "think tank."

In Judaism, institutes of higher learning do more than just educate—they create the fabric of thought from which Jewish communal life finds meaning. Furthermore, these institutions help determine who can declaim on Jewish life and practice. Presently, Messianic Judaism has no such institutions, so it only takes a poorly designed web page or a self-published book to gain a hearing from those who are less informed. If Messianic Judaism is going to mature, it will need its own educational institutions to set high standards for credentialling, education, information dissemination, and to develop platforms for theological and halakhic disputation and consensus building. Of course, the investment of financial and human resources to develop such institutions will be great, but relative to the collective cost of avoiding this endeavor, the price is miniscule.

## Questions for Discussion

- How much emphasis should be placed on historical Jewish thought (i.e., *Mishnah*, Rashi, and Maimonides) in a Messianic Jewish education?
- How much emphasis should be placed on historical Christian writings (i.e., the Greek fathers and the church reformers)?

- How much should a Messianic Jewish rabbi learn about *halakhah*? How much training should a Messianic Jewish rabbi receive in Jewish liturgical practice and lifecycle events?
- Do you think higher critical thought is an important element in a Messianic Jewish education?

✡ ✡ ✡

Rabbi Paul L. Saal is the spiritual leader of Congregation Shuvah Yisrael in West Hartford, Connecticut, where he resides with his wife, Robbie, and their four daughters. He received his ordination through the Union of Messianic Jewish Congregations and has served on its Steering Committee as Planter Chairman since 1996. Rabbi Saal is the Editor-at-Large of *Boundaries* and is a former editor of *Kesher: A Journal of Messianic Judaism.*

# MESSIANIC JEWISH CHILDREN'S EDUCATION AND CHURCH RESOURCES

—Eva Rydelnik

## The Jewish Value of Children's Education

Teaching our children to love and obey the God of Abraham, Isaac and Jacob is so important that the Talmud says, "A village without a school should be abolished" (Sabbath 119a). The education of our children one of the highest values of the Jewish people.

The *Tanakh* emphasizes the responsibility of teaching our children to love and obey the Lord. The *Sh'ma* commands us to teach our children diligently to love the Lord with all their heart (Deut. 6:4–9). Each year at *Pesach*, we are reminded of the importance of instructing our children in all the details of the festival and of observing *Pesach* forever (Exod. 12:24–27). Proverbs instruct us to "train up a child in the way he should go, even when he is old he will not depart from it, " (Prov. 22:6 NASB). The concept of early education is echoed in the *Midrash* when it says, "If you don't teach an ox to plow when he's young, it will be difficult to teach him when he is grown" (*Midrash Mishlei*, 22).

Children were important to the Messiah Yeshua. He gave them priority, even after a long day of ministry, when the disciples wanted to send the children away. Yeshua, said: "Let the little children come to me, and do not hinder them, for the kingdom of God belongs to such as these" (Mark 10: 13-16 NASB). On the *Shavu'ot* immediately after the Messiah's ascension, Peter spoke powerfully to the crowds who had come up to Jerusalem for the festival. As he challenged this Jewish audience to recognize Messiah, Peter said, "For the promise is for you and your children" (Acts 2:39 NASB). How are our children to know of the Promise, unless they are taught?

## The Messianic Movement and Children's Education

The Messianic movement is faced with the issue of how to best teach our children about the Messiah. Of course, each family is to instruct their children in the Scriptures "as we talk about them when we sit at home, walk along the road, when we lie down and when we get up." However, we must be diligent to provide high quality Messianic education in Messianic Synagogues as well.

## Christian Publishing Houses as a Resource for Messianic Children's Education

There is a wealth of educational material available to Messianic congregations that is often overlooked. In order to broaden their educational resources, Messianic congregations should consider using traditional Sunday school material prepared by one of the Christian publishing houses. These classic church based materials could be used as supplements to Messianic educational materials that focus on the Jewish holidays.

Messianic congregations do not need to "reinvent the wheel" in children's education. These Christian publishers have been producing children's educational material for decades, and have produced a wealth of excellent lesson plans and teaching resources that cover almost every aspect of the Scriptures—from the Creation to the Second Coming. Although some of the lessons are not culturally relevant to the needs of a Messianic synagogue, much of the curriculum is useful and should not be overlooked when we are searching for educational resources.

When choosing a church based curriculum, all publishing houses are not equally suitable for Messianic needs. Of the dozens of Christian publishing houses, many are too denominationally focused, while others are generally insensitive to Jewish issues—making them unsuitable for our use. However, two publishers in particular have proved especially sensitive to Jewish needs. They are a good option for augmenting Messianic education.

David C. Cook Communications has excellent graded Sunday school materials. The lesson books for children are colorful and the crafts are well explained. There are resource packets for each quarter (three-month period) and the instruction books for teachers are easy to follow. The lessons are designed to teach through the major events of the whole Bible in a three-year cycle. They have lesson plans and materials for nursery age through high school.

Gospel Light Publishers also has exceptional material that is suitable for Messianic use, and is perhaps the stronger of the two resources. Gospel Light provides excellent biblical background in the form of maps and archaeological insights. They often include information about the Jewish holidays. The illustrations of Bible characters are appropriately Jewish, but not stereotypical in appearance. The language used is generally sensitive to Jewish concerns. Another advantage of Gospel Light is that the weekly handouts are not dated (e.g., Sunday, January 4) but are designated with sequential numbering (e.g., Spring #4). Thus, the material is useful for Friday or Saturday services, and allows for interruption of the curriculum for teaching special Jewish holiday lessons without falling behind printed dates on the handouts. Gospel Light has a wide variety of teaching resources available, including curricula for nursery through high school. These include easy to use instruction books for teachers, resource packets, and hands-on learning materials for students.

## Messianizing and Adapting Church Based Materials

When using a church based curriculum, certain adaptations must be made. By taking the following steps, these church based materials can be helpful and effective for Messianic use. The following strategy for Messianizing the materials can make them workable in any Messianic setting. This will take some extra effort on the part of the education director and the teachers, but it is well worth the effort to make use of these valuable educational resources.

To begin, read through the curriculum and be sure that the lesson plans coincide with the Jewish calendar. If the curriculum has the Passover lesson plan for November, hold it back and teach those lessons in the Spring at *Pesach*. Likewise, if teaching about Ruth is scheduled in the curriculum for winter, move those lessons to *Shavu'ot*. In the same way, watch for stories about Esther and have them taught at *Purim*. Hold the Jonah lesson for *Yom Kippur* and the creation lesson for *Rosh HaShanah*. This keeps the curriculum in line with Jewish calendar. Of course, these church based lessons will not include all the necessary materials for complete Jewish holiday lessons. Special effort must be made to teach about all of the Jewish holidays in our Messianic congregations.

Always use Jewish terminology when teaching. Speak of the *Scriptures* or the *Tanakh* and the *B'rit Hadashah*, instead of the *Old* and *New Testaments*. Focus on the Atonement and Redemption. Avoid using the term *saved*. Talk about the *Jewish people* specifically—not generically, as "a special people." Avoid the term *Christian*, which may be confused with *Gentile*. Instead, speak of *Messianic believers, believers*, or *followers of Messiah*. Watch out for the word *church*, and instead, teach about the *congregation, synagogue*, or *fellowship*.

Use the Hebrew name *Yeshua*, instead of *Jesus*. Always say *Messiah*—not *Christ*. The words are parallel, yet *Christ* is strongly linked to the history of anti-Semitism. Most church materials will use the words *Jesus* and

*Christ.* These expressions can be easily adapted by the teacher and corrected in the resources and the handouts so as to read *Yeshua the Messiah*, or *Messiah Yeshua*.

Carefully screen all crafts and games to eliminate any pictures of the cross. Often, stars of David or other meaningful Jewish symbols can be substituted in the crafts or handouts. Watch for pictures of churches with steeples, and substitute synagogue style buildings instead.

When the geography of the Middle East is part of the lesson, identify the Land of Israel. Do not merely teach about "God's special place" or whatever vague term may appear in the curriculum. Do not call the land *Palestine.* Since this is the name of the area before 1948, sometimes, it still crops up in church materials. Instead, remember to always use the biblical name—*Israel.* Always connect the biblical land of Israel (Judaea, Zion, Canaan) as well as place names such as Jerusalem, Galilee, Jericho, and so on—with the ancient and modern State of Israel (*Eretz Yisra'el*). It is helpful to have a map of modern Israel in the classroom to keep the children oriented to the Land. Put up posters of modern Israel and Israeli cities.

Watch for insensitive words in the teacher's lessons or children's handouts that could be offensive to Jewish people. Watch for negative comments about "Jacob the cheater," for example, as a stereotype of all Jewish people. Carefully correct any lesson that places blame on the Jewish people for the death of Yeshua. Clarify the fact that Yeshua died for all people and rose again— proving he is God.

Look for opportunities to focus on God's faithfulness to Israel and the Jewish people as the stories from the Scriptures are taught. This may not be the emphasis of the church based lesson for that week, but it is easily customized to fit the focus of a Messianic congregation.

## Learning, Learning, Learning

Our children must grow up to know God's word and to value their Jewish identity and heritage. As Ahad HaAm said, "Learning, learning, learning: that is the secret of Jewish survival." Learning God's word and about our Jewish heritage should be a joy for our children. Messianic educators should not overlook the wealth of resources that lie outside the traditional Messianic circles—resources that can be found in classic church based curriculum. We must ensure a bright future for our children (and the Messianic movement) by instructing them in the word of God and helping them grow in knowledge and appreciation of their Messianic Jewish heritage.

## Questions for Discussion

- Why is it important to teach the Scriptures to our children?
- Some Christian educational materials are good resources for Messianic congregations. Do you agree or disagree—and why?
- What precautions should be taken when selecting Christian educational materials?
- What adaptations can be made to prepare a Sunday school curriculum for Messianic Jewish congregational use?

✡ ✡ ✡

Eva Rydelnik is an adjunct professor at the Moody Bible Institute and the Chicago Area Coordinator for Chosen People Ministries. She has a Diploma in Jewish Studies from The Moody Bible Institute, a B.A. from Azusa Pacific University, and an M.A. from Wheaton College Graduate School. She is married to Michael Rydelnik. They have two sons.

# EACH GENERATION MUST TEACH THE NEXT

—Jeffrey E. Feinberg

What could be more bizarre than to educate a child, born into the tribe of Judah, that he must no longer value that membership if he chooses to accept Yeshua, born of the tribe Judah, as King of the Jews? Yet, religious Judaism and religious Christianity have joined ranks to construct a middle wall of partition. Ironically, both sides accuse Messianic Judaism of erecting the barriers: the Christians suspect that Messianic Judaism will value Judaism over Yeshua, and the Jews of Judaism loudly proclaim that bowing to the King is an idolatry that Judaism cannot tolerate. Such false dichotomies erect obstacles for the child who insists on the simple truth that it is natural to remain within Judaism while worshipping the King of the Jews!

The nature of Messianic Jewish education must be Messiah-centered, yet distinctly Jewish. It is the task of Messianic Jewish education to transmit a Jewish heritage that integrates an understanding of *Tanakh* and *B'rit Hadashah* into the context of a Jewish community. This chapter will discuss the purpose of Messianic Jewish education and how it can be informed by the historic vision that has guided Judaism from its inception. As a Judaism, Messianic Judaism must find its place among other Judaisms. Broadly speaking, the spectrum of traditional Judaisms accord distinctive honor to the *Torah* and to the holy calling of the Jewish people at Sinai; whereas modernistic Judaisms focus on the challenge of living Jewish lives within the context of modern culture. This chapter will conclude with ways that Messianic Jewish education can assist Messianic Judaism to transmit an ageless Jewish heritage to the coming generation of New Covenant priests.

## The Vision of Judaism

Israel, as a people, first entered into covenant relationship with God at Mount Sinai. God validated his servant *Moshe* and spoke the Ten Words to a "called out" people fenced off from a holy mountain. Seventy *z'keynim* ascended to celebrate a covenant feast under the feet of the Almighty. Higher still climbed *Aharon* and his sons, *Nadav* and *Avihu*. These *kohanim* (priests) represented a people called to be a Kingdom of Priests and a Holy Nation (*mamlechet kohanim v'goy kadosh*). *Moshe* and his successor *Y'hoshua* continued on; but *Moshe* alone penetrated the heavenly cloud veiling the presence of the *Sh'chinah* on Sinai's summit, where heaven touched earth. Judaism transmits this picture of the Jewish people, called to ascend the mountain of God's holiness. This "called out" people, set free from the servile labor (*avodah*) of Egypt, are now offered the transcendent *avodah* of priestly service and worship, led by its great prophet, its High Priest (*Kohen Gadol*), its priests, its seventy elders, and its people (*am ha'aretz*).

## Imparting the Vision

Transmitting Jewish identity across generations clashes directly with the formidable forces of the American melting pot. Former U.S. Assistant Secretary of State Elliot Abrams writes that Jews are doomed as an ethnic, cultural, or political entity in the face of "a society seeking relentlessly to include them within larger groups of citizens who do not share their religious heritage" (193). Without a religious community that builds a hedge from within, the Jewish people could be cut in half within a generation or two. But what kind of religious community lends itself distinctively to a Messianic Jewish education? Can it be a Traditional Judaism that recognizes *Torah* as God's revelation that the Jewish people are called out and set apart to function as a holy kingdom of priests (*mamlechet kohanim*) among the nations? Can it be a Conservative Judaism that recognizes the synagogue and promotes the day school as an institution that will preserve the Jewish people? Can it be a Reform Judaism that cultivates values deriving from Sinai, the Jewish people's call to covenant with the God of Israel? Each approach raises its own questions. Messianic Jewish education must advance the vision of Judaism across generations, by equipping and training its members to live as New Covenant *kohanim* in a religious community that stresses equality of spiritual status in matters of race, class, nationality, and gender.

## Comparisons to Traditional Judaism

Traditional Judaism emphasizes *Torah* as revelation, the supernaturally revealed word of God in our midst. Jews must learn Hebrew, read *Torah*, don priestly garments (*tallit*), maintain a state of ritual purity, ascend the *bimah* (platform), and appropriate the *Torah* as a heritage passed from one generation to the next, forever. For traditional Jews, *halakhah* regulates a lifestyle that eats and breathes holiness. Each generation learns to read *Torah* for itself, as interpreted over the years by the traditions and texts of the rabbis.

The priest/*tzaddik* is called to draw near to God. The immense amount of learning begins in the households and later in the *beyt midrash* (place of religious study), day school, and *yeshiva*. Every member of the priesthood must be equipped to lead or participate in the *minyan* (quorum of ten required for certain prayers), that Jewish corporate community (*beyt knesset*) which assembles to celebrate the vision at Sinai where God first called Israel to be His people (*Parashat Yitro*, Exod. 19:6).

But is the priesthood still valid today, when God's manifest *Sh'chinah* is absent? Is the sheer quantity of learning practicable for a generation raised on video and sound bites? Do the pace of life and the shortness of people's attention spans force changes on traditional methods of transmitting and celebrating Judaism's heritage from Sinai? Can every Jew become a *ba'al k'riah* (master of the reading), raised to ascend the mountain? Or is this calling only practical for the holy sons of *Aharon*, *Elazar*, and *Pinchas*?

Conservative Jews also raise their members as priests in a religious Jewish community. They walk a fine line, however, between the traditional demands for holiness and relevancy to the people living in greater society. Schools assume the burden for imparting Jewish education to the membership (to make up for lapses in the home, cf. Deut. 6:4–11; *Bava Batra* 21a). Following the Orthodox lead, the day school has increasingly become the bulwark for Conservative Judaism's effort to assist the synagogue in transmitting the heritage of a priestly Judaism. Rabbi Jacob J. Schacter, at a recent conference of the Partnership for Excellence in Jewish Education (PEJE), set the price tag for a movement of day schools at one billion dollars (see *Forward*, 22 Sept. 2000). With only $15 million currently channeled to fund day schools, and nearly three-quarters of a billion being given annually, the private Jewish family foundations can help make progress toward the goal. But will the outcomes of day school efforts justify the costs?

Lloyd P. Gartner points to the paradox that functional illiteracy among Jews rises with affluence (33). His observation accords with the teachings of *Torah*, warning against the dangers associated with wealth:

Be careful not to forget ADONAI your God by not obeying his *mitzvot*, rulings and regulations that I am giving you today. Otherwise, after you have eaten and are satisfied, built fine houses and lived in them, and increased your herds, flocks, silver, gold, and everything else you own, you will become proud-hearted. Forgetting ADONAI your God—who brought you out of the land of Egypt, where you lived as slaves. (Deut. 8:11–14)

Abrams responds, "it can be proved with statistics that Judaism and Jewish schooling maintain Jewish identity and enable Jews to pass their faith on to their children" (196). Notwithstanding the need for massive funding, Schechter schools have succeeded in raising a second generation of teachers, rabbis, and community leaders to found and endow schools. Forty percent of children receiving formal Jewish education presently attend day schools (see Wertheimer 49). Perhaps financial sacrifice can reverse the trend that affluence and functional illiteracy increase together.

## Comparisons to Modernistic Judaism

Perhaps Reform, Reconstructionist, and Humanistic Jews will consider it unfair to be lumped together. But from the perspective of the priestly Judaisms, these approaches appear to take a lighter view of the inspiration and authority of *Torah*, in order to accommodate Judaism to American society and serve the greater community.

The majority of Jewish children enrolled in formal Jewish education attend supplementary school (up to 14 hours/week). These schools assist the home in transmitting significant cultural, religious, and social heritage through a knowledge of history, literature, customs, and religious practices. But are these efforts enough to unlock the Hebrew language and lead to reading *Torah* as a way of life? How can the next generation choose to bond with Jews from the past or with Jewish people in other lands, including Israel? Hebrew language is the very lifeblood of Jewish culture and identity. Its loss cuts off continuities across generations along with the ideals that have empowered those generations. Such a loss distances Jewish people from their God, His Temple, the Land, and the call of the people to be a priestly nation among the nations of the world.

How then shall we live? Writing in *The Forward*, "Reform rabbi R. Jan Katzew summarizes the role of supplementary schooling: "The success of Jewish schooling is not only how much the graduates know, or even how much they are able to do, but also how they choose to live."

## Fulfilling the Vision of Messianic Jewish Education

Messianic Jews must never lose sight of their calling to transmit the Jewish heritage of membership in a priestly community. Each generation must teach its children to appropriate *Torah* and live out God's word for themselves. If this requires knowledge of Hebrew, literacy, *trop* (*Torah* cantillation), and liturgy, then we must embrace the task—utilizing tutors, mentors, cantors, supplementary schools, or even day schools as necessary. Messianic believers, as New Covenant priests, must follow *Moshe*'s lead, ascend the mountain of God's holiness, and enter the cloud to stand before God Himself. The awe of this moment lingers as individuals choose to go out and serve God, the community, and the world. *Ahavat Tzion* (love of Zion), *bikkur holim* (visiting the sick), *hiddur p'nay zaken* (respecting the elderly), *ma'akhil re'evim* (feeding the hungry), *hakhnasat orhim* (welcoming guests), and the praxis of other *mitzvot* maintain the continuities between the *Torah* and the New Covenant in distinctly Jewish ways.

Holy people sanctify time by celebrating holy days, and the Messianic Jewish community needs to instill these holy days in the bones of each new generation. Sanctifying *Shabbat* and setting it apart from scheduled tasks frees up time to appreciate one's family and one's Jewishness. The day should be devoted to *tz'dakah* (righteousness, acts of charity), reading *Torah* as the foundation of the New Covenant, and worshipping as a holy community.

Sanctifying other holy days binds the worshipping community to its past and its future. The spring festivals of *Pesach* and *Shavu'ot* celebrate our redemption from servile labor and calling to covenant relationship and priestly service. The fall festivals look with anticipation to the future. Christianity has no holy day devoted to Messiah's return, but Messianic Judaism has four! *Rosh HaShanah* and *Yom Kippur* bid a priestly community to purify itself and prepare for the days when all souls are resurrected. The *B'rit Hadashah* says that Messiah will be Judge on this day. *Sukkot* climaxes the Ingathering of all nations with the establishment of Messiah's thousand years as King of kings. *Sh'mini Atzeret*, that most final of holy convocations of *Torah*, welcomes the day when the nations go home from Jerusalem and the King bids his faithful entourage of holy priests to tarry an extra day. These men and women, these Levites from among the Jews and Gentiles, these rich and poor abide in the Glory of His Presence.

In conclusion, Messianic Jewish education must kindle in the coming generations a passionate desire to know Hebrew and read *Torah* weekly as New Covenant *kohanim*. Observing the weekly reading cycle attaches the Messianic Jewish community to Jewish communities everywhere. The community must raise consciousness of liturgy, so that its members can join corporate worship in synagogues throughout the world. Celebrating the holy days and entering festal worship as a priestly community radiate a holiness that influences nations.

Integrating understandings of the *B'rit Hadashah* with the *Torah* opens one's eyes to the abiding riches of the Jewish heritage—to reign when Yeshua comes. On that day, we will greet him in Jerusalem with the words, "*barukh haba b'shem ADONAI*" (Matt. 23:39). And he will say to his royal priesthood, "*G'shu-na elai. Atsru!*" ("Draw near to me. Tarry!") Tarry an extra day.

## Questions for Discussion

- Empowerment: How can someone be sanctified to hear God's word for himself?
- Practicality: How can Messianic Jews train and equip their children to regularly read scripture in the original languages, know Yeshua, and maintain a priestly life?
- Community: How can Jewish people construct a religious community that is broad enough to be inclusive, yet narrow enough to remain holy to God?
- Transformation: How can God's word be appropriated, internalized, lived, and passed on as an everlasting heritage for generations to come?

## Bibliography

Abrams, Elliot. *Faith or Fear: How Jews Can Survive in a Christian America*. New York: The Free Press, 1997.

Gartner, Lloyd P., ed. *Jewish Education in the United States*. New York: Teacher's College, 1969.

Katzew, R. Jan. "How We Can Make Hebrew Schools Work Again: With the Right Priorities, Learning in the Home Becomes the Primary Focus." *Forward*, 19 Jan. 2001.

Staff article. "Educators Put Billion-Dollar Price Tag on Day Schools," *Forward*, 22 Sept., 2000.

Wertheimer, Jack. "Who's Afraid of Jewish Day Schools?" *Commentary* 108.5 (December 1999): 49–53.

✡ ✡ ✡

Dr. Jeffrey Feinberg has chaired Education at the Union of Messianic Jewish Congregations for more than a decade. He leads Etz Chaim Congregation of Buffalo Grove, Illinois and has five earned degrees including an M.Div. and a Ph.D. from Trinity International University. He and his wife, Pat, have written extensive Messianic Jewish curriculum materials, used by more than a hundred congregations throughout the world. Ordained by UMJC, Jeff teaches *Torah* at the UMJC Yeshiva.

# INTERMARRIAGE CAN HAVE A POSITIVE EFFECT ON MESSIANIC JUDAISM

—David Rudolph

Intermarriage between Jews and non-Jews in the Messianic Jewish movement is a hotly debated issue, not only because of its social and theological implications, but also because of the emotion that surrounds it. Some leaders decry intermarriage as an agent of assimilation and an impediment to generational continuity. Other leaders contend that intermarriage can make a positive contribution to Messianic Judaism, and that we need not fear adverse consequences if scriptural standards are maintained. The latter position, being the author's view, is advocated in this essay.

## The Permissibility of Intermarriage

Scripture is the yardstick of faith and life for Messianic Jews. It is highly significant, therefore, that Scripture not only permits intermarriage, but also sets forth restrictions for its governance. Shaye Cohen, Professor of Judaic Studies at Brown University, concurs:

> A general prohibition of intermarriage between Jews and non-Jews does not appear anywhere in the *Tanakh*. Leviticus lists numerous sexual taboos (Chapters 18 and 20) but fails to include intermarriage among them. Exodus 34:15 and Deuteronomy 7:3–4 prohibit intermarriage with the seven Canaanite nations, and Deuteronomy 23:2–9 prohibits four additional nations from *entering the congregation of the Lord*—perhaps (but probably not) a prohibition of marriage. But neither Exodus nor Deuteronomy prohibits intermarriage

with all non-Israelites, and both of them prohibit intermarriage with Canaanites only because it might lead to something else that was prohibited (idolatry). (260–261)

As an example of divinely sanctioned intermarriage, the book of Numbers records that, on one occasion, 32,000 virgins from among the Midianites were added to Israel's number by the Lord's command (Num. 31:25–47; cf. Deut. 21:10–14). The Scriptures generally permit intermarriage as long as the spouse in question is not from a forbidden nation or Canaanite-like (Ezra 9:1–2; see Cohen 243–244, 261). This was the difference between Moses' intermarriage with Zipporah and Ahab's intermarriage with Jezebel. The Gentile spouse was expected to live in accordance with the laws of Israel (Num. 15:15–16).

## Caveats to Intermarriage

To the above, I would add three qualifications in light of the Messianic Jewish context under discussion:

1.  Intermarriage is not preferable to marriage between two Messianic Jews. The scriptural witness is that intermarriage is the exception and not the rule in Israel. Sharing in common a Jewish heritage and family goes a long way toward maintaining the chain of Jewish identity.

2.  Knowledge of the pros and cons of intermarriage is insufficient to guide Messianic Jews in deciding whether to intermarry. Personal prayer and the leading of the *Ruach HaKodesh* (Holy Spirit) are essential.

3.  Not all types of intermarriage are beneficial for Messianic Jews, and two types are especially problematic. The first of these is the marriage of a Messianic Jew to a Gentile who is not a follower of Messiah Yeshua. This is prohibited by New Covenant *halakhah* because the deepest loyalties of the couple will be divided (2 Cor. 6:14). The second of these is the marriage of a Messianic Jew to a Gentile follower of Yeshua, who prefers a church environment to a Messianic synagogue, and a Christian lifestyle to a Jewish one. This kind of intermarriage places Jewish continuity at risk.

## Conversionary Intermarriage

Only two kinds of intermarriage are beneficial for Messianic Jews; they are (1) marriages in which the non-Jewish partner has a formal conversion, and (2) marriages in which the non-Jewish partner has an informal conversion. A formal conversion is one in which a non-Jew joins the nation of Israel through a course of study culminating in a conversion ceremony. An informal conversion is one in which covenant words are spoken or even prayed privately where, like Ruth, the intended convert declares: "Your people will be my people and your God will be my God" (Ruth 1:16). What makes these two kinds of intermarriage appropriate for Messianic Jews is that the non-Jewish spouse has committed to live in accordance with the laws of Israel. [Note: Throughout this essay, I continue to refer to the converted spouse as "non-Jewish" or "Gentile" to emphasize the intermarriage aspect.]

Some may argue that Jewish/convert marriages are not intermarriages at all, since a Jew-by-birth marries a Jew-by-choice. What must be appreciated, however, is that marriage is not only a joining of individuals, but a joining of two families; the convert brings into the marriage his or her non-Jewish family and non-Jewish cultural upbringing. Looking at it in this way, marriages between Jews and converts are certainly intermarriages (see Petsonk and Remsen 10; Schneider 4–5).

Because of the ongoing debate in the Messianic Jewish community over formal conversion, the vast majority of conversionary intermarriages are presently informal. While these Gentile spouses may lack official recognition as converts they, nevertheless, are converts to Judaism in every sense of the word. They pray as Jews, keep Jewish households, and raise their children as Messianic Jews. Given the opportunity, they would not hesitate to formalize their commitment to their adopted people Israel.

My opinion, having been part of the Messianic Jewish community for over twenty-five years, is that informal conversionary intermarriage can be as successful in perpetuating Jewish identity as its formal counterpart, or even Jewish-Jewish marriages. It all depends on the degree to which the couple is spiritually motivated, active in their local Messianic synagogue, involved in the broader Jewish community, and committed to Jewish education. Jewish-Gentile couples who are serious about these areas will make a far greater contribution to the future of Messianic Judaism than Jewish-Jewish couples who attend services once a week but are apathetic about Messianic Jewish life in the home.

## Intermarriage Benefits the Messianic Jewish Community

Intermarried couples already exert a profound and positive impact on the Messianic Jewish movement in a variety of ways.

### 1. Enhanced Numbers and Resources

The vast majority of Messianic Jews in the United States are intermarried. If all of these couples (and their children) were suddenly transported to heaven, the Messianic movement would shrink to less than half its present size. Such is the numerical priority of intermarried couples in the Messianic Jewish community. They represent the core of the movement at the present time and their significance will surely increase in the future. Two reasons can be given for this: (1) The American Jewish intermarriage rate has risen to fifty-two percent and shows no sign of abating (see Kosmin 13–16); and (2) Messianic Judaism is an attractive option for intermarried couples.

Dan Cohn-Sherbok links the growth of Messianic synagogues with the growing interest of intermarrieds in the Messianic Jewish option:

> No doubt the high rate of intermarriage between Jews and Christians in contemporary society has greatly contributed to such growth. Messianic Judaism provides a home for those couples who seek to integrate Jewish living with belief in Jesus. (xii)

Carol Harris-Shapiro concurs. In her book, *Messianic Judaism: A Rabbi's Journey Through Religious Change in America*, she states that the Messianic Jewish community is attractive to intermarried couples because it provides them with "a place where both their faith and cultural needs are fulfilled" (183). Intermarried couples bring to the Messianic movement their enthusiasm, spirituality, wisdom, creativity, time, and material resources. The Messianic Jewish community benefits from all of these contributions.

## 2. Jewish Continuity

In contrast to the mainstream Jewish community where intermarriage usually leads to assimilation, Messianic intermarrieds are generally successful in perpetuating Jewish heritage (see Abrams 109–112). This is not to say that every Messianic Jewish marriage is a success story, but relative to the Jewish world, Messianic Jewish intermarried couples excel in commitment to their Jewishness. A principal reason for this is that intermarried Gentiles in a Messianic Jewish congregation are committed to living a Jewish life.

> Messianic non-Jewish spouses in the movement often times demonstrate far more of a commitment to Jewish life than Jewish unbelievers. Furthermore, their children, by and large, are expressing an interest in maintaining a Jewish heritage. (Klayman 134)

Similarly, Rich Nichol, a former President of the Union of Messianic Jewish Congregations, maintains that "often, the most committed, hardworking members of Messianic Jewish synagogues are non-Jews" (23).

Why are non-Jewish spouses of Messianic Jews so committed to living out and conveying Jewish identity? An important contributing factor is that the Gentile spouse finds spiritual fulfillment in the Messianic Jewish faith and lifestyle. This enables the spouse to be an advocate of Messianic Judaism. In addition, since Messianic Judaism is faith-based, intermarried couples are typically motivated by spiritual zeal in expressing Jewish life.

The Jewish spouses of Messianic intermarriages are also committed to Jewish continuity. Few people realize that the 1990 National Jewish Population Survey (NJPS) interviewed Messianic Jews as well as members of the rest of the Jewish community. One of the survey questions was: "Is being Jewish very important in your life?" The results were compiled by the North American Jewish Data Bank and sponsored by the Council of Jewish Federations. Professor Sergio DellaPergola of Hebrew University tabulated the results and presented these findings.

### *Percent of Respondents Agreeing That "Being Jewish is Very Important in Your Life"*
By Denomination, USA, 1990 (weighted sample)

| Respondent's Denomination | % Agree |
| --- | --- |
| Messianic | 100 |
| Orthodox | 77 |
| Multiple denomination | 61 |
| Conservative | 58 |
| Reconstructionist | 49 |
| Reform | 40 |
| Just Jewish | 29 |
| Jewish + other religion | 27 |
| Christian | 21 |
| Don't know | 21 |
| Secular | 16 |
| Non-participating | 13 |
| Other religion | 5 |
| No answer, refuse | 4 |
| Agnostic/atheist | 0 |

According to the above data, one hundred percent of all Messianic Jews interviewed said "yes" to the survey question, thereby indicating that being Jewish was "very important" in their lives. This was higher than any other Jewish group interviewed (see DellaPergola 86). DellaPergola sums up the significance of this data as follows:

Not unexpectedly, the perceived importance of being Jewish is highest among those who consistently manifest their identity via a religious definition and a clear denominational preference. The expected gradient among the major denominations (Orthodox,

Conservative, Reform) emerges. Jews who are consistently secular display far lesser interest for being Jewish. The amount of interest is quite variable, though generally low among other sub-groups with the survey population, including ex-Jews. *One small group with extremely high percentages of interest in Judaism is those preferring the Messianic denomination.* (84, emphasis added)

While it is not known what proportion of the Messianic Jews in the study were married, of those who were, over seventy percent of them were likely intermarried (see Adelstein 53; Eaton 46). Their commitment to Jewish identity is an important indicator of the Messianic Jewish community's success in promoting Jewish continuity.

An example of how this translates into religious practice is that Messianic Jewish intermarrieds are usually faithful in attending *Shabbat* services weekly at their Messianic synagogue. By contrast, the average intermarried couple in mainstream Judaism attends synagogue services only once or twice a year or not at all (see Cohen 111). In ways such as this, Messianic Jewish intermarried couples exert a positive influence on Jewish continuity in the Messianic Jewish movement.

## 3. Compatibility of Marriage Partners

Many Messianic Jews in their twenties and early thirties face a limited pool of potential Messianic Jewish marriage partners. Compounding the problem is that it is a violation of New Covenant *halakhah* for a Messianic Jew to marry a Jew or Gentile who is not a believer in Messiah Yeshua (2 Cor. 6:14). Moreover, it is not expedient to marry a Gentile Christian who lacks Messianic Jewish convictions. What then, is a young Messianic Jewish man or woman in search of a future marriage partner to do? A hard line against intermarriage could result in their not marrying at all.

There is a second problem. The average Messianic synagogue is made up of fifty percent Gentiles (see Feher 165; Bernstein, 1997), some of whom are unmarried and face the same dilemma as Jewish members in finding suitable marriage partners. New Covenant *halakhah* forbids them from marrying anyone who does not believe in Messiah Yeshua, and it is also counterproductive to their calling for them to marry Gentile Christians who do not share their Messianic Jewish vision. As posed previously concerning Messianic Jews, what are these young Messianic Gentile men and women to do? If they maintain their convictions, they may not marry at all.

It is my contention that supporting intermarriage between Messianic Jews and Messianic Gentiles is an ideal solution to the above conundrum. If Messianic Jews marry Messianic Gentiles, the marriage pool doubles, young persons have a greater likelihood of finding suitable marriage partners, and Jewish continuity is not compromised because the spouses share a common background and calling to remain in the Messianic Jewish world. Additionally, by marrying within the community, they strengthen it with their commitment and experience, and their children receive the benefit of having two parents with a Messianic Jewish identity. In these and other ways, intermarriage between Messianic Jews and Messianic Gentiles contributes positively to the future of Messianic Judaism.

## 4. Mitigation of Prejudice

Besides intermarried couples, every Messianic synagogue includes Jewish-Jewish couples, Gentile-Gentile couples, and unmarried members; the intermarried couples among them are important in forming relational links between all the other segments. I wish I could say that prejudice against Gentiles did not exist in the Messianic Jewish movement; but realistically, prejudice exists in every religious community. Recognizing this, Reform rabbi Steven Foster wrote:

> All Jews still have prejudices and those negative reactions are often hurtful to others as well as to our self perceptions. We need to actively change our language that still refers to Gentiles as "*goyim* and *shiksas*" . . . So long as these attitudes of superiority exist, our synagogues will not be the welcoming places they need to become. (113)

Intermarried couples serve a vital role in minimizing prejudice within the Messianic Jewish community. This is because Messianic Jews who are intermarried are protective of their own spouses and refuse to tolerate insensitivity toward other Gentile members as well. In this way, the presence of intermarried couples helps to eliminate the prejudice rooted in ethnic pride that can arise from time to time.

## 5. A Broader Perspective

A final benefit of intermarriage is that it helps Messianic Jews to gain a broader perspective on the day-to-day issues that make up Messianic Jewish life. Even mainstream Judaism increasingly recognizes that synagogue members from non-Jewish backgrounds bring new kinds of creativity to the community. Gary Tobin writes in *Opening the Gates*:

> Because they come from other faith traditions or none at all, they can ask probing questions and push individual Jews to think more about what it means to be a Jew. They bring into Jewish life what has worked (and what has failed) from other faith traditions and institutional venues . . . An infusion of new individuals who come

from outside the Jewish community brings along their experience and knowledge to help build institutional strength inside the Jewish community. (140)

Intermarriage causes Messianic Jews to bring forth perspectives that would not otherwise be evident in an entirely Jewish community. Intermarried Gentiles help Messianic Jews see issues through different cultural lenses, and be more discerning (in an evaluative way) of traditional Jewish perspectives. Non-Jewish spouses can exhibit a unique frame of reference in their approach to Messianic Jewish history, theology and culture because they ask questions that Messianic Jews frequently do not ask. They also tend to focus on areas that Messianic Jews often take for granted, and this leads to a deeper understanding of Messianic Judaism itself.

## Conclusion

The case in support of intermarriage rests on the premise that God allowed intermarriage in the first place because it could benefit his people. In the Messianic Jewish movement, this benefit is manifest in a variety of ways including enhanced numbers and resources, Jewish continuity, compatibility of marriage partners, mitigation of prejudice, and broader perspectives. On the cautionary side, intermarriage does entail certain risks that should not be taken lightly. This notwithstanding, formal and informal conversionary intermarriage has made a vital contribution to Messianic Judaism, and promises to do so in the future.

## Questions for Discussion

- What kind of intermarriage does Scripture permit? What kind is prohibited?
- What two types of intermarriage are problematic for Messianic Jews? Why?
- What two types of intermarriage are appropriate for Messianic Jews? Why?
- What are the five ways in which intermarriage can benefit the Messianic Jewish movement?

## Bibliography

Abrams, Elliot. *Faith or Fear: How Jews Can Survive in a Christian America*. New York: The Free Press, 1997.

Adelstein, Amy. "U.S. Jewish Believers Surveyed." *Mishkan* 1 (1984): 52–54.

Bernstein, Howard. "Evangelizing Jews: Messianic Jews Versus Jews for Jesus." Annual meeting of the Association for the Sociology of Religion, Toronto. Aug. 1997.

Cohen, Shaye J. D. *The Beginnings of Jewishness: Boundaries, Varieties, Uncertainties.* Berkeley: Univ. of California, 1999.

Cohen, Steven M. *Content or Continuity? Alternative Bases for Commitment.* New York: American Jewish Committee, 1991.

Cohn-Sherbok, Dan. *Messianic Judaism.* London: Cassell, 2000.

DellaPergola, Sergio. "New Data on Demography and Identification Among Jews in the U.S." *Jewish Intermarriage In Its Social Context.* Ed. Paul Ritterband. New York: The Jewish Outreach Institute & The Center for Jewish Studies, The Graduate School of the City Univ. of New York, 1991.

Eaton, Tony. "Forum: Should Messianic Jews Intermarry?" *Kesher: A Journal of Messianic Judaism* 9 (Summer 1999): 32–64.

Feher, Shoshanah. *Passing Over Easter: Constructing the Boundaries of Messianic Judaism.* Walnut Creek: AltaMira, 1998.

Foster, Stephen. "Outreach and the Synagogue: Preparing for the Future." *Outreach and the Changing Reform Jewish Community: Creating an Agenda for Our Future.* New York: UAHC, 1989. 111–113.

Harris-Shapiro, Carol. *Messianic Judaism: A Rabbi's Journey through Religious Change in America.* Boston: Beacon, 1999.

Klayman, Seth. "The Messianic Jewish Youth Experience: Our Past, Present and Future." *Kesher: A Journal of Messianic Judaism* 11 (Summer 2000): 117–141.

Kosmin, Barry, Sidney Goldstein, Joseph Waksberg, Nava Lerer, Ariella Keysar and Jeffrey Scheckner. *Highlights of the CJF 1990 National Jewish Population Survey.* New York: Council of Jewish Federations, 1991.

Nichol, Rich. "But Will Your Children Be Jewish?" *Boundaries* (March/April 1999): 19–23, 31.

Petsonk, Judy and Jim Remsen. *The Intermarriage Handbook: A Guide for Jews & Christians.* New York: Arbor House, 1988.

Schneider, Susan Weidman. *Intermarriage: The Challenge of Living with Differences Between Christians and Jews.* New York: The Free Press, 1989.

Tobin, Gary A. *Opening the Gates: How Proactive Conversion Can Revitalize the Jewish Community.* San Francisco: Jossey-Bass, 1999.

✡ ✡ ✡

David J. Rudolph is the editor of *Kesher: A Journal of Messianic Judaism* and of *The Voice of the Lord Messianic Jewish Daily Devotional.* He is the author of *Understanding Messianic Judaism* and a forthcoming book from Messianic Jewish Publishers on the subject of intermarriage. David has served as the leader of Shulchan Adonai Messianic Congregation. He and his wife, Harumi, are intermarried and are raising their two daughters as Messianic Jews.

# INTERMARRIAGE CAN HAVE AN ADVERSE EFFECT ON MESSIANIC JUDAISM

—Michael Schiffman

Jewish life is a precious, yet delicate commodity. It is fragile because of all the factors that come against it in the world in which we live. Jewish life, culture, and faith is at the heart of the intermarriage issue, and consequently, the issue of intermarriage is complicated by the factors of other issues in the Jewish world; assimilation, patrilineal descent, and conversion of non-Jews to Judaism. Considering the effect of all these factors, and the present early stages of Messianic Judaism's development, intermarriage can have an adverse affect upon Messianic Judaism.

## Intermarriage and Assimilation

Since the emancipation in the time of Napoleon, the influence of assimilation has had an eroding effect on the Jewish community all over the world, relegating Jewish identity to a peripheral part of life, rather than its central focus. The more open any society has been for Jewish people, the stronger the attraction toward assimilation has made Jewish lifestyle at best, difficult, and at worst, abandoned. Yet, assimilation is not the only threat Jewish life faces. A stronger force is Intermarriage.

Intermarriage is understood to be the marriage of a Jew to a non-Jew. A Jew is a descendant of Jewish parents, regardless of how religious or non-religious the upbringing may have been. Being Jewish is not merely a religious affiliation, and not merely an ethnic background, but a blend of both, and anyone seeking to grapple with intermarriage must consider both factors in their understanding.

There was a time, less than fifty years ago, when intermarriage between a Jew and non-Jew was a very rare thing. Today the rate of intermarriage is over fifty percent in America, and higher in other countries of the Diaspora. It is no wonder, that the world wide Jewish community is worried. As Messianic Jews, it should also be a concern of ours.

According to Sidney Goldstein, as quoted by Nathan Glazer, "Jews, once 3.7% of the American Population, are now only about 2%" (8). Elliot Abrams, in his important book on the current state of the American Jewish community, *Faith or Fear*, states, "One-third of all Americans of Jewish ancestry no longer report Judaism as their religion. Of all Jews who have married since 1985, the majority have married non-Jews, while the rate of conversion of non-Jewish spouses is declining. Only 29 percent of the children of intermarried couples are raised as Jews. Demographers predict a drop of anywhere from one million to over two million in the American Jewish population in the next two generations" (1–2).

The issue of intermarriage is not simply about two star-crossed lovers from different sides of the tracks who fall in love but whose families do not approve of the union. It is about future generations. Abrams reports, "A three-generational study of the Jews of Philadelphia found that no grandchildren of mixed marriages continued to identify as Jews" (111).

When people from different religious and ethnic backgrounds get married, the bottom line question they will need to deal with is, "How will the children be raised?" Will their children see themselves as Jews or non-Jews, and will they go on to have Jewish homes and raise Jewish children themselves? In ancient times, there was an attitude of inclusiveness towards outsiders becoming Jewish.

There are many cases of Jews who were widowed or divorced, and later in life, married non-Jews. Their children (now adults) balked because the parents did exactly what they told their children not to do. The parent's response was "this marriage is for companionship and not for starting another family, so it's not an issue anymore." This scenario illustrates the issue that future generations are at the heart of the intermarriage debate. The Messianic Jewish movement has a very high percentage of intermarriage within its constituency. This is not because Messianic Judaism advocates intermarriage, but that many intermarried couples have found a home in its midst for good reasons. Messianic Judaism provides a place where the Jewish partner feels he or she is on home turf regarding his or her background, while the non-Jew finds they can still connect to belief in Yeshua, while adjusting culturally. While neither partner may have had any Messianic Jewish involvement before their marriage, they find more comfort in a Messianic synagogue than in a traditional church or a traditional synagogue. Many such couples are otherwise lost to churches or simply cut all affiliations and raise their children with some syncretistic blend, but in such cases, the children usually do *not* go on to live Jewish lives or choose Jewish spouses.

While it is a good thing for Messianic Judaism to be reaching out to intermarried couples—both for its own growth, and also to assist intermarried couples in creating and maintaining Jewish continuity in their lives for themselves and their children—this does not mean that Messianic Judaism should encourage intermarriage.

## Intermarriage and Patrilineal Descent

In the wider Jewish world, the topic of intermarriage has been the starting point for other discussions—most recently, the halakhic issue over patrilineal vs. matrilineal decent; whether the children of a Jewish father and non-Jewish mother are to be considered Jewish. Over the millennia, traditional *halakhah* has maintained that the children of a Jewish mother were to be considered Jewish regardless of the father's Jewish status, but the children of a Jewish father and non-Jewish mother were to be considered to be non-Jews.

In the past decade, this halakhic position was challenged by the Reform movement, and has been at odds with the rest of the Jewish world ever since. The position was taken to reach out to intermarried families, and bring their children into the fold instead of leaving them outside. Messianic Judaism, has concurred on this issue with the Reform movement, and considers the children of intermarriage Jewish regardless of whether their Jewish status is through the father or mother.

While on one level it is easier to go along with the traditional halakhic view, because it is most widely accepted, it is hard to do so in real life situations. There are many cases of Jewish children who are Jewish on their mother's side or on both sides, yet they walk away from their Jewish identification, considering themselves to be agnostic or atheist. There are also instances of children who have Jewish fathers and non-Jewish mothers, who are deeply drawn to their Jewish heritage, and want to embrace it, yet are spurned from traditional circles and considered to be non-Jews.

When I was visiting Russia, I became friendly with a young Jewish man in his early thirties, an attorney, who was very drawn to Jewish prayer. When he found out that I prayed and donned *t'fillin* each morning, he asked if I could teach him to *daven* (pray). I had a Russian-Hebrew *siddur* with me. I showed him which prayers to pray and lent him my *t'fillin* to wear during the prayers. I was touched by how much it meant to him. Later he told me that his father is Jewish, but not his mother, and when he tried to go to the Orthodox synagogue, they told him to not come there, because they didn't consider him to be a Jew. He said he was also acquainted with the Reform Synagogue in the city, and knowing they accept people of patrilineal descent, I encouraged him to go there.

Upon reflection, I realized that being Jewish is not only a matter of descent, but is also rooted in what has been called the *pintele Yid* (the spark of

Jewish being). If someone is of Jewish descent, through either parent, and manifests a spark of Jewish being, a love of Jewish people, Jewish faith, and Jewish culture, they should be embraced, and not rejected.

The position of inclusiveness is more complicated than simply affirming the Jewish status of children with a patrilineal Jewish background. That is only the starting point. The main question remains. How will the children be raised, and what will be the way they perceive themselves? Will they go on to live Jewish lives, choose Jewish spouses and make Jewish homes, or will they see being Jewish as something their father or mother was, but consider it something not relevant for their own lives? This is not simply a Messianic issue, but one with which the entire Jewish world wrestles. The goal of a Jewish household is to produce Jewish children who will go on to live Jewish lives. Whatever Jewish identity is passed on to future generations, will be learned in the home and in the religious community, not merely from a family tree.

The first step is that the couple must agree that they will have a Jewish household, and that their children will be raised Jewish. If the parents are not committed to this, their children will grow up confused, not sure of what they are. They will not fit in anywhere. When the parents agree, they need to communicate this to their parents. This is academic until the children are born. Once the children come into the world, the Jewish relatives are looking for a *b'rit milah* and the non-Jewish relatives are looking for a baptism. Intermarriage means the parents are caught between their parents and in-laws.

I know an intermarried family where the mother is Jewish and the father is Irish Catholic. They decided to raise their children as Jews, as the father was not a religious man and did not mind his wife's religious convictions. His mother is a religious Catholic and when the children were born, she tried to put pressure on her daughter-in-law to convert or to at least have the children baptized as Catholics. The Jewish woman refused, and said her children will be raised as Jews. Because she stood her ground, and she and her husband were in agreement, they raised their children as Jews, were members of the synagogue, and her in-laws even helped chauffeur the children back and forth to Hebrew school. While this is a mixed marriage situation, it was made easier by the resolve of the parents to be of one mind on the issue, in spite of parental pressures.

Ultimately, while it is fine to advocate that the Messianic Jewish community should embrace intermarried *families*, it should not in any way endorse intermarriage as a practice that should be embraced. It is entirely possible to love and accept intermarried families without having to affirm intermarriage as good and ideal. The main reason is Jewish survival. We want our people to go on. If a person takes a cup of coffee and puts a few ounces of water in it, it is still a cup of coffee. But if a person takes that cup of coffee, puts it under a faucet, and runs the water for thirty seconds, there may be some coffee left in the cup, but it is no longer a cup of coffee. If intermarriage as a practice is endorsed and encouraged in Messianic Judaism, in a few generations, Messianic Judaism will become a movement of people with one remote or imagined Jewish ancestry. There will be coffee in the cup, but it will not be a cup of coffee.

If Messianic Judaism is, as it maintains, "a Judaism," then it must be seeking to produce Jews. It is right and good to draw intermarried couples to Messianic Judaism, but this does not mean that intermarriage as a principle should be advocated and supported. On the other hand, it should not be completely forbidden either. There are some very fine couples that are intermarried, who have stable home lives—better than some couples that are not intermarried. *Shalom bayit* (peace in the home) is an important concept, in any marriage, but especially in intermarriage. This should be strongly encouraged. If the Jewish and non-Jewish spouses can agree that their children will be raised as Jews. If they endeavor to be involved in a Messianic Jewish community, celebrate *Shabbat* and Jewish holidays in their homes, as well as in the synagogue—they will have peace in this matter. Their children will grow up with a *sense* of who they are, instead of *confusion* over who they are.

## Intermarriage and Conversion

Another part of a solution to the intermarriage issue should be encouraging the conversion of the non-Jewish spouse to Messianic Judaism. According to Dr. Lawrence J. Epstein, in his paper, "Why the Jewish People Should Welcome Converts," [the ancient writer Philo made reference to the] " . . . conversion of gentiles who lived among the Jewish people, including, many children abandoned by their gentile families; and through marriage of a Jew to a gentile. Such efforts were deliberately not intrusive. They did not characteristically include belittling the beliefs of others, or the creation of a widespread exclusively missionary occupation."

While the Messianic Jewish community as a whole is not now, or ever has in the past advocated the conversion of gentiles, it would do well to reconsider this option for the sake of family continuity and *shalom bayit*. If the non-Jewish spouse is willing and wanting to make this step, it would go a long way towards cementing the Jewish identity of the family, and help remedy the situation of the non-Jew feeling like an eternal outsider. If a non-Jewish spouse converts, they are no longer a non-Jew, and the marriage is no longer an intermarriage. Conversion involves not only a holding to Jewish beliefs, but also a commitment to the Jewish people. Being Jewish is not merely holding to certain beliefs or enjoying a culture. A Jew must be concerned for all other Jews. Conversion is marrying the whole Jewish people. A person must not convert as a means to get married to a Jew, but they must be willing to take upon themselves all that it means to be a Jew.

According to research by Ergon Mayer, "Only 24% of children of mixed marriages identify as Jews, while 84% of the children of conversion do. 86% of conversion couples joined synagogues, only 38% of their children did. Only 24% of converts say they would discourage intermarriage" (24).

Intermarriage may indeed be "when worlds collide," but the collision can be softened, and even remedied. Intermarriage can have an adverse affect upon Messianic Judaism. Messianic Judaism can not sit by and watch our people dissolve. As *Mordechai* the *Tzaddik* said to Queen Esther, "For if you remain completely silent at *this time*, relief and deliverance will arise for the Jews from another place, but you and your father's house will perish. Yet who knows whether you have come to the kingdom for *such a time as this?*" (Esther 4:14). Messianic Judaism must be part of the solution.

## Questions for Discussion

- How can an intermarried couple nurture Jewish identity in their children?
- What are ways in which a couple can be connected to the Jewish world outside their home?
- How can a non-Jewish spouse feel more connected and welcome in our midst?
- Why is it important to pass on Jewish identity and heritage to our children?

## Bibliography

Abrams, Elliot. *Faith or Fear*. New York: The Free Press, 1997.

Epstein, Lawrence. "Why the Jewish People Should Welcome Converts." *Judaism*, Vol. 43, No. 3 (Summer 1994). <http://www.convert.org/judaism.htm>.

Glazer, Nathan. "New Perspectives on American Jewish Sociology." *American Jewish Year Book*. New York: American Jewish Committee; Philadelphia: Jewish Publication Society, 1987.

Mayer, Ergon. *Children of Intermarriage*. New York: American Jewish Committee, 1989.

Michael Schiffman grew up in a traditional Jewish family in New York. He has earned three degrees including a D.Min. The author of *Return of the Remnant*, over the past two decades, he has been the leader of three Messianic Jewish congregations. Dr. Schiffman lectures on a variety of Jewish subjects in the UMJC Yeshiva and is an Adjunct Professor of Rabbinic Literature at Fuller Theological Seminary in association with the Messianic Jewish Theological Institute.

# A CASE FOR JEWISH LEADERSHIP

—Tony Eaton

When modern Jewish believers in Yeshua of Nazareth chose to designate their faith practice as Messianic Judaism the choice was made to identify first and foremost with the Jewish people, their history, values, and tradition. Inherent in all of that is the notion that who we are, and how we relate to God is inextricably connected to our identity as the Children of Israel. As Michael Wyschogrod eloquently states in his book *The Body of Faith*, "Israel's symbol of the covenant is circumcision, a searing of the covenant into the flesh of Israel and not only or perhaps not even primarily, into its spirit. And that is why God's election is of a carnal people. By electing the seed of Abraham, God creates a people that is in His service in the totality of its human being and not just in its moral and spiritual existence" (Wyschogrod 67).

If this is so then it must be reflected in the way our congregations are constituted. If we see ourselves as a Jewish movement primarily oriented towards the Jewish people, then the leaders of our movement and our congregations must be primarily Jewish men and women. This may seem like an obvious statement to most, yet it has been less obvious to some in our movement. It depends largely on how one sees the purpose and calling of Messianic Judaism. If we are a universal body, uniting Jew and Gentile into one, then whether our leaders are Jewish is a matter of total indifference. If, on the other hand, we are indeed a Jewish movement for Jews, we must face the thorny issue of the role of non-Jews in the leadership of our congregations, most especially at the level of Spiritual Leaders and Rabbis.

At its most fundamental, the word *rabbi* means "my master." But as with so much of human language, it is where an idea is and is going rather than where it has come from that matters most, and nowhere is this more evident than in the meaning of the word *rabbi*.

An interesting and unique phenomenon of Jewish history is the veneration, not of military and political figures, but the religious leadership of the Jewish world. While all the kingdoms of the Earth remember with awe the great conquerors of their pasts, the Jews have reserved that kind of attention for their rabbis. The importance of the relationship between master (also known as teacher, Pharisee, and later as rabbi) and disciples took root during the Second Temple period. Thus began the age of the great sages—teachers, who upheld the covenant, and built a precautionary fence around the *Torah* to prevent a breach. Every aspect of life was discussed, debated, and hammered out by these sages until all meaningful existence fell under the sacred canopy of the law. It was these learned and experienced men, from within the community who not only taught but also practiced, that were looked to as the spiritual leaders.

This notion of the term *rabbi* as being an exclusively Jewish appellation is evident even in modern American pop culture. A famous joke starts out, "A priest a minister and a rabbi are on a desert island..." Notice that no qualifiers are needed to indicate who is being spoken of. Who the Jew is in this story is clear from the use of the term *rabbi*.

Jacob Petuchowski, in his book, The Heirs of the Pharisees states, "'Rabbi' may be the highest title, which Judaism has to confer. But much depends upon when and where that title is being conferred. In the final analysis, it is the bearer of the title who confers honor and dignity upon the rabbinical title, and not vice versa" (83).

So for some, the word *rabbi* stirs up images of the great sages of our past. For others it is their Hebrew school days—toiling over their Haftarah portions longing for the torture to be over—or perhaps the stern somber senior who greeted them on High Holy days. However people view their rabbis, ultimately, they are the ones who are looked to as the guardians and leaders of the community.

In 1981, my wife and I, both products of marginally religious Jewish homes, had our son Jared. Despite the fact that we were, by that time, utterly non-observant, in fact completely secular in outlook, our first thought was to call "our rabbi" to arrange for the *b'rit milah* of our son. However he would choose to live his life, at least he would start life out as a Jew!

I tell this story to illustrate a point about those to whom we look for anchors in important times in life. We look to those we know, or at least perceive that we know, understand what these things mean and can guide us through because of their long experience, and because we as a community have given them permission to lead us. Again, Petuchowski says, "The formula of ordination, yoreh, yoreh, yadin, yadin, (he may teach, he may judge), implied permission to render decisions in ritual and civil law" (77).

The implication here is that those who practiced the ritual and civil law of Israel—were Jewish. For how does one declaim on such matters for a community if one is not of the community? Stated another way, it is the community itself which imputes the authority to an individual to declaim, and those they choose will invariably be from among their own. No community chooses its leadership from outside.

One may think that I am reasoning myself out of a job. After all, Jewish Messianic congregational leaders are no more legitimate to the wider Jewish community than are non-Jews in that role. Yet, despite our status in the wider Jewish community, we will as a movement—continue to see more progress in moving toward the mainstream. As indications of this trend, I offer the recent studies of our movement by prominent members of the wider Jewish community (Feher, 1998; Harris-Shapiro, 1999; Cohn-Sherbok, 2000). These treatments, most especially the latter, represent great progress in our relationship to the community. I am convinced that the more we work towards normalizing our relationship with the wider community, and see ourselves as primarily serving the Jewish community, sharing in its life and its values, the more Jewish people will understand that we are not "other." It is in this atmosphere—that our people will be able to see the magnificence of our Jewish faith centered in Messiah Yeshua.

Recently, I sat down to lunch with a prominent local rabbi. We were discussing membership for my congregation in the Interfaith Council of our city. At the meeting, there were other prominent clergy persons of various faiths. Among the things discussed was my own, and my congregation's claim to Jewishness. It was because we were joining the group as a Jewish organization and not a Christian one that our application was being called into question. It struck me then and does so now—that my position would have been untenable had I not been a Jew. How could I have convinced the rabbi or the others there that Messianic Judaism's claim to be a legitimate Judaism is valid if I were not a Jew myself? The discussion would have been an absurd one.

The rabbi and I discussed all the traditional questions attendant to the larger question of "Who is a Jew?' We spoke about the question of matrilineal or patrilineal descent, one's practice of Judaism, and conversion. While I held my ground well on the first two points, (the rabbi was from the Reform tradition) it was on the third point that I knew we were weakest.

It was clear from that discussion that if we are to maintain our integrity as a Jewish movement—our congregational leaders and rabbis must be Jewish. After all, how do you shape a Jewish institution without Jews? It is impossible to do so without those who have a "Jewish memory." Those who have experienced and have some understanding of Jewish life and can synthesize that experience with their faith in Messiah Yeshua into a religious expression deeply rooted in the Jewish experience, and filled with God's Spirit through faith in our king.

But what of the men and women who now serve our congregations in these capacities who are not Jews by birth? I can personally testify of their ability, love, faithfulness, and calling as they serve our people and our Messiah. I am convinced that they belong among us, that they have been called by God to serve Israel, and that without them our movement would be greatly diminished. But is that enough?

Dr. Michael Schiffman, in an article for *Kesher*, identifies a problem in Messianic Jewish leadership culture when he says, "As a pioneering endeavor the Messianic Jewish movement has struggled to generate excellence in every area of its formation. Messianic Judaism's leadership emerged through the same 'learn as you go' situations in which the movement itself was formed. Messianic leaders arose from positions of lay leadership into congregational leadership, reflecting the theological discipleship in which they themselves were nurtured. This leadership for the most part lacked professional ministry training. Some even said that all that was required to be a Messianic leader was a beard and a Bible!" (123). This casual approach to the choosing of leadership extends even to the trickier notion of the claim to Jewishness of that leader. Because of our association with the evangelical, free, church movement, and our embracing of the more universalistic messages of the New Covenant, we have rendered the historical understanding of rabbis as "Jewish" leaders of our congregations as unimportant and unnecessary. This notion, for reasons that I have already stated, renders our identities as Jews a matter of indifference.

However, nowhere in the Bible is Jewish identity trivialized. Indeed, the distinctions between Jew and Gentile are pointed out vividly in the portion called "The Jerusalem Council" (Acts 15). Here the first Apostles (all Jews), come together to discuss the role of Gentiles in what was for them a Jewish faith. Ultimately their decision is that Gentiles remain Gentiles, and Jews remain Jews. In other words while Yeshua came to break down barriers between Jews and Gentiles. He did not come to obliterate all distinctions in peoples.

If we are to keep our claim to being a Jewish movement legitimate, it is imperative that we develop a rite of passage that formalizes the relationship between our non-Jewish constituency and the Jewish people. Yet, not all in our movement agree.

Scott Moore, in addressing the issue of committed Gentiles in Messianic Jewish congregations offers this, "I propose that Gentiles who adopt such a lifetime commitment, whether married to a natural born Jew or not, be considered proselytes after the manner of Ruth. . . . 'Ruthian' proselytes would be those Gentiles who, make a lifetime commitment to identify with the Jewish people and observe biblically Jewish practices along with the Jewish cultural practices of the congregational environment in which they dwell. They would circumcise their sons as Jews, and they and their children would be considered Jews" (113).

Moore, while acknowledging difficulties with this approach, never the less feels that this approach is correct. However, it circumvents the traditional ways in which people join a community. As I have written elsewhere,

" . . . conversion or more generally a rite of passage is and has been the historically accepted way in which those who were outsiders in a community were allowed to enter into that community without being marginalized. A well defined, rigorous rite of passage will also ensure that the candidate will be fully equipped to live out the life that they are pledged to" (Eaton 57).

Can we ever expect acceptance from the wider Jewish community if we insist on bypassing the way that people have for centuries, been received into the community? I suggest that it is not possible for us to go back to some ancient place and time and adopt a practice that even in Yeshua's time was long out of currency. Instead, what we must do is enter into dialog with the history, tradition, and normative practice of Judaism as it now is, and there find the answers to our problem. If we do, it will address the other difficulties Moore's approach raises.

For instance, he asks the question, "What prevents a proselyte from reversing his or her direction when the going gets tough?" (Moore 114). Even conversion is no guarantee against this possibility. A well defined, rigorous rite of passage will do much to test the commitment of any candidate for conversion. Right now, we ask only for a person's word, if that. What we need to do is follow the advice of *Ya'akov* when he says, "But someone will say that you have faith and I have actions. Show me this faith of yours without the actions and I will show you my faith by my actions" (James 2:18).

The challenge for our movement as we enter the new millennium is to develop and institute a conversion process for our non-Jewish members. Without this process, we will find it difficult—perhaps impossible—to justify ourselves as a Judaism to the wider Jewish community, the wider world, and perhaps in time, even to ourselves.

## Questions for Discussion

- When you hear the word *rabbi*, what kinds of images come to mind?
- Who should have the right to call themselves "rabbis"?
- A Jewish leader has more of an opportunity to guide the Messianic Jewish community into a better relationship with the wider Jewish community. Do you agree or disagree—and why?
- Yeshua came to break down barriers between Jews and Gentiles. He did not come to obliterate all distinctions in peoples. How is this truth demonstrated in your congregation?

## Bibliography

Cohn-Sherbok, Dan. *Messianic Judaism*. London: Cassell, 2000.

Eaton, Tony. "Should Messianic Jews Intermarry?" *Kesher: A Journal of Messianic Judaism* 9 (Summer 1999): 32–64.

Feher Shoshanah. *Passing Over Easter: Constructing the Boundaries of Messianic Judaism.* Walnut Creek: AltaMira, 1998.

Harris-Shapiro, Carol. *Messianic Judaism: A Rabbi's Journey Through Religious Change In America.* Boston: Beacon, 1999.

Moore, Scott. "Gentiles and the Spirit of Adoption." *Kesher: A Journal of Messianic Judaism* 11 (Summer 2000): 102–116.

Petuchowski, Jacob. *Heirs of the Pharisees.* New York: Basic Books, 1970.

Schiffman, Michael. "Authority to Lead: What is the Source?" *Kesher: A Journal of Messianic Judaism* 4 (Autumn 1996): 123–136.

Wyschogrod, M. *The Body of Faith.* Northvale: Jason Aronson, 1996.

Tony Eaton is the congregational leader of Simchat Yisrael Messianic Jewish Synagogue, located in West Haven, Connecticut, and the Northeast Regional Director of the UMJC. He is enrolled in the UMJC Yeshiva program and is pursuing *s'mikhah.* Tony teaches adult theological education at The Gateway School of Ministry. He and his wife, Merryl, reside in Hamden, Connecticut. They have three children.

# EQUAL PARTICIPANTS IN THE COMMUNITY

—Patrice Fischer

The "modern" Messianic Jewish movement has a complex and chaotic interrelationship with Gentile Christian churches and with other non-Jewish individuals and subgroups. These interrelationships form complicated subsystems that are difficult to analyze. Individual Messianic congregations began to emerge out of Gentile Christian (Protestant) church groups in the early 1970s. These "new" congregations were made up of both Messianic Jews and fellow Gentiles who wished to worship the God of Israel in uniquely Jewish ways.

To worship in Jewish ways has seemed easy and logical for many Jewish believers. However, the path of Gentiles who wish to worship and live in Jewish ways is difficult to trace. It does not overstate the fact to say that the Messianic movement's handling of its Gentile participants is critical. "Messianic Gentiles" can be called on to be in leadership within Messianic congregations if they follow the worship and lifestyle of the Godfearers of the first century C.E. The prime example is Cornelius from the book of Acts. However, if we choose to grow without the assistance and participation of solid and committed Gentile families, Messianic congregations may dwindle and die—part of a well-meaning but doomed experiment left over from the social upheavals of the 1960s.

## Coming Out of the Churches

The modern Messianic movement began as a rebellion of Jewish believers in Yeshua from within largely Protestant congregations in the late 1960s and early 1970s. Jews within churches found that Gentile Christians did not understand their need to identify with their childhood culture. As part of the social upheavals of the 1960s, "foreign" Christians from places such as Laos, Korea, and Viet Nam came to the United States and established congregations which were centered around their home cultures. Messianic Judaism was another example of cultural expression on the part of people who had a shared understanding of their Jewish heritage and culture (see Schiffman, 1996).

Jewishly-based congregations sprang up and prospered in Philadelphia, Chicago's northern suburbs, Baltimore, and Minneapolis—literally all across the country during the 1970s. The Jewish believers, who left churches in order to form a "new" type of congregation, brought their Gentile spouses with them to these new congregations. There were other Gentiles, not related by marriage to Jews, who came to these new Jewish services—Gentiles who wanted to participate in these congregations.

## Getting Established

At first, the leadership of these groups was unsure of the intentions of these Gentiles. The non-Jewish spouses seemed linked to the Jewish congregations in a natural and well-defined way. However, there was also an under-the-table issue of how the Gentiles who were also attracted to the Jewish worship would be treated. The easiest way to prevent a slippage back into Gentile Christianity (so it seemed to these early pioneers) was to make sure that there were few or no Gentiles in charge of the meetings. Gentile leadership would create Gentile congregations, while Jewish leaders would *ipso facto* create Jewish congregations.

However, much of what passed for "Jewish worship" at these early meetings was little different than the average Protestant service that many Jewish believers had become comfortable with. Peppy Jewish-flavored music, Israeli folk dancing, and the recitation of the *Sh'ma* were added to a central sermon given by a male leader. If congregations met on Friday evenings, there may have been a candle-lighting ceremony, since this ceremony required a woman who knew the Hebrew blessing. Other formal Jewish prayers and responses found at *Shabbat* services were almost non-existent in these proto-congregations.

From a sociological point of view, this should not be surprising. The "rebels" had rebelled yet again. The same Jews who had found fulfillment in naming Yeshua as their Messiah had left their home synagogues (and in some cases, the Jewish community) to meet and be acculturated within Gentile churches. Now they would leave the Gentile churches to meet with others that wanted, in theory, to live life Jewishly. As a group, there was an urgency to "re-acculturate" —back into a more identifiably Jewish worship style and family lifestyle.

Unfortunately, many of these rebels did not have a broad experience or understanding of weekly Jewish worship, so there was little or nothing of the *siddur* to be found in their meetings. Important Jewish holidays such as Passover and *Purim* were celebrated with gusto within more informal large-family settings. The emphasis was on broadly educating the participants rather than on formal propriety. This push toward learning how to "live Jewishly," along with the de-emphasis on formal Jewish worship (highly formulaic worship was pejoratively labeled as "dead ritualism") fits in with the milieu of American society in general. It was widely followed by many groups, both religious and non-religious, during the 1970s and early 1980s.

Added to these negative perceptions about formal Jewish worship was a positive underlying commitment to see the modern nation of Israel as an active focus in communal life—something not normally found in Gentile churches at the time. Large groups of Gentile churches (usually those grouped as evangelical and/or charismatic, as opposed to Christendom in general) and almost all Messianic Jewish congregations viewed world events as hurtling inevitably towards the apocalypse which would be coming around the year 2000. This viewpoint was easy for them to agree on, and again, was a reflection of a common societal attitude during that time. However, Messianic Jews felt (and still feel) that the establishment and defense of the modern State of Israel constitutes a major act of God in our world—something that will determine the future of all Jews worldwide. Some Gentile churches feel various levels of commitment to the real-life State of Israel, and do not bind up their future "peoplehood" along with Israel.

## Where Do Gentiles Fit In?

As individual congregations within Messianic Judaism flourished, both Jews and Gentiles within them were sitting shoulder-to-shoulder on Friday nights or Saturday mornings—worshipping the same God in the same way and sharing identical spiritual world views. However, the actual status of Gentiles within individual congregations was not (and still is not) overtly spelled out. Each congregation had unwritten rules about what (exactly) Gentile participants are and are not allowed to do. These unwritten rules seemed to be based on fears and misconceptions that were not brought out into the open—for fear of offending the congregants. Even the designation of individuals as either a Jew or a Gentile could be fuzzy and vary from group to group.

The wide opinion within the movement crystallized in the early 1970s around the definitions of "Jewish" and "non-Jewish" as stated by groups such as the International Hebrew Christian Alliance. Founded in the early 1900s, when the vast majority of Jews who believed in Yeshua worshipped in churches, this parachurch alliance of individuals used as its criteria of membership that any Jew who believed in Yeshua, or the spouse of such a Jew, could belong. (Its name was changed in 1975 to the IMJA). How would a person's claim to be Jewish be proved? Based on that person's statement that it was so (this is called "self-report" in scholarly circles).

The process of labeling groups of people invariably becomes messy—there are always "exceptions." The status of children who had only one Jewish parent was unclear. In 1975, the appeal of a Gentile family (who had formally converted to Orthodox Judaism) to join the IMJA— was soundly denied. Based on unwritten rules, any Gentile who converted to Judaism was to be seen as suspect and that conversion was not acceptable by Messianic groups if the conversion was revealed to them. If a Gentile had converted to Judaism (or if a self-reported Jew had a mother or a father who converted to Judaism), it was not to be admitted publicly if a person wanted to be fully accepted by the Messianic Jewish community.

These unwritten rules were not just for the rank-and-file membership in congregations. Jewishness based on parents' identity was the most important criteria for leadership in Messianic congregations and fellowships—sometimes superceding gender in importance. In real life, this meant that a Jewish woman could have more of a voice in matters than a Gentile male within the early groups. However, spousal privilege was also seen as important. In couples where one spouse was Jewish, the loyal spouse who worshipped in the Messianic synagogue and participated whole-heartedly in a Jewish home, achieved, in practice, the same level of respect as married couples where both partners were Jewish. Labels on individual Gentiles who had married Messianic Jews could be downplayed in average congregational functioning. This could be seen in statements such as, "You would never know that Beth is not Jewish—she is so committed to the congregation!"

But what of other Gentiles who are not married to Jews—what about them? Under what rules were (are) they allowed to function within a Messianic synagogue? Again, it varies from synagogue to synagogue, with almost no rules overtly written down. Some congregations will not allow a Gentile in main leadership positions (i.e., they would not be permitted to serve as a ruling council or eldership member). Some will allow those married to a Jew the same rights and privileges as a Jew. Teenagers that attend national Messianic Jewish conferences are sometimes told that Jewish kids should date only Jews and Gentiles should date only Gentiles. (The identity of those who are applying the labels on these children is never discussed. It is assumed that everyone can tell who-is-who). Incredibly, there are currently some fine leaders of Messianic congregations who have no Jewish DNA at all (if such a thing can be proven to exist).

The situation is confused and confusing for those Gentiles who have aligned themselves with Messianic congregations. There now exist hundreds of Gentile families who attend and support Messianic congregations without one (provable) drop of "Jewish blood" in them. Why do they come? Why do they feel a part of the Jewish people? Each family would give its own unique answers, but in common, they feel that they have "come home" to the Jewish way of life and worship. Many say that they have gone to Gentile churches for years—being contented until they "woke up" and began to seek out Jewish worship and Messianic Jews for themselves. Once they started to go to a Messianic synagogue, they became deeply dissatisfied with their former Gentile-based worship. One common word that many of them use is that they felt "called" to be one with the Jewish people. They bring their spouses to Messianic congregations along with them, and they also bring their children to be religiously educated side-by-side with the Jewish children.

## Our "Righteous Gentiles"

Of course, not all of these Gentile families stay committed to Messianic synagogues. They stay for a while and then move on to some other place to worship. Granted, some of these families are "flaky" (lacking in social skills), but Gentiles of varying levels of commitment are commonly found within Messianic Judaism. Each congregation seems to have one or more Gentile families who have shown by their lifestyle that they could qualify to be Jews. They have proved their unity with the Jewish faith and lifestyle, investing their time and effort into living as Jews among the Jews. Yet, there was and still is no formal way to identify them within the Messianic community.

There have been those Gentile individuals and families who have wanted to go further still in their commitment to the Jewish people and have inquired about conversion (i.e., formal attachment to the Jewish people). As intimated above, conversion to Judaism is roundly condemned by most within the Messianic movement. It cannot be pursued openly by these Gentiles without backlash from many quarters within the movement. There is an underlying fear that stems from the early days of the movement—Gentiles bring with them "Gentile ways."

One issue that the Messianic movement has never openly discussed is the existence and status of these "Righteous Gentiles" in our midst. They came to the Messianic movement as adults, having chosen the Jewish lifestyle as adults, rather than at their parents' knees. This group of Gentiles most emphatically does not bring "Gentile ways" with them. They have entered our congregations to be taught about the Jewish ways of life and worship. They have taken steps to read and learn and experience the Jewish way of life as a free choice, rather than have it "forced" on them by their parents. In the movement's infancy, people were naive enough to believe that all Jews know and appreciate Jewish ways of worship and life—more than all Gentiles. Further experience and history have shown us that this is not so.

There are Messianic Jews that have little or no grounding in Judaism (or little or no grounding in *living* Judaism, at any rate). There are Messianic Jews that border on being anti-Semitic in word and deed. There are Messianic leaders who are Jewish, but bring with them into the Messianic movement reactions from individual childhood events and negative impressions which they attribute to all Jews. This makes sense, again, when realizing that if an individual was completely happy and satisfied with the faith of his/her parents, they would probably not have chosen to identify with Yeshua as the promised Messiah of Israel. It is usually the dissatisfaction that a person has with the status quo of Judaism that leads them to investigate belief in Yeshua as a possible remedy to that dissatisfaction.

## Blocks to Openly Accepting "Righteous Gentiles" As Equals

There are several reasons why the open acceptance of "Righteous Gentiles" has been an "uncomfortable" issue without formal discussion within the Messianic movement. They can be outlined as follows:

1. There is an incomplete or incorrect understanding (on the part of both leaders and Messianic congregants) of the place of Gentiles (both their theological place and their practical place) within our congregations.
2. Some Jews (including leaders) were raised in nominally Jewish homes and do not have a strong background or experience in the varieties of Judaism. Some Jewish leaders may be threatened by Gentiles who know more about Judaism than they do.

There is an unwritten rule that states that the only definition of "who constitutes a Jew"—which is acceptable to the Messianic movement—is a Jew who has "Jewish DNA," or who marries someone with "Jewish DNA." Formal conversions to Judaism by the larger Jewish community are portrayed at a public level within the Messianic movement as undesirable at best and heretical at worst. Therefore, those "Righteous Gentiles" who pursue conversions are shunned by many in the Messianic movement. Other reasons for the lack of acceptance are:

3. There may be a truncated and/or misguided understanding of the existence and goal of Gentile conversion to Judaism both historically and today.
4. There may be a truncated and/or misguided understanding of the passages in the New Covenant which deal with the primary identification of Jewish and Gentile "positions" in the hierarchy of God's plan as described by *Rav Sha'ul*.

These are some of the issues that should be dealt with as a matter of community discussion in order to make a way for these "Righteous Gentiles" to be handled equitably within local congregations. These discussions will also serve to highlight and enhance the rights and responsibilities of Gentile participation at a larger level within local congregations and regional Messianic organizations.

One underlying issue that affects all parts of the issues surrounding Gentile participation in Messianic Judaism concerns the inadequate levels of formal training for current Messianic leaders within the movement. Many Messianic leaders were discipled and/or trained by those who used primarily Gentile Christian definitions of Judaism. These leaders learned theology that is based on negative Christian stereotypes of Jews and Judaism. Consequently, these leaders have a personal operational theology—and even world view—that presents a Gentile Christian understanding of Judaism as a "dead" or lifeless religion without Yeshua. Some leaders are "self-taught" through the reading of random theologically-based books that may or may not establish a knowledge base that is accurate or even helpful for the congregation leader. Leaders who are inadequately taught the requisite Jewish backgrounds of the Messianic faith will allow their congregations to ignore or even discriminate against Gentiles in their midst.

## A New Covenant Example: The Godfearers

There is a pattern in the New Covenant that can guide the theology and practice of establishing the rights and responsibilities of Gentiles as full participants within Messianic congregations. As investigated in more detail in "Modern-Day Godfearers: A Biblical Model for Gentile Participation in Messianic Congregations," the book of Acts describes the practices of a group of Gentiles who had an integral part in the establishment of the first Messianic synagogues. There, the "Righteous Gentiles" have a specific and unique name: Godfearers. As exemplified by Cornelius (Acts 10:1), these Gentiles followed primary Jewish laws such as the keeping of the Sabbath, basic kosher laws, and the celebration of the Jewish holidays. It was this group of whom *Shimon* (Peter) was made aware in the pivotal vision described in Acts 10:10–16 (where he was convinced of God's total acceptance of the Godfearers' worship).

Investigating the first Godfearers' religious practices and way of life can give us a strong pattern for basing Gentile participation within today's Messianic congregations. If a Gentile family can faithfully (and without reservation) adhere to the Godfearers' way of life as described in the book of Acts (and other contemporaneous accounts)—then there would be no reason to forbid them from actively participating in the life of the Messianic synagogue as equal partners with Messianic Jews. Understanding and applying the Godfearers' life principles would prevent discrimination within local congregations, and help Gentile participants to feel fully accepted by the congregation. There would be very little reason to fear that Godfearing Gentiles would "take over" Messianic congregations. A Gentile family would not feel a need to "prove" that they have a rightful place within the Messianic movement.

Many issues need to be discussed when the topic of future Gentile participation in Messianic synagogues is broached. There continues to be distrust and silence regarding Gentiles who feel committed to the Messianic movement. There are many conflicting answers to the question of "Who is a Jew?" within the modern Messianic movement—a question that needs to be openly addressed. Messianic leaders need to educate themselves as to the issues and needs of their Gentile congregants. Messianic Gentiles who are acting the part of Cornelius in today's world can be fully accepted as congregants and even as active parts of congregational leadership.

We are now entering the second generation of Messianic Judaism. The topic of Gentile participation has been ignored or even eliminated from discussion. It is important to start to resolve this central question in a biblically reasoned manner. If the Messianic movement wants to be able to retain hundreds of valuable Gentiles in our own congregations, we owe them this consideration.

## Questions for Discussion

* Why were Jewish believers wary of active Gentile participation in Messianic synagogues during the infancy stage of Messianic Judaism?
* In what ways might Gentiles feel "left out" if they choose to attend a Messianic synagogue?
* Do Messianic Jews need Gentiles in their synagogues? Why or why not?
* How could settling the "Gentile question" help the children of Jewish-Gentile marriages?

## Bibliography

Fischer, Patrice. "Modern Day Godfearers: A Biblical Model for Gentile Participation in Messianic Congregations." *The Enduring Paradox: Exploratory Essays in Messianic Judaism*, Ed. John Fischer. Baltimore: Lederer/Messianic Jewish Publishers, 2000. 171–181.

Schiffman, Michael. *Return of the Remnant.* Baltimore: Lederer/Messianic Jewish Publishers, 1996.

Patrice Fischer and her husband, John Fischer, were founding members of Congregation B'nai Maccabim in Highland Park, Illinois. She has three earned degrees, including an M.A. in Cross-Cultural Communications. Her thesis topic was "The American Jewish Community's Response to Organized Christian Evangelistic Outreaches in the 1970s." She is a Ph.D. candidate at the University of South Florida and has taken additional coursework at Princeton Theological Seminary, the Institute of Holy Land Studies, and Hebrew University.

# CONVERSION OF THE GENTILES—"NO WAY!"

—Michael Wolf

Some in our Messianic Jewish movement have been considering a process for the conversion of Gentiles to Messianic Judaism. When I hear such discussion, my response is to wonder, "What needs to be discussed?" There is no basis in Scripture for our Messianic Jewish institutions to entertain such an idea. Furthermore, the practice would bring great confusion to our movement and accusation from those we are seeking to reach. Nevertheless, since the issue of conversion is being seriously considered by some in the Messianic movement, these points are worth expanding in some detail.

Other writers on this subject have often offered ambiguous observations and conclusions, shifting back and forth between the subject of a Messianic Jewish conversion process and Gentile Christian conversion to Judaism in general. One writer starts advocating a Messianic conversion process and then subtly switches to a defense of any kind of Jewish conversions, calming (imagined) fears that Christians will be forced by Jewish *beyt din*s to renounce Yeshua as Messiah. I must make it clear at the outset that the primary focus of this chapter is not the wider subject of conversion to Judaism. While I will point out that the biblical foundation for full conversion to Judaism might be questionable, this is not the controversial issue that concerns me. Simply put, the issue under discussion is not conversion of Gentiles to Judaism but conversion of Gentiles to Messianic Judaism facilitated by Messianic Jews.

## The *Ger* in the *Torah*

When discussing the foundation, or lack of it, for a Messianic Jewish conversion process, the Jewish Scriptures are a reasonable place to start. The *Torah* provided no means for the conversion of Gentiles to Judaism. Though some have contested that intermarriages after the Exodus resulted in *de facto* conversions, there is no evidence for this in the Scripture. Even Ruth was identified with Moab throughout the book. Her children were seen as fully Jewish (although not Ruth herself). This same principle would apply to the "mixed multitude" that left Egypt. The *Torah* provided no way for the Egyptians who left with the Israelites to become full citizens as Jews. However, by the time the people enter the Promised Land, there is no reference to a mixed multitude. This does not imply a process of conversion for the Gentiles. All it implies is that the children of the original mixed marriages were recognized as Jews. The word *ger* always designated a foreigner who joined himself to the people of Israel.

Options concerning observances seem to have existed, even in biblical times, for Gentiles living amidst Israel, so that some participated in all *Torah* observance, beginning with circumcision. Some elected not to participate (although the basic laws of justice applied to all living in the land). However, there is no evidence that the individual *ger* ever lost his or her identity as a *ger* or took on the complete identity of an Israelite.

Later, the rabbis made a differentiation between the proselytes (*gerim*) of the gate who were not circumcised and did not fully participate in *Torah* observance, and the proselyte of righteousness who was circumcised and adhered to all of the Jewish laws. (The word *proselyte* is simply a translation the word *ger*.) To the *gerim* of the gate, they applied the following verse:

> Ye shall not eat of any thing that dieth of itself: thou shalt give it unto the stranger that is in thy gates, that he may eat it. (Deut. 14: 21 KJV)

The circumcised proselyte was referred to as a *Ger Tzedek*, (Righteous Alien). This formal differentiation went beyond the intent of Scripture and established the foundation for formal conversion to Judaism.

In fact, the term *Ger Tzedek* hints at some disagreement between the rabbis during the Second Temple period concerning the standards for accepting a full conversion. There is much discussion about this subject in the *Mishnah*. The term implies respect and acceptance, as well as the acknowledgement that the *ger* is still "outside," distinguished from the native born Israelite.

Nevertheless, a process for conversion developed amidst the struggle for agreement concerning standards. During the Second Temple period, this biblical choice was seen by some leading rabbis as the difference between a stranger in the midst of the people and a full Jewish citizen.

> An alien living among you who wants to celebrate the LORD's Passover must have all the males in his household circumcised; then he may take part like one born in the land. No uncircumcised male may eat of it. (Exod. 12:48 NIV)

Although this passage shows that Gentiles could choose to observe Jewish life, they were still called *gerim*.

Again, although there may be evidence for an historic rabbinical conversion process that was in accordance with *halakhah*, there is no clear biblical process for making a *ger* into a former *ger*, outside of the assimilation of the children and grandchildren of an intermarriage. This is a very important point for the Messianic Jewish movement to consider. Our movement lacks the biblical precedent or authority to perform conversions.

## An Exception in the Book of Esther?

In the book of Esther, reference is made to Gentiles becoming Jews. "And many people of other nationalities became Jews because fear of the Jews had seized them" (Esther 8:17 NIV).

Some use this one verse to prove the existence of a conversion process in the Persian Jewish community before the Babylonian Captivity, or at least, to give evidence that a process developed that early. However, the text reveals no process for conversion. Did the people merely identify as Jews in order to avoid being slaughtered by that community, which had been given the sword to deal with their enemies? The part of the verse that deals with the fear of the Jews suggests this as a motivating factor. There is no evidence that the Jewish religious authorities did anything to make them Jews. In fact, some rabbis in the *Mishnah* questioned the legitimacy of their conversion. An example is given in *Yevamot* 24b.

> Nor the proselytes of Mordecai and Esther are proper proselytes unless they become converted at the present time.

Perhaps these Persians entered the community and eventually assimilated through the next generation or two. That would follow the same biblical pattern that had existed since Mount Sinai. Were they received, instead, through some kind of formal conversion process? We do not have enough evidence in this one verse to conclude that they were.

## Traditional Jewish Conversions

At this point, someone might ask, "Are you saying that Messianic Jews don't accept conversions done by the traditional Jewish community?" First, there is no consensus in the Messianic Jewish community on traditional Jewish community conversions, whether Orthodox or otherwise. While the IMJA and its affiliated national alliances do not accept converts to Judaism as full Jewish members (however, the Gentile spouse of a Messianic Jew can be a member of the Jewish membership organization), other Messianic organizations do.

Second, as the focus of this chapter is not the wider subject of conversion to Judaism, the discussion will be limited to the conversion of Gentiles to Messianic Judaism, facilitated by Messianic Jews.

Third, I honor traditional Jewish conversions in my synagogue. This is because the Jewish community embraces these converts. Therefore, I embrace them too—even if the process was never outlined or sanctioned in the *Torah*. This brings me to my main concern about Messianic conversions: the resulting break with the Jewish community, which we can also call peoplehood of Israel. This argument will comprise the rest of the chapter.

## Authority to Convert

Sometimes, fairly strong language is used to support a conversion process in the Messianic Jewish community. One interesting argument likens a conversion-less Messianic Judaism to a mule. With similar language to what one might use to describe the unnatural beliefs of the Shakers, who forbade marriage, a Messianic movement without a conversion process is seen as sterile, stunted, and unable to reproduce itself. These same conversion proponents hold very high standards for candidates, which would result in only a sprinkling entering into full Jewish status, even over a long period of time. Yet, their language implies that the whole future of the movement is stake here.

In addition, they state that no true legitimate Judaism exists without the authority to convert. This argument implies that Messianic Judaism, without a conversion process, is contrary to the standards of God for Judaism. Yet, as we have shown earlier, God did not provide a law or process for conversion in the *Torah*, when he had every opportunity to do so. Such strong language about this controversial issue may make good rhetoric, but its dire predictions about a Messianic Judaism without a conversion process have no basis in fact.

## The Peoplehood of Israel

The peoplehood of Israel is a theme that runs through the Bible (both Old and New Covenants), as well as through writings and discussion in the modern era. The concept speaks of a distinctive community that has a Jewish identity and calling in common.

In the Jewish community, there is hot disagreement about the subject of conversion. Some of this controversy has recently reached secular news audiences in the form of items about the Israeli Orthodox exclusions of certain non-Orthodox conversions. In fact, in our movement, we probably would not be considering a conversion process so seriously if the mainstream Jewish community was united on the subject of conversion—if there were a process that was agreed upon by all of the mainstream branches of Judaism.

Are we, perhaps, using the lack of unity on this issue in the mainstream Jewish community to our own advantage? Are we saying, "We have a conversion process too, just like the Reform movement does? We don't need everyone to accept our converts."

The Jewish community is in crisis precisely because there is no agreement on which conversion process makes legitimate Jews. However, this crisis is not an open door for us. We must remember that the entire Jewish community sees Orthodox conversions as legitimate. And although some of the Orthodox do not consider Conservative, Reform, or Reconstructionist conversions to be legitimate, *no one* in the mainstream Jewish community would consider our process legitimate. The *Messianic Jewish converts* would never be considered Jewish by any branch of Judaism.

If one allows for this fact, and therefore considers Messianic Jewish conversion to be a limited conversion for the Gentile candidate—a conversion not to Judaism, but merely to the particular Judaism called Messianic Judaism—then we are creating a new entity. In doing so, we confirm that, indeed, we are not part of the historic Jewish people, but rather, part of a new and previously unknown entity called Messianic Judaism. This is a very important point, and should be underscored. There are some things we cannot and should not undertake to do on our own apart from our connection to our people as a whole.

Some argue that even those in the Messianic community who are born Jewish are often not seen as Jews—so why let the non-acceptance of these Messianic Jewish converts stop us from declaring them Jews? However, those who argue along these lines forget the importance of biblical definitions, especially in the Messianic Jewish community, which upholds the Scripture as the final arbiter of our identity. The point is this: When certain segments of the Jewish community say that they do not consider Messianic Jews as Jewish any longer, we know that the Scripture and our hearts teach contrary to that. For the same reason, we can embrace patrilineal Jews (those with a Jewish father and a non-Jewish mother) although a large segment of the Jewish community does not.

Many Jewish leaders recognize that the teachings of the Bible, and even rabbinical writings, do not exclude Messianic Jews from being Jews. These leaders may say that we are *meshumed*s (traitors) but not ex-Jews. However, the utter lack of acceptance in the Jewish community of the Gentiles we would convert, added to the lack of a clear scriptural model for our authority to convert Gentiles, produces a disassociative factor in relation to the Jewish community. In other words, there is no touch point of commonality or understanding anywhere in the Jewish community concerning these Gentiles.

In short, conversion of Gentiles to Messianic Judaism does not confirm our belonging to the peoplehood of Israel (as some may suggest) but, instead, further distances us by creating a distinct entity not connected with the rest of the people. In fact, the strongest argument against Messianic Jewish conversion is that this practice would be counterproductive to our unity with the whole peoplehood of Israel. Moreover, that unity is a spiritual reality that our Messianic Jewish community must affirm and be committed to—regardless of the response of the Jewish community at large. We are, from God's point of view, part of the peoplehood of Israel, no matter what some in the mainstream community may say.

In closing, let us consider the example of a Gentile leader of a Messianic congregation who is converted through a Messianic Jewish conversion process. Some, in fact, have suggested that Gentiles in Messianic leadership would be prime candidates for conversion. Let us say that this man attends a Jewish function and introduces himself as a Messianic Jewish rabbi. The community does not know that he is a convert because he appears to be Jewish. (The experience of many Messianic Jewish leaders has been that they find themselves accepted as individual Jews at various Jewish functions, even though some members of the Jewish community often have trouble accepting the validity of Messianic Judaism as a movement.) In our imagined scenario, after accepting this man as a Jew, the Jewish community discovers that this person has no Jewish blood on either his father or mother's side, and that his whole claim to Jewishness is through a Messianic Jewish conversion. At this point, all areas of unity and agreement fade away. The old charge of deception gains credence. The link, the connection to the rest of the Jewish people dissolves and in many circles, we would be seen as a cult.

## Questions for Discussion

- What is the only way provided in *Torah* for Gentiles to be assimilated into the Jewish community as Jews? What were the two basic options for *gerim* as outlined in the *Torah*?
- What were the names given to the two kinds of *gerim* by Second Temple period rabbis?
- Why is the controversy in the Jewish community concerning non-Orthodox conversions not an open door for a Messianic Jewish conversion process?
- How would a Messianic Jewish conversion process threaten our identification with the peoplehood of Israel?

Rabbi Michael Wolf has served as the leader of Beth Messiah Messianic Jewish Synagogue since 1977. Born into a Conservative Jewish home in Philadelphia, he became a Messianic Jew in 1971. After graduating from Temple University, Rabbi Wolf was trained at Beth Yeshua Messianic Synagogue in Philadelphia under Rabbi Martin Chernoff. He is a past President of the MJAA and presently serves on the organization's executive committee and administrates the organization's Yeshiva program.

# THE LEGITIMACY OF CONVERSION

—John Fischer

Messianic Judaism has tended to be a future-oriented movement from its first appearance (or re-emergence) on the stage of modern history. This future orientation has two aspects: generational and eschatological. We are concerned that we not only have Jewish children, but Jewish grandchildren and great grandchildren as well. As we pray daily in the synagogue, "as for me, so also for my descendants," we want them to live and love their Jewish heritage, traditions, and faith. However, as there is a clear anticipatory dimension in classical Judaism, so also it is with us. We eagerly await the arrival of the *Olam HaBa*, the Messianic Age, and the reign—for us, the return—of the Messiah. This is the core of our vision for the future—and to some degree or other, it shapes the vision of our future.

As the ancient prophets of Israel pictured an important role for the Gentiles as part of that future, so should we. At both the beginning and end of his prophecy, Isaiah (2:3–4 and 66:22–23) predicted a time when Gentiles would worship according to the principles of *Torah* and in keeping with the Jewish traditions alongside the Jewish people at the Temple in Jerusalem. Zechariah not only mentioned Gentile nations observing holidays such as *Sukkot* (14:16–19), he described a striking situation (8:20–23). People around the world ask to accompany Jewish people to Jerusalem to worship God together with them. It appears that some of the Gentiles would worship not only with Jews—but *as* Jews; they would have "a place and a name" among Israel (Isa. 56:5).

Isaiah's and Zechariah's prophecies are part of our future, as many of us understand it. Since that is so, it should also become an essential part of what we envision for Messianic Judaism. This includes, for the Gentiles, "a place and a name" among us. However, in order to envision the future properly, we should consider the past and present as well.

In 1978, several people from our Messianic synagogue pursued Judaic studies at a well-known Jewish college. Many professors knew we were Messianic Jews. One professor, a rabbi, suggested that the Messianic Movement would demonstrate it was a credible part of Judaism when it had a viable, active process of conversion. Some within the Messianic movement would argue that it is high time for this. Others—as indicated by the UMJC majority position "Conversion of Gentile Believers"—have serious difficulty with this proposal. They raise several objections to conversion.

Since this paper—along with Stuart Dauermann's paper, "Conversion: Surely Not Now," remains the most clearly articulated Messianic argument against conversion, it is appropriate to address their concerns. The first objection raised states: "Despite inferential, contrary arguments, a clear biblical emphasis plus serious practical problems should prevent the UMJC from promoting any such conversions." Several things need to be noted. First, the arguments against conversion are just as "inferential" as those supporting it. Unfortunately, "inferential" is therefore a highly prejudicial term as used here. Second, to label one's own position "clear" and "biblical" is soothing, but it is also self-serving. Those supporting the opposing position would also argue that their own position is based on "a clear, biblical emphasis." Third, "serious practical problems" must be addressed, but they can be overcome.

The second concern addresses conversions through other forms of Judaism, and so is largely tangential to the issue discussed here.

The third point cites 1 Corinthians 7:18 as evidence that "specifically addressed the issue of conversion." While many use this passage in this way, it by no means, "specifically addressed the issue of conversion"! The context and commentators are quite clear on this. Verses 1–7 deal with whether to marry and with marriage responsibilities. Verses 8–11 include recommendations to both the unmarried and married regarding marriage. Verses 12–16 instruct people how to deal with unbelieving spouses. Verses 17–24 give the underlying rationale (with several types of examples) for remaining married if possible. Verses 25–28 include *Rav Sha'ul*'s suggestions to the unmarried. Verses 29–35 contain his reasons why to remain unmarried. Verses 36–40 conclude with guidelines for those who do get married. In other words, the entire chapter deals with marriage, *not* with conversion. In addition, if verse 18 is an instruction not to convert, then by implication and context, verse 21 counsels slaves *against* obtaining their freedom. In that case, in Philemon, *Rav Sha'ul* then contradicted himself because he urged the very opposite, that the slave Onesimus should be freed! 1 Corinthians 7:18 ff. is simply counseling that Yeshua's followers be content in whatever circumstances they find themselves (vv. 20–24). This is precisely the message of Philippians 4:10–19 as well. Further, if 1 Corinthians 7:18 ff. truly instructs Gentiles not to become Jews, then the passage, in context (v. 24), also equally strongly instructs the unmarried to remain so. In other words, if this text is used against conversion, it must also be used against marriage—and we should therefore counsel *all* the unmarried among us to remain so. Finally, if 1 Corinthians 7:18 is a directive against conversion and circumcision, *Rav Sha'ul* himself violated it when he had Timothy circumcised.

The fourth objection to conversion states: "There is no example in the *B'rit Hadashah* of a Gentile believer becoming a Jew." It then describes Timothy's circumcision (Acts 16:1–3) as a "pragmatic measure." Whether a pragmatic measure or not, it remains *just* such an example! To argue that Timothy was half-Jewish because of his mother—as the position paper does—misses an important matter. In the Second Temple period, Jewish males were circumcised; very simply, Jews circumcised their sons. If they were not circumcised, they were not Jews. This was one of the things the Maccabees had fought for, and in fact established after their Hanukkah-producing victory—the right and responsibility of Jewish parents to circumcise their sons. Every Hanukkah celebration reinforced this principle. Earlier God himself had set the precedent. Abraham had to be circumcised (Gen. 17:10–14). In order to be part of God's covenant with Abraham, each male *must* be circumcised. If they were not circumcised, they were not part of the covenant. This was Timothy's situation. In fact, when Moses neglected to circumcise his son, the Lord threatened his life (Exod. 4:24–26)! In addition, the term "circumcision" is used throughout the Newer Testament as a synonym for being Jewish (1 Cor. 7:18; Phil. 3:3). So, when *Rav Sha'ul* had Timothy circumcised, he had him "officially" converted to Judaism. As to the fact of his being "raised according to the Scriptures," implying that he was raised Jewishly, Gentile "Godfearers" of that time did the same for their children (Fischer, P. 172).

With the fifth concern of the UMJC position paper there should be no disagreement: "Gentile believers who feel a strong identity with Jewish people may join Messianic synagogues, participate in congregational life, and thus express a high degree of identification without actually becoming Jews." Conversion *is* unnecessary. But that does not make it unbiblical.

The sixth objection indicates that Messianic conversions "would not be recognized in Israel nor among the majority of the Jews" outside Israel. This is undoubtedly true. But then again, it is these very same people who do not recognize Messianic synagogues as synagogues or Messianic Jews as Jews. In fact, some Jewish leaders are beginning to argue for the recognition of Messianic Judaism as an authentic part of the mainstream Jewish community (Harris-Shapiro, 1999; Cohn-Sherbok, 2000). As indicated earlier in this chapter, there *are* those in the larger Jewish community who expect, and even encourage, this process.

If it is argued that the rest of the Jewish community does not even fully accept its own converts now, it must be admitted that this is sometimes the case. However, there have also been many (and maybe, many more) cases where converts have been warmly welcomed and fully accepted. As traditionally understood, "the convert is worthy of even greater honor than the one Jewishly born!"

The seventh point raises the issue of "a two-class mentality among Gentiles in Messianic synagogues." Without sound instruction, there is that possibility. However, as numerous Gentiles in the Messianic Movement have related, in many circumstances they presently feel like "second-class citizens." Because they feel this way does not mean we should do away with Messianic synagogues or Jewish identity. In the same way, the "possibility" of a two-class mentality among Gentiles because of conversion should not keep us from making conversion available. Sound, consistent teaching solves both problems. Consequently, rather than erecting a barrier between Jews and Gentiles in our congregations, the opportunity to convert may well go a long way toward tearing down the subtle one that already exists in many circumstances. For example, how readily would a Gentile be accepted as a congregational leader or ordained as a rabbi?

The final concern of the UMJC paper addresses a significant problem: "Even a non-obligatory conversion of Gentiles would be viewed as heretical by many in the churches." However, many already view the Messianic Movement this way simply because of the existence of Messianic synagogues, the emphasis on Jewish identity, and the continued observance of Jewish tradition. On the other hand, as a the editors of a *Kesher* article, "Halacha in Action," perceptively reflected, while the concern is valid, it ". . . should not be weighed too heavily. If there is a clear biblical basis for a given policy, we must pursue it, even if many of our Christian brothers and sisters would misunderstand. We need to be careful that our halacha does not drift from the clear teaching of Scripture, as it seeks to accommodate the realities and limitations of modern life" (95).

So the question remains: Is there any teaching of Scripture, or are there any precedents within it that would commend allowing for the conversion of Gentiles? As it turns out, there is.

First, the *Torah* makes provision for "conversion." In Exodus 12:48–49, the "alien living among you" (the *ger*) is given an opportunity to fully participate in Jewish life and observance if he so chooses. However, this requires a "conversion" process. He must be circumcised (v. 48). After this, "the same law applies to the native-born and the alien living among you." In other words, both are now part of the *same* community. By this process, the alien has joined with—and has been joined to—the native-born. Together they live by the same standards ("the same law"). Deuteronomy 21:10–14 describes an analogous process for women (shaving her head, trimming her nails, and putting aside her old clothes). As the NIV Study Bible perceptively notes at this point, these procedures are "indicative of leaving her former life and beginning a new life" (269). In other words, she has become an integral part of a new people and a new community. This was undoubtedly the process—

since it is mandated by the *Torah*—Rahab later went through that enabled her to become part of Israel (Josh. 6:25) and part of David and Yeshua's ancestry. Certainly Ruth followed the same path in carrying out her promise: "your people will be my people, and your God will be my God" (Ruth 1:16). She too, became part of the ancestry of David and Yeshua. In fact, from a classical Jewish perspective, "the most famous convert in the Bible is Ruth" (Epstein 29). This conversion-addition and its consequences are the point of Rabbi Eleazar's statement in the Talmud. He teaches that God predicted that Ruth "would be grafted onto the tree of Israel," who in turn would benefit ("be blessed") by this (*Yevamot* 63a).

Building on the *Torah*, the prophets anticipate the times when large numbers of Gentiles would follow the lead of Rahab and Ruth. Isaiah 56:3–8 speaks of the "foreigner" who "binds himself to the LORD" (v. 3), "keeps *Shabbat*" (v. 4), "holds firmly to my covenant" (v. 4), and offers acceptable sacrifices in the Temple (v. 7). The practices cited here are distinctly *Jewish* observances. Further, these people are not "excluded from his people" (v. 3), but are "gathered to the exiles of Israel" (v. 8). In fact, these Gentiles are given "a place and name" among Israel (v. 5). These terms indicate that they have a portion both in Israel the land and in Israel the people. Clearly, they have become fully part of Israel; they have converted. Earlier Isaiah had predicted (14:1ff.) that "aliens will *join* Israel and unite with the house of Jacob." Moreover, this was forecast in a Messianic-millennial setting and context. In other words, there is a large-scale conversion of Gentiles still to come! Ezekiel 47:22–23 takes Isaiah's eschatological picture a step further. The "aliens" who have become part of Israel receive land among the twelve tribes and an "inheritance" as part of Israel; they are completely and thoroughly incorporated into Israel. When in the time of Esther "many people of other nationalities became Jews" (8:17), that served as a precursor of things yet to take place.

Some well-intentioned people might object that the foregoing comes from the Older Testament (OT). Therefore, it no longer applies today. However, several of the passages discussed previously predict times and events still in our future. And, perhaps more importantly, the words of Yeshua and *Rav Sha'ul* are to the point. Yeshua reminds us that he does *not* set aside *Torah* and that *none* of the Scriptures (OT) will be set aside "until everything is accomplished" (Matt. 5:17–19). Not only does *Rav Sha'ul* say that Scripture (OT) is for our "instruction" (Tim. 3:16), but he informs us that observing *Torah* is part of honoring God (Rom. 2:23) and living according to the Spirit (Rom. 8:4). Therefore, since the Older Testament is still valid, then conversion is valid.

Acts 15 and the book of Galatians may seem to present difficulties for this position. However, it is important to note that the issue there was *mandatory* circumcision (conversion) of the Gentile; the issue under discussion here is their *voluntary* conversion. *Allowing* Gentiles the opportunity to convert is far different from *expecting* that they do so. It should be further noted that denying the appropriateness of conversion to Judaism subtly suggests that Jewish identity has an essential qualifying (or disqualifying) genetic or racial component. That is simply not true. Anyone who strolls through the streets of modern Jerusalem will encounter Jewish people from nearly a hundred different ethnic or racial backgrounds! In addition, if it is acknowledged that conversion is legitimate for the larger Jewish community, then it is equally so for Messianic Judaism. If it is valid for Gentiles to become Jews in the former situation, then it is as well in the latter.

Throughout this discussion, one issue must be kept clear.

> The issue is not whether Gentiles should or must become Jews to attain full status in the Body of Messiah. All Messianic Jews agree this issue was settled by the Apostles and Elders in Jerusalem...The issue is whether or not it should be possible for willing Gentile believers to identify more closely with the Jewish people by voluntarily converting. (UMJC position paper)

In other words, the issue is not, as often inaccurately portrayed, that the Messianic Movement should "promote" conversions. The issue is whether they should *allow* for legitimate conversion and recognize it.

There are numerous Gentiles who have thoroughly associated themselves with Messianic synagogues—often with considerable sacrifice. Some have even been ridiculed and shunned by their families for taking their stand with us. A considerable number of Gentiles have made significant contributions to the life and growth of our synagogues. Most of them are quite comfortable and satisfied with participating in synagogue life and activities as Gentiles. However, as a result of their involvement in Messianic life, some have been more deeply drawn to the Jewish traditions and observances, as the ancient godfearers were. In many cases, they have evidenced a higher level of Jewish commitment and observance than many of the Jewish people in our synagogues. They long to identify with our people in a more thorough way—and they sense a calling from God to do so. For such people, who have demonstrated their commitment, have invested their lives in the Messianic Movement, and are clear about the call of God, there *should* be an accepted means of acknowledging their call, commitment, and longing. There should be a recognized way for them to more completely identify with us as a people. Such a conversion would in no way convey a higher level of spirituality or acceptance by God, and all those involved must be very clear about this. However, this process would allow such individuals to identify more closely with the Jewish people. Perhaps, a natural consequence may even be the clarification of Jewish and Gentile identity issues. It would then be clearer as to just who is defined as Jewish among us. This in turn might reduce the danger of the blurring Jewish-Gentile distinctives and distinctions that could threaten the identity and integrity of the Messianic Movement.

There is this further consideration. The Messianic Movement can continue to deny to mature, committed Gentiles the possibility of following the leading of the Spirit of God by converting. However, by doing so, we risk the danger of appearing, and being, like an exclusive club based on genetic/racial qualifications. We may well be perceived as saying: "Jewish identity is just for us; you can't have any!" In this way, we may just "project" elitism and exclusiveness toward others.

What would—or should—be the impetus for a Messianic Jewish conversion? As argued above, there is legitimate biblical precedence. And, it is a Jewish thing to do. In *Proselytism in the Talmudic Period*, Bernard Bamberger traces the history of the conversion process in Judaism and the enthusiasm with which it was practiced until its abolition by the Christianized Roman Empire in the talmudic period. The influential and respected Rabbis Yohanan and Eleazar concur that the reason God allowed the exile of the Jewish people from Israel was to multiply the number of converts! In other words, conversion is viewed as a very desirable and positive outcome of the Diaspora. Although forcibly dormant for centuries, this positive opinion of active conversion to Judaism has re-emerged in recent Jewish history as well. In 1978, Rabbi Abraham Schindler, then President of the Union of American Hebrew Congregations, challenged Jewish people to reach out religiously to their non-Jewish neighbors in a sensitive but active way. This call was reissued by his successor, Rabbi Eric Yoffie, in 1996. More recently, the website of the Jewish Outreach Institute suggested that conversion is good for the Jewish community. Further, inviting Jewish people but not non-Jews into the Messianic Movement may well reinforce the sense in the Jewish community that Messianic Judaism is simply a deceptive front for converting Jews out of the Jewish community and into Christianity. An authentic process of conversion to Judaism, in that case, would convey a commitment to Jewishly strengthen the community rather than diminish it.

Although a case can be made for conversion, care must be taken to prevent a "bandwagon effect" and to deal with those for whom Jewish identity is simply a fad or "fashionable." Strict guidelines must be established, and stringent checks must be applied to test commitment. In this process, we would do well to be as rigorous and selective as the Orthodox. That would filter out immature or over-enthusiastic believers who may be tempted to convert and "play Jewish" for a while for whatever incorrect, hasty, or shallow reason that might spur them on. And, following the pattern of traditional conversion, leaders could repeatedly discourage initial inquirers to filter out the more casual and less committed and to test the commitment and call of the serious-minded and Spirit-led.

Further problems and issues may arise along the way, but within this guarded and carefully monitored framework of conversion, they can be addressed as they are encountered. It appears that it is certainly time for Messianic Judaism to take a step toward its future, a step toward fulfilling Isaiah's prediction (14:1) that Gentiles "will join Israel and unite with the house of Jacob."

## Questions for Discussion

- In what ways does 1 Corinthians 7 impact the discussion of conversion? What does this chapter teach?
- How does Timothy's conversion contribute to the discussion?
- What are the biblical precedents and principles that allow for the possibility of Gentile conversion to Judaism? What might be the possible impetus or motivation for conversion to Messianic Judaism?
- How could the conversion process be safeguarded from possible abuses?

## Bibliography

Bamberger, Bernard. *Proselytism in the Talmudic Period.* Hobokern: KTAV, 1968.

Barker, Kenneth., ed. *New International Version Study Bible.* Grand Rapids: Zondervan, 1985.

Cohn-Sherbok, Dan. *Messianic Judaism.* London: Cassell, 2000.

Dauermann, Stuart. "Conversion: Surely Not Now." Hashivenu Forum. Skokie. 19 Oct. 1999.

Dauermann, Stuart, Barney Kasdan, Rich Nichol and Russ Resnik. "Halacha in Action." *Kesher: A Journal of Messianic Judaism* 5 (Summer 1997) : 91–95.

Epstein, Lawrence. *Conversion to Judaism: A Guidebook.* Northvale: Aronson, 1994.

Fischer, Patrice. "Modern Day Godfearers: A Biblical Model for Gentile Participation in Messianic Congregations." *The Enduring Paradox: Exploratory Essays in Messianic Judaism,* Ed. John Fischer. Baltimore: Lederer/Messianic Jewish Publishers, 2000. 171–181.

Harris-Shapiro, Carol. *Messianic Judaism: A Rabbi's Journey Through Religious Change In America.* Boston: Beacon, 1999.

UMJC Postion Paper. "Conversion of Gentile Believers," September 1983.

*Intermarriage + Outreach = Jewish Population Growth.* Fall 1999. <http://www.joi.org>.

Dr. John Fischer is rabbi of Congregation Ohr Chadash in Clearwater, Florida; Vice President for Academic Affairs at St. Petersburg Theological Seminary; and Executive Director of Menorah Ministries. He serves on the Executive Committee of the International Messianic Jewish Alliance, and is Rosh Yeshiva of Netzer David International Yeshiva, and President of the Association of Messianic Believers. A founder of the Union of Messianic Jewish Congregations, he has six earned degrees, including two doctorates.

# WOMEN CAN BE IN LEADERSHIP

—Ruth Fleischer

## In the Beginning . . .

God created male and female and placed them in *Gan Eden* (the Garden of Eden). They sinned. He expelled them. Thus, the story of humanity began. Throughout history, there has been a sense of competitiveness between the sexes but also, at the best of times, a sense of cooperation, of working together for a common goal and purpose. That is what this chapter is about— harmony of the sexes within God's plan. Not the elevation of one sex over the other, not the servitude of one sex under the other, but a program that utilizes the gifts and calling of each, individually, and as men and women, to advance the kingdom of God. The purpose of this chapter is to provide biblical, historical, Judaic, and Christian support for this position.

The Reader's Digest Oxford Complete defines "harmony" as "an apt or aesthetic arrangement of parts" (683). I believe that God's intention from the beginning was that man and woman should form just such an arrangement, not just as husband and wife, but also within the larger community. His plan for husband and wife is clearly put forward in Ephesians. Rabbi *Sha'ul* tells his *talmidim* (disciples) that the balance of the home is accomplished when (1) a man leaves his father and mother and loves his wife in such a way that he places her needs before his own as Messiah did when he gave his life for us and (2) a woman submits to her own husband as to the Lord. Neither of these statements, which are so apt for the home, applies to the community at large, where we are to submit to one another in the fear of the Lord.

If we set before us the example of the orchestra, it is easy to see how harmony works. The conductor directs all the instruments. Each instrument has its own special place within the orchestra. The violin cannot play the same notes as the kettledrum, nor can the French horn operate in place of the flute. One is not better than another simply because it is stringed instead of percussion. Each of us is an instrument, with God as our Conductor. He has provided the orchestration and we must play what he has set before us, some leading and some following, according to his plan. If we do this, we have harmony, and we fulfil the role he has properly provided through the "instrument" (or gift) he has given each of us. Harmony in the Body of Messiah brings honor and praise to our King.

## Women in the Bible

Throughout time, God has gifted women with a variety of talents. He has called them to a wide spectrum of roles, not just the obvious ones of "wife" and "mother," which parallel "husband" and "father" for men. He chose to use women in positions of leadership and authority on numerous occasions, as the following examples demonstrate.

*Devorah* (Deborah) both prophetess and judge, was used by God to lead Israel to victory over their enemies. She did not wake up one morning and say, "I'd like to be a judge and a prophetess" —God *chose* her to lead his people. We know that she was married, yet hear nothing about her husband, certainly nothing which suggests that he was the one who *really* heard from God. No doubt within their home, Deborah was a godly wife, but Deborah was also prepared, called, and directed by God to accomplish precisely what God had laid out for her to do as the leader of Israel.

God chose Huldah, the prophetess, for a special role (2 Kings 22:14–20; 2 Chron. 34:22–28). Again, we know little about this woman except that she was the wife of Shallum, who was "keeper of the wardrobe." When Hilkiah found a *Torah* scroll in the Temple, King Josiah sent for Huldah, a known prophetess, to attest to the authenticity of the "book." She prophesied national destruction because the people had abandoned God's instructions and commandments. Largely because of her authoritative pronouncements, Josiah carried out many godly reforms.

*Hadassah* (Esther) was brought by God to a place of influence to deliver her people from yet another enemy. When the Jewish people in the Persian Empire were faced with destruction, God used her to influence the king. In doing so, she became a leader of her people in the first Diaspora.

Lydia, a wealthy woman engaged in business. Originally from Thyitira, she was a probably a proselyte to Judaism. She was the first person in Europe that Rabbi *Sha'ul* led to faith. Previously, she led a prayer group, which met by the river. Her home became the location of the first congregation in Philippi, and she, herself, became its patroness.

In Romans 16:1, Phoebe is named as a "*diakonos*" by Rabbi *Sha'ul*. Interestingly, this word, defined as "missionary" or "minister" when used of male leaders, has been translated as "servant" or "deaconess" when describing Phoebe. Obviously, she served in the same capacity as the others thus designated, who were men. *Sha'ul* also calls her "a helper of many." This term, *prostatis*, is used in other passages (1 Thess. 5:12; 1 Tim. 3:4) to relate the activities of elders in positions of authority (see Silberling, 1993; Keener 237–240). Phoebe was a significant enough personage to be given the responsibility of transporting *Sha'ul*'s letter to the Romans, was recommended by him to them, and given authority to explain and expound upon the letter she carried.

Sha'ul mentions a Jewish woman named Junia (Rom. 16:7), possibly a relative, and refers to her as an "apostle." She apparently served as such with her husband, Andronicus, and was imprisoned with him along with *Sha'ul*. He knew this woman well and commended her to others.

There are women of note throughout the Scriptures. Some served as leaders in supportive roles, such as Miriam, the sister of Moses and Aaron. God called others to positions of singular authority. It is absurd to deny either role as characteristic of women. Rather, we should see that the gifts and calling of God were used as they were given, for purposes which God declared, by their presence in that particular individual. It should be no more difficult to accept this premise for a woman than for a man. Calling has always been God's provenance, and not the choice of either man or woman.

## The Historic Role of Women

If what has been is what must be, we, of the modern Western world, would not have democratic governments with voters from all walks of life. (Many of the founders of the United States thought only landowners should be allowed to vote.) We would not allow people from certain national or geographic origins the rights of citizens and we would still employ children in manufacturing and agriculture. Fortunately, things have changed. For example, although the Bible allows for slavery, we no longer accept slavery as an appropriate element in our economy. Although the Bible suggests that gold jewelry and braided hair are inappropriate for *talmidim* and head-coverings should not be seen on men, most men and women wear gold rings and earrings, some of each sex braid their hair, and men wear *kippot*. Yet, many of those who have no problem with these changes believe that women should continue to be marginalized within the body of Messiah and the Messianic Jewish Movement. I would suggest that this attitude is a product of history rather than the consequence of biblical instruction.

Until modern times, indeed, until the twentieth century, men largely regarded women as chattel, as possessions that might be traded, bought or sold, or given by parents in return for a consideration. Baby girls were a liability in ancient Greece, and elsewhere, often left to die on mountaintops.

Girls were seen as less capable of intellectual activity, of physical prowess, and of self-control. Yet, women have been outstanding scholars, rulers, writers, doctors, scientists, and artists, especially in the last few hundred years as more and more doors are open to them.

## The Position of Women in Judaism

Within Judaism, women have existed in much the same condition as women in the world surrounding them. That is, far from being an outpost of biblical truth, Judaism has treated its women, especially for the past two thousand years, as the *Goyim* have treated their women. As in the Gentile world, there have been exceptions of women who were given opportunities to learn and to do. However, these examples are rare.

However, with Jewish emancipation, women began to examine their lot, to reflect on the changing role of women in the Western nations, and to consider their options. In 1889, journalist and Jewish community activist Mary M. Cohen asked, "Could not our women be ministers?" (1). (In that day, the term "ministers" was used commonly of those in the rabbinate.) The thought was that women who were wholly committed to Judaism and who were competent to lead could be one in the same!

While the Orthodox, a declining community in the United States and elsewhere, continued to force women into the mold of previous centuries, Conservative and Reform Judaism began to consider the possibilities for women in leadership. In the 1920s, five women in the United States and one woman in Germany spent enough time in rabbinical schools to urge Jewish leaders to respond to their request to become rabbis. The past won this debate. The decision was made that since it had not been before; it should not be now. The claim was also made that ordination of women would break the bond between the various branches of Judaism. This did not stop women from pursuing rabbinical education and ordination (see Nadell 1998).

On the secular front, women like Henrietta Szold (who had applied to study rabbinics under Solomon Schecter in 1902), Golda Meir, and Trude Weiss-Rosmarin rose to positions of significance and influence in the Jewish world. Other Jewish women followed. It became clear that women who had been gifted with intellectual and leadership abilities should look elsewhere than the synagogue for a place of service. This reaction began to challenge the bastions of tradition.

Women first served as synagogue presidents and then as rabbis in Reform Judaism as early as the 1950s (U.S. and U.K. according to Nadell). In 1972, Hebrew Union College ordained Sally Preisand as the first woman rabbi. The debate continued within Conservative Judaism until 1985, when Amy Eilberg, a graduate of Jewish Theological Seminary, became "*Ha'Rav*

*Chana Beyla*, rabbi, teacher and preacher in Israel" (Nadell 214). Today there are many fully qualified women in the Reform and Conservative rabbinate, in the United States, the United Kingdom, Israel, and Europe.

The Orthodox continue to discuss possibilities, as scholarly Orthodox women pursue ordination. Although no woman has been officially ordained, women now serve in superior leadership positions within the Jewish community. The question of ordination for women will not go away.

## The Changing Role of Women in the Church

As with the role of women in Judaism, the place of women in organized Christianity was largely one of subservience, ignorance, and powerlessness. This, too, began to change to women's emancipation. In 1947, the Presbyterian Church, again, took up the debate over women's ordination, and in 1955, its General Assembly voted in the affirmative. The first female minister in the Presbyterian Church (U.S.A.) was ordained in October 1956 (see Nadell 129).

Since that time, most Protestant and "non-conformist" denominations have begun to train and ordain women to the role of senior minister or pastor. Even evangelicals allow women to occupy the pulpit. In the 1990s, the Church of England followed suit and now has many women priests, vicars, and ministers. The Roman Catholic Church has not, however, seen fit to begin the practice of ordaining women as priests.

## Conclusion

As a movement, Messianic Judaism has not yet seen fit to ordain women as rabbis. Yet, there are at least two properly ordained Messianic women rabbis. Leaders within the movement have various reasons for excluding women from ordination. Some continue to believe that Rabbi *Sha'ul's* teaching about women was for eternity, and not for his own time and place. However, the majority of Christians now ordain women (this brings us back to the question of men wearing head-coverings and anyone wearing gold jewelry). Others feel that ordaining women would break with Jewish tradition and would gain the movement nothing but disdain—although most main branches of Judaism today practice female ordination.

Some within our movement believe that we should be the head and not the tail in Judaism, and yet, in this area, we are assuredly not leading the way. I am not suggesting that we should encourage women who are not clearly called by God, to apply for Messianic ordination. Instead, as with the men in our community, we should examine those who feel called to lead—not on the basis of sex, but from the perspective of calling, first, and then of education, background, and suitability for ordination. If ordination, from the biblical perspective, is the recognition of the calling God has already placed on someone's life, then we should be willing to accept this as the soundest basis for rabbinical ordination for men or women.

If we choose to go the way of the Orthodox and of the Roman Catholic Church, we risk losing qualified and called women that are needed in our movement, to other avenues of service and other pursuits outside of the Messianic community. There are few enough leaders to go around as it is without rejecting a handful (there will never be huge numbers of women who want to be Messianic rabbis!) because—and only because—they are women. It is time to re-think history and to note what is happening around us.

Could we be wrong? How will our children and grandchildren judge us on this issue? Will the traditional Jewish community praise us for holding the line on female ordination or will the Reform and Conservative communities count this as yet another area in which we are unwilling to confront the present and cling to "Christian" modes? Will we encourage and motivate women within the movement or will those who are educated and knowledgeable leave us for greener pastures? What does God's nature really say about his calling upon the lives of individuals, male and female?

## Questions for Discussion

- Is the present Orthodox Jewish view of women and their role the result of scriptural, talmudic, or historical thinking?
- What are the best models in the Bible for the roles of men and women today?
- Is concern for *role*, the best way to estimate the place of the individual in the modern Messianic paradigm?
- How do you think Messianic Judaism will change if women are openly accepted as rabbis, teachers, cantors, and congregational leaders?

## Bibliography

Cohen, Mary M. "A Problem for Purim." *Philadelphia Jewish Exponent.* 15 Mar., 1889: 1.

Keener, Craig S. *Paul, Women & Wives.* Peabody: Hendrickson, 1992.

Nadell, Pamela S. *Women Who Would Be Rabbis.* Boston: Beacon, 1998.

Tulloch, Sarah, ed. *The Reader's Digest Oxford Complete Wordfinder.* Oxford: Oxford Univ., 1998.

Silberling, Kay. "Leadership/Ordination of Women." Paper presented to the Theology Committee of the International Alliance of Messianic Congregations and Synagogues, 15 Oct., 1993.

Dr. Fleischer is rabbi of the London Messianic Congregation and Executive Director of Yeshua Ministries and Conferences. A second-generation Messianic Jew, she holds degrees in Social Science, European History, and Ecclesiastical History. She serves on the boards of the Messianic Jewish Alliance of America, the International Alliance of Messianic Congregations and Synagogues, British Friends of the International Messianic Jewish Alliance, and is Chair of the British Union of Messianic Jewish Congregations.

# MALE LEADERSHIP AND THE ROLE OF WOMEN

—Sam Nadler

Some have said that since women have served with the Lord and his emissaries (apostles), and have judged, prophesied, preached and prayed as effectively as any man, suffered for Yeshua more than many men, sacrificed and invested as much as any man for the Good News—then it seems quite unfair to exclude them from senior leadership in a Messianic congregation. The issue of whether women should be in senior congregational ministry is not an issue of orthodoxy regarding a major doctrine of Scripture. Therefore, it should be considered (by those who differ on the matter) a discussion point among brothers and sisters in Messiah and not an opportunity to "refute heretics." To understand the issue let us start with looking at the various scriptures that describe women in ministry in general as well as in congregational ministry, specifically.

## Several Scripture Portions
*(Note: Certain words and phrases have been italicized for emphasis.)*

### Women in Ministry Support Roles

> Soon afterwards, he began going around from one city and village to another, proclaiming and preaching the kingdom of God; and the twelve were with him, and *also* some women who had been healed of evil spirits and sicknesses: Mary who was called Magdalene, from whom seven demons had gone out, and Joanna the wife of Chuza, Herod's steward, and Susanna, and many others who *were contributing to their support out of their private means.* (Luke 8:1–3)

And when she and her household had been baptized, she urged us, saying, "If you have judged me to be faithful to the Lord, come into my house and stay." And she prevailed upon us. (Acts 16:15)

And they went out of the prison and entered the house of Lydia, and when they saw the brethren, they encouraged them and departed. (Acts 16:40)

I commend to you our sister Phoebe, a shamashah (deaconess/diakonon) of the assembly at Cenchreae. (Romans 16:1)

Clearly, women were used in various support roles. It is likely that they handled some administrative responsibility but there was no indication that assistance and service had ever made one a congregational leader.

### Women in Ministry Pray and Prophesy

And Miriam the *prophetess.* (Exod. 15:20)

Now Deborah, a *prophetess,* the wife of Lappidoth. (Judg. 4:4)

Huldah the *prophetess,* the wife of Shallum the son of Tikvah. (2 Kings 22:14)

And there was a *prophetess,* Anna the daughter of Phanuel. (Luke 2:36)

These all with one mind were continually devoting themselves to prayer, along with *the women, and Miriam* the mother of Yeshua, and with his brothers. (Acts 1:14)

When the day of *Shavu'ot* had come, they were all together in one place. And there appeared to them tongues as of fire distributing themselves, and they rested *on each one of them.* . . . And they were *all filled* with the Holy Spirit and began to speak with other tongues, as the Spirit was giving them utterance . . . but this is what was spoken of through the prophet Joel "And it shall be in the last days," God says, "that I will pour forth of my Spirit on all mankind; and your sons and your daughters shall prophesy, and your young men shall see visions, and your old men shall dream dreams . . . even on my bondslaves, both men and *women,* I will in those days pour forth of my spirit and *they shall prophesy."* (Acts 2:1, 3–4, 16,18)

But every *woman* who has her head uncovered *while praying or prophesying* disgraces her head. (1 Cor. 11:5)

Now this man (Phillip) had four virgin *daughters who were prophetesses.* (Acts 21:9)

Evidently, where there are prophets there are also prophetesses. God did not limit his prophetic word to and through men. It is true that seventy elders also prophesied (Num. 11:16–30), but these were all "men" ("*ish*" in Hebrew). Though there were prophetesses, there is no evidence that there were any female elders in Israel; when there is any description of elders it is always "men" as noted above.

### A Woman as a Judge in Israel

"Now Deborah, a *prophetess,* . . . was judging Israel at that time" (Judg. 4:4). Indeed, women were not restricted from the role of judge, as in the case of Deborah. But, it does not follow that because one is a judge they could therefore be an assembly leader. Jephthah was a judge, but because of his illegitimate birth (Judg. 11:1–2), he could neither receive an inheritance nor enter the assembly (cf. Deut. 23:2). Although one might be otherwise disqualified from assembly leadership, this does not mean that they could not serve adequately in some other place of leadership. Therefore, a woman could serve as judge although she could not serve as an assembly leader.

### Women in Ministry Teach and Testify

*Older women* . . . are to . . . *teach* the younger women. (Titus 2:3–4)

From that city many of the Samaritans believed in him because of the word of *the woman who testified,* "He told me all the things that I have done." (John 4:39)

But when *Priscilla and Aquila* heard him, *they took him aside and explained* to [Apollos] the way of God more accurately. (Acts 18:26)

Women could teach and were encouraged to teach in women's ministries (see the book of Titus). Many women missionaries have been used—as the Samaritan woman was—to bring the Good News to a previously unevangelized community. Priscilla, at least, assisted in the teaching Apollos, a man, though this was done in conjunction with her husband. It is true that one of a senior congregational leader's main responsibilities is to teach and preach the word of God (Acts 6:2, 4; 1 Tim. 5:17), but it does not follow that all teachers are congregational leaders. Though women teach (and often, quite well) it does not mean that biblically, they were elders, overseers, pastors, or rabbis in a local congregation, since none are ever mentioned.

### Women in Ministry Are Persecuted for the Good News

But Saul began ravaging the congregation, entering house after house, and *dragging off men and women*, he would put them in prison. (Acts 8:3)

If [Paul] found any belonging to the Way, both men and *women*, he might bring them *bound* to Jerusalem. (Acts 9:2)

I persecuted this Way to the death, binding and putting *both men and women* into prisons. (Acts 22:4)

Help these *women who have shared my struggle* in the cause of the gospel. (Phil. 4:3)

Struggling and suffering for Messiah is not limited to men. Women were every bit as "spiritually infectious" and therefore "dangerous" to the unbelieving world as men when it came to sharing the Good News (cf. John 4:39). Though suffering has everything to do with being an identified member of the people of God (Exod. 3:7, 2 Cor. 1:5–7; 2 Tim. 3:12; 1 Peter 4:13), it has nothing to do with the senior leadership role in the congregation.

### Women in Ministry Are Generally Single

The *woman who is unmarried, and the virgin*, is concerned about the things of the Lord, that she may be holy both in body and spirit; but one who is married is concerned about the things of the world, how she may please her husband. (1 Cor 7:34)

Now she who is a widow indeed and who has been left alone, has fixed her hope on God and continues in entreaties and prayers night and day. (1 Tim 5:5)

Probably, for practical concerns, it is easier and more convenient for single women to serve in ministry. The same argument can be made for men (1 Cor. 7:31–33). But interestingly, there is a group of singles in a congregation for which there seems to be no parallel benefit, widows and widowers (1 Tim. 5:3–16). It is assumed this benefit (probably financial) is for women (widows) only. A man would be excluded—since a woman is all that is spoken of—and a man could not fulfill the qualification of being "*the wife of one man*" (vs. 9). So also, as men can be excluded from this aspect of congregational involvement, it does not seem too improbable that women might be excluded from another (i.e., senior congregational leadership).

### *In the Congregation, Women Are Limited in Ministry to Men*

> The women are to keep silent in the congregations; for they are not permitted to speak, but are to subject themselves, just as the Law also says. (1 Cor 14:34).

It can be argued from the immediate context (1 Cor 14:35) as well as from elsewhere within the book (11:5), that the issue was actually women asking questions of their husbands in a service where women did not sit with men (as in Orthodox Jewish congregations). "But I do not allow a woman to teach or exercise authority over a man, but to remain quiet (1 Tim 2:12)." In this verse, it seems that the problem of men "not stepping up to the plate" (see discussion of 1 Timothy 2:8 below) led to women asserting their leadership in the congregation (perhaps out of perceived necessity). Paul corrects this issue by mandating male leadership in the service and congregation (1 Tim. 2:8; 3:1–2).

## Some Scriptural Principles

In light of these portions of Scripture, several reasons and principles can be considered concerning the exclusion of women from the position of senior congregational leader.

1.  There are no biblical models of women as senior congregation leaders. All elders and pastors/rabbis in the Scriptures were men. Though many women were faithful and sacrificial to Yeshua (Luke 8:1–3) and gifted to teach in general (Acts 18:26, Titus 2:4–5), still, we find no women appointed to senior congregational leadership in the biblical record. There may one indication of a female leader in a New Covenant congregation (cf. Rev. 3:20). However, the only insight this would provide would be that it is a sign of disorder.

2.  There is no biblical authorization given for women to be senior congregation leaders. All instruction regarding women and their role is meant to restrict them from senior congregational leadership (1 Tim 2:12).

3.  All instruction assumes that men are to be the overseers. All positive instruction for elders is addressed to men. It seems questionable whether a woman could be included in all the character issues of an overseer (*episkopais*) since the list includes "the husband of one wife," literally, "a one-woman-man," (1 Tim 3:2). Paul's instructions are clear. He wanted "the men in every place to pray (1 Tim. 2:8)." It is not that women cannot pray publicly, for elsewhere it is permitted (1 Cor 11:5). In context, it seems the situation in Ephesus was one where many men were caught up in strange teachings (1 Tim. 1:3–7). The normative congregational priorities (especially prayer, 1 Tim. 2:1) were evidently being handled by the faithful women. Therefore, Paul was trying to straighten out this congregational disorder (1 Tim 3:15) —especially problems in leadership (see 1:3–7; 2:1–14; 3:1–15; 4:6–16; 5:17–22; 6:3–12). His instruction for "*the men in every place to pray*" was to have men in the profiled and senior congregational leadership role as opposed to the women.

4.  In the home, the husband was always the leader, even if he was disobedient to the word (1 Peter 3:1–2). The home was seen as the microcosm and training ground of the congregation (1 Tim 3:4–5). Therefore, it would seem to be incongruous, to the point of absurdity, to have a women in a senior leadership position in the congregation when she could not have such a senior leadership position in her own home.

## A Scriptural Position

### Gender in Congregational Ministry

There are a large number of gifted and highly talented men and women Messianic congregations. We desire to make good use of all the resources that God brings to the body in a way that improves our effectiveness and also remains consistent with biblical principles, with regard to the role of women in ministry.

### Equal Standing before God

The Bible is clear in stating that men and women are equally valued by God. In Genesis 1:27 we read, "So God created man in his own image, in the image of God he created him; male and female lie created them." Men and women are both equally created in the image of their Maker. In Galatians 3:28 we read, "There is neither Jew nor Greek, there is neither slave nor free man, there is neither male nor female; for you are all one in Messiah Yeshua." Thus, men and women have equal spiritual status before God. They are equally forgiven and equally valued by him. All believers, we are told, are equipped and gifted for ministry. In 1 Corinthians 12:7 we read, "Now to each one the manifestation of Spirit is given for the common good." Nowhere, in any of the passages relating to the gifts of the Spirit, is there any indication that gifts are given to one gender and not the other. All of us—both male and female—are to submit our gifts to God for the common good of the body.

### A Biblical Gender Distinction

A central statement bearing on leadership and gender is 1 Timothy 2:12 where, in the context of instructions about congregation leadership, Paul wrote, "I do not permit a woman to teach or have authority over a man." There are those who believe this is an instruction that applies specifically to the first century congregation at Ephesus and not to the present day congregation in American culture. This could be a plausible understanding were it not for Paul's mention of Adam and Eve and a creative order. This would suggest that Paul was not only concerned with his particular culture, but with our human nature. God is a God of order and structure and this can be seen other ways. In the Godhead, Father, Son, and Holy Spirit, there are three distinct personalities, all God and all equally God. Yet, there is a recognized authority—the Father, to whom the others willingly submit. In marriage, where husband and wife are equal spiritually before God, God establishes authority and places it in the man. That authority is to be used only for the benefit and welfare of those he serves—never selfishly. When sin entered the world, while Eve was the first to sin, it is Adam that God holds ultimately accountable. Thus, while men and women are equal before God, men are given authority and special accountability before God.

### Authority for Congregational Leadership

Men do not earn the authority for leadership of the congregation due to an inherent superiority; God ascribes it to them. In a similar way, the Levites did not earn their role as priests among the twelve tribes of Israel, but had it ascribed to them by God. The role ascribed to men pertains to the leadership of the congregation as a whole. This includes setting the overall direction of the congregation, keeping the congregation in line with biblical principles, and seeing that the congregation is spiritually nurtured. These are the functions of the *z'keynim* in our congregation. Not all men are suited for the role of elder. In selecting elders from among the men, we seek to follow the biblical criteria set forth in 1 Timothy 3:1–7 and Titus 1:6–9 as well as the demonstration of leadership in the congregation.

## Other Leadership Opportunities

The *z'keynim* fulfill only part of the needs for leadership in the congregation. In light of this, apart from holding the office of and serving as elders, women are needed and encouraged to lead in the various ministries of our congregation. The *shamashim* (deacons and deaconesses—both Hebrew and Greek transliterated terms mean "servants") assist the *z'keynim* in ministry and in administration of the congregation. Leaders are needed for various ministries and administrative functions (e.g., small groups, *Shabbat* school, to serve as role models, and to act as shepherds and mentors among their acquaintances).

## Teaching Ministry

All teaching in the congregation, whether by individual *z'keynim* or non-*z'keynim* must be done in harmony with the principles laid out for the congregation by the *z'keynim*. All teaching is to be carried out under the authority of the elders. This applies equally to men and women, regardless of the gender of those they are teaching. Speaking in harmony with the *z'keynim* and in deference to their leadership is what demonstrates submission to the authority ascribed to the elders by God. An elder need not be present when a non-elder is teaching. Thus, we will state explicitly, that women are allowed to teach men without an elder present (e.g., a special *Shabbat* school class or a financial counseling session). Because pulpit teaching is seen as an authoritative ministry of the congregation, this function is set apart primarily for the congregation leader (i.e., the teaching elder) or his designee.

## A Female Leadership Staff Member

Our policy of male headship through the *z'keynim* allows women to be hired onto the leadership staff. In fact, we expect and hope that there will be women on our leadership staff serving by exercising their gifts. In Ephesians 4:11 we read, "It was He who gave some to be apostles, some to be prophets, some to be evangelists and some to be pastors and teachers, to equip the saints for work of service." This list of gifts is given without regard to gender and is why we would allow women to be part of our leadership staff. They would not, however, hold the office of elder. In the *Tanakh* as well as the New Covenant, though women were both prophetesses and teachers (Judg. 4: 4; Acts 18:26) they were never considered *z'keynim*. Outside of the congregation leader and associate leaders, all remaining leadership staff, both male and female, would not be considered elders. They would be invited to join the *z'keynim* in their meetings as nonvoting participants.

### *Diversity of Opinion, Unity in Policy*

In our congregation, we are unified in affirming male headship in the congregation as well as in the homes represented in this congregation. We acknowledge that other believers and evangelical congregations have reached conclusions of biblical interpretation that allow for women *z'keynim*. On the other hand, we acknowledge that some do not allow women to even pray or testify in public. Our decision and policy applies specifically to our own congregation. We do not want this to become an issue that divides our congregation or the body of Messiah at large. We seek as the higher principle of love and unity. Differences between our congregation and others in this matter will not prevent us from remaining in fellowship with those congregations.

God has entrusted us with an abundance of resources for ministry, including his *Ruach* and the particular gifts imparted to each of us. It is vitally important to the congregation that each man and woman actively seeks to discern his or her gifts and to fully exercise them for the edification of the body, the evangelization of the community and to exaltation of *Adonai* Yeshua.

## Questions for Discussion

- Define the phrase *male headship* as it pertains to the home and congregation.
- How did women exercise their gifts in the *Tanakh* and in the New Covenant?
- How are women involved in the ministry of your congregation? Are there any areas where they might serve that they are not serving in now?
- What congregational roles are women *uniquely* qualified to fill? Why?

✡ ✡ ✡

Raised in a traditional Jewish home in New York City, Sam Nadler came to faith in Yeshua in 1972. He received his theological training at Northeastern Bible College and has been involved in Jewish ministry for almost thirty years. A past President of Chosen People Ministries, he is the congregational leader of Hope of Israel Congregation in Charlotte, North Carolina and President of Word of Messiah Ministries.

# THE TRADITIONAL JEWISH MISSION AS A MODEL

—Mitch Glaser

I am the leader of a traditional mission to the Jewish people and believe the future for organizations like ours is bright. Our organizational structure and the model upon which it is based is effective, biblical, and uniquely suited to carry out our mission statement: *to evangelize and disciple Jewish people and to equip others to do the same.* In fact, our mission continues, in vision and structure, much as we started over one hundred years ago.

In 1892, Rabbi Leopold Cohn, a recent immigrant from Hungary, became a believer in Jesus. Soon thereafter, he went to Scotland to receive his theological education and training. While in Scotland, Rabbi Cohn learned about his faith as well as how to establish a traditional mission effort to reach his fellow Jews with the gospel. When he returned to America, he began the Brownsville Mission to the Jews and employed the traditional British mission model he had discovered in Scotland. Today the ministry maintains this structure with only a few modifications to meet the needs of the modern era. It is a structure that is both biblical and effective. Along with other approaches to God's work, this ministry model will play an important role in the future of Messianic Judaism. Eventually Cohn's mission would move to Williamsburg, Brooklyn, and then to Manhattan. The mission, known as the American Board of Missions to the Jews for many decades, changed its name to Chosen People Ministries in the mid-1980s.

## The Biblical Basis for the Traditional Jewish Mission

The Bible teaches that there is only one true Church made up of Jews and Gentiles who have accepted Jesus as their Messiah. However, there are structures within the Church that serve God's various purposes in the world. The local church, the modality, is the Church stationary and the sodality is the Church on the move. Both entities carry out the Great Commission, but one conducts its primary ministry in a local area while the other breaks new ground in a geographic and cross-cultural dimension. There is one Church, but two structures by which God accomplishes his work.

One of the best examples we have of the mission structure is the apostolic band led by the Apostle Paul (first seen in Acts 13:1–3). This mission structure began to break through cultural barriers in presenting the gospel to various people groups. However as early as Acts 10, in the conversion of Cornelius, we see the gospel was already penetrating through Gentile cultural barriers. Then, in Acts 11:19–20, the disciples who were scattered after the stoning of Stephen were "gossiping" the gospel to Jews and non-Jews as they fled.

The result of the work of the mission structure was often the establishment of local fellowships or churches. There are, in fact, many indications of interrelationships between the mission structure and the local church. Not only was there sharing of personnel (2 Cor. 8:16–24) but also sharing of resources. One example is the occasion when Paul collected money from believers in Asia Minor for the saints in Jerusalem.

The traditional Jewish mission is a continuation of this legacy of apostolic bands that crossed cultures and countries to bring the Good News to Jews and Gentiles alike. This is why Jewish missions like the Mildmay Mission to the Jews, though founded and based in Great Britain, was able to establish work in Russia. It also explains why the British Barbican Mission was able to start a ministry in Greece. Like their counterparts among non-Jews, the China Inland Mission and other similar mission agencies crossed boundaries to fulfill the mandate of world evangelism given by Yeshua before his ascension.

There are various types of traditional Jewish missions. Some represent denominations and others represent state churches—although today, most are independent missions. However, the great commonality among Jewish missions lies in the dominant methodology utilized by most of the traditional missions during the past two hundred years.

## The Traditional Mission Model

The model for the Jewish mission station developed by Rabbi Cohn was not much different than the other missions of his day. A station might include everything from housing for the missionaries and colporteurs (those who distributed literature from house to house), to a chapel, offices, school for children, vocational training school, Bible school for adults, and a medical dispensary. The pioneer agency of modern Jewish missions, CMJ (Church's Ministry among the Jews, established in 1809 as the London Society for the

Propagation of the Gospel Among the Jews), established similar mission stations around the world, from Israel to Iran, as well as locally, on the East End of London. The United Church (and Free Church) of Scotland Missions to the Jews, which Cohn experienced first hand, established compounds across the globe as well, in Israel, Hungary, and Turkey.

## The Methods Employed by Traditional Jewish Missions

The Jewish Mission Stations that were established around the world by CMJ, the British Jews Society, and others followed a similar pattern to that of other missions. The station served both the spiritual and physical needs of the Jewish people. The missionaries and volunteers also distributed tracts, held street meetings, did personal visitation, engaged in Scripture distribution, or convened children's meetings. Uniquely, Leon Rosenberg maintained a successful orphanage in Poland during the 1930s, along with the medical, educational and other mercy ministries of his mission. Some missionaries were particularly effective in reaching the destitute among the Jewish community. All missions conducted special meetings for the Jewish holidays and followed the pattern of holding regular Sabbath services and Bible studies with unbelievers being invited.

Missionaries also traveled to smaller cities and even to villages which had limited Jewish populations. For example, Victor Buksbazen (who led the Friends of Israel ministry in the United States for many years) established a center in Krakow while serving with the British Jews Society. However, because of the extraordinary number of Jewish people in the surrounding area, he itinerated regularly among them, preaching the gospel and particularly visiting all known Jewish rural villages. His basic method of outreach was the distribution of tracts and portions of Scripture, as well as street preaching in the public squares.

## The Model on the Move

This British model was imported to Eastern Europe and adapted by the various missions to meet their needs. Later, when the European missionaries traveled to the United States, they established this mission station approach wherever they went. For example, Rabbi Cohn established gospel preaching services, children's classes, a medical dispensary, sewing classes, English classes, citizenship classes, and a residence for Messianic Jews who were asked to leave their homes on account of their faith.

When the social conditions of the Jewish people improved, these various ministries of the Mission were discontinued. Rabbi Cohn established a medical clinic at the Mission Center in Williamsburg, Brooklyn. However, when public and private medicine improved in the United States, the clinic was no longer necessary. The heart of the traditional approach was rooted in a holistic vision to meet the needs, social and spiritual of a particular Jewish community. This structure was also able to flex with the times and the particular needs of the Jewish community and continues to be effectively utilized today.

## Messianic Congregations and the Traditional Mission Approach

In addition to the varied evangelistic, social, and educational ministries of the traditional Jewish mission, a worshiping community was usually established as part of the mission station. The worshipping assembly—now described as a Messianic congregation—was a vital part of the work of the traditional Jewish mission—especially in Europe.

It is a mistake to think that Messianic congregations are a new idea and that traditional missions did not start Messianic congregations. For example, CMJ (also known as the London Jews Society, LJS) established a large mission station and center in Warsaw. The work of the LJS in Warsaw reached its height during the decade before the war. The staff included Director H. C. Carpenter, J. I. Landsmann, Benjamin Jocz, and many others. The Center included the mission house, Emanuel Church, and a training hall. In 1926, the foundation stone of a new mission building was laid for the LJS and the building opened the following year. This meeting hall, named Emanuel of Warsaw, was dedicated soon thereafter (British Jews Society Annual Report 1927–28:30). The Emanuel Hall housed the Emanuel congregation, which was in effect a Messianic congregation, had a part in the spiritual growth of great 20th century Messianic leaders like Jacob Jocz (Benjamin's son) and Rachmiel Frydland.

The congregation outside of Bucharest led by Isaac Feinstein, who served with the Norwegian Israelite mission, is well known by students of the period. The congregation of Peter Goroditch in Kiev lasted into the 1920s until the Red army forced it to disband. These are just a few examples.

The congregations addressed a number of concerns. First, it was understood that congregations were to be an effective means of evangelism. Secondly, they were created as a source of fellowship for Jewish believers, especially for those uncomfortable in attending an evangelical church. Often, the Jewish congregations would be attached to a denomination or national church body. There was little difference in Jewish expression between those congregations that were attached to missions and those that were independent.

The Messianic congregations were common and their validity was not debated within the mission community. Perhaps the differences between

Jews and Gentiles were so obvious that it went without saying that a congregation that was Jewish in character was deemed necessary. The congregations, denominational or not, promoted the maintaining of Jewish identity by Jewish believers. The congregations celebrated the Jewish holidays and the services were usually in Yiddish. The leaders were often well trained in rabbinical studies. The liturgy, language, and practice of customs varied. Some varied because of the region. Others were influenced by the church or missions structure to which they were attached.

To affix the label *Hebrew Christian*—and in doing so imply that the Jewish believers had renounced their Jewish identities—is based upon false assumptions. They were called *Hebrew Christians,* as that was the terminology of the day. However, the strength of their Jewish identity cannot be questioned. To imply otherwise ignores the modern history of our movement and diminishes the testimony of those who died in the Holocaust as Jews and as believers in Yeshua.

For a brief time, a few traditional Jewish missions, primarily among American fundamentalist groups, shied away from starting Messianic congregations during the post-war period. However, this is certainly not true of the majority of traditional Jewish missions around the world. Chosen People Ministries, in fact, has started more than twenty Messianic congregations in the last twenty years. What is new is that Messianic congregations are being started without the help of the traditional mission structure. This adds a delightful and exhilarating new dimension to God's work among his Jewish people.

## The Enduring Qualities of the Traditional Jewish Mission

The traditional Jewish mission, like the apostolic band of the Apostle Paul, crossed cultures and countries, establishing mission stations and congregations in various languages around the globe. Unlike a local congregation, the traditional Jewish mission follows this apostolic pattern. The mission to the Jews is able to maintain its effectiveness throughout time. The traditional model demonstrates four organizational characteristics, which makes it uniquely suited to fulfill the Great Commission among Jewish people in the twenty-first century.

### Global in Structure

We live in a global society and serve a people who live in many different countries around the world. Society in general is more mobile and the traditional Jewish mission is perhaps more necessary than ever today. Since the Jewish community is geographically fluid, it is necessary for a mission to remain global in structure. The global nature of a traditional mission to the Jews brings many challenges—including personnel, language, financial support, and governance. Jewish missions require a unique structure to be successful. The more traditional model is proven in its ability to meet the geographical challenges. In fact, some contemporary Messianic congregations have realized this and formed organizations that follow the more traditional model.

### Flexible in Methodology

From mission schools in Romania to vocational and language training in Brooklyn—the missions have always tried to meet the needs of a local Jewish community. It is foolish to view these ministries as non-evangelistic. This service-oriented outreach not only demonstrates the love of God to the Jewish people within the community but also enables thousands to hear the gospel. This is part of the reason for the fruitfulness of Jewish missions, in post World War I Europe, as the more socially oriented ministries spoke the gospel louder than any direct evangelistic approach.

Another way in which the traditional mission to the Jews showed great flexibility of methodology was in their response to the Holocaust. The Swedish Mission to the Jews Center in Vienna was used to save thousands at the start of the *Anschluss*. After the Holocaust, many missions, including Chosen People Ministries, established "soup kitchens" and other ministries that served the needs of Holocaust survivors.

The traditional Jewish mission has also utilized technology faster than most other groups. Chosen People Ministries was one of the first Jewish ministries to use newspaper ads to preach the gospel in its Smiling Faces ad campaign in the early 1970's. The traditional mission has been anything but "stodgy" in its approach to worldwide Jewish outreach. The traditional mission has usually been on the *proverbial cutting edge* of missions, developing new and dynamic methods and strategies to fulfill its worldwide mission.

### Attuned to Contemporary Jewish Culture

The traditional mission to the Jewish people has always been more sensitive to various expressions of Jewish identity. David Baron, one of the great leaders of a traditional Jewish mission in the last century (with the Hebrew Christian Testimony to Israel), was an early and ardent Zionist. He attended all of the initial Zionist conferences and attempted to share the gospel with Theodor Herzl.

The missions to the Jews were some of the first to recognize that the recent immigration of Russian Jews around the world was unique and demanded a response. Chosen People Ministries has established work among Russian Jews within the former Soviet Union and within the communities of Israel, Brooklyn, Germany, and Australia. The flexible nature and outreach drive of the mission has caused the staff and leadership of the traditional mission to pay close attention to the geographic and cultural changes within the worldwide Jewish community. The flexible nature of the structure usually allows the mission to quickly respond.

There are many other changes in today's world. The growing alienation among Jewish youth, the increase of elderly Jews, the move to the Sun Belt, and many other demographic and social trends are carefully watched by traditional Jewish missions. These new directions within the Jewish community worldwide will have a determinative effect on strategies in the days ahead.

### Self Governing and Self Supporting

The traditional Jewish mission is not dependent upon a geographically defined area for its governance or financial support. This enables the organization to begin work in areas that are not able to govern or support such an endeavor. For example, ministry in the former Soviet Union and Israel is difficult to support. The traditional model, which raises funds outside of its sphere of actual ministry, has been able to meet the challenges in areas that offer little financial support. Some of these new works are able to become self-supporting after a time, but it is difficult to begin without some form of outside support. This support, in the form of personnel, expertise, leadership, and funding has usually been provided through a traditional mission structure.

## The Future of the Traditional Jewish Mission

Perhaps, more than any other organizational form, the traditional mission to the Jews is well equipped to face this new millennium of opportunity to bring the message of Yeshua to the Jewish people. The very nature of the traditional Jewish mission—especially as described with these four enduring qualities—will stand the test of time. One of the important steps to a bright future of ministry among the Jewish people will be the uniting of hearts and strategies between the traditional missions and the new Messianic congregations. This must be an item on the agenda for the future of the Messianic movement. Both congregations and missions must recognize their respective validity in fulfilling God's plan—that Jewish people around the world hear the gospel and come to know Yeshua as Messiah.

Traditional Jewish missions like Chosen People will continue to utilize a variation of the Center approach—and a part of that strategy will be to establish Messianic congregations. In fact, when Messianic congregations seek to plant additional congregations across geographic and cultural borders, they could benefit greatly from the partnership of traditional Jewish missions. The unity of our messianic movement must include those who are part of the traditional Jewish missions community.

## A Final Word

This time-tested structure of the traditional Jewish mission is not only biblical—it has proven itself effective in meeting the needs of diverse Jewish communities across the globe. The future is bright for the traditional mission to the Jewish people. The precise structure and form of the traditional Jewish mission structure will keep changing as new challenges present themselves. As it has been in the past, the traditional model will continue to be successful and effective in the future due to its unique and enduring qualities.

## Questions for Discussion

- How did the combination of the "Social Gospel" and the evangelism of the Jewish mission structure lend itself to success in the post-World War I setting?
- What impact did the Holocaust have on the mission movement in Europe in the years following World War II?
- Due to the success of the Jewish mission structure in meeting various needs of the people, what lessons could single-driven organizations learn to meet the physical and spiritual needs of people today?
- What is the long-term forecast of the effectiveness of the Jewish mission structure in reaching out with the message that Yeshua is the Jewish Messiah?

✡ ✡ ✡

Born into an Orthodox home in New York City, Mitch Glaser received Yeshua as his Messiah in 1970. Since 1997, he has served as President of Chosen People Ministries. An alumnus of Northeastern Bible College, he holds a Master of Divinity degree from Talbot Theological Seminary and a Ph.D. in Intercultural Studies from Fuller Theological Seminary. Dr. Glaser is the co-author of *The Fall Feasts of Israel* with his wife, Zhava.

# MESSIANIC *KERUV*: GATHERING IN, REACHING OUT

—Kay Silberling

> The eminent scholar of Christian origins welcomed his Duke University graduate students to his seminar on Paul with detailed bibliographies, extensive references to *Pirke Aboth* 1.1 and personal greetings to all participants. At one point during such introductory matters, he interrupted his greetings with ". . . and, ah, a Jewess." I looked around quickly: there's a Jewess in the room! Get a fly swatter, a butterfly net, an archivist. An etymologist or an entomologist . . . It took a moment before I realized he was talking about me.
>
> —Amy-Jill Levine

This anecdote by a Jewish scholar of the New Testament brings to mind the pitfalls and hazards that we encounter when we breach the boundaries between Christianity and Judaism. Language is a boundary marker. And the two worlds of Judaism and Christianity have used language to construct themselves as sharp polarities—as binary opposites on the social and historical stage. Those who dare to violate these boundaries are thus marked by both groups as dangerous and threatening. Those who breach the boundary threaten the dominant group's own identity and thus elicit comments that single them out as unusual specimens to be marked and noted.

A new social group has entered this sharply polarized world—one that is in its own process of identity-formation—Messianic Judaism. And, like any other social group, it has legitimate concerns for self-perpetuation and self-expansion—concerns for *keruv*, a Hebrew word that means "ingathering"—the process of perpetuating a group's existence and its very survival into the next generation by attracting others with its message. But this is the rub. While those Messianic Jews who identify primarily with the Jewish world have a legitimate desire for self-proliferation, their efforts at communicating with that group—a group that deeply informs their own identity construction, are blocked because of how the larger Jewish world perceives them. This perception, as I will demonstrate, is deeply embedded with elements of power and domination. This is the fundamental impediment to Messianic *keruv*, and it is this impediment that must be addressed before all others.

Traditional Jewish and Christian elites characterize Messianic Jews as Christians and not Jews. In this way, the social boundaries that the elites construct appear fixed and immovable. The dominant Jewish group, because of its greater social power, is able to impose its own definition of normalcy onto the weaker Messianic Jewish group and thus to "define out" Messianic Jews in the process. In this power-charged environment, communication between the groups becomes greatly hampered. With respect to membership in the Jewish polity, as far as the elites are concerned, Messianic Jews have no legitimate claims. This characterization is repeated as a mantra until even Messianic Jews despair of ever successfully contesting it.

Given their position as objects of this pattern of alienation and disenfranchisement, it is incumbent upon Messianic believers, as they negotiate their way between the cracks and fissures that mark out the boundaries of the two dominant groups, to call for new methods of communication and reaching out that reject current models of power and supremacy. There are alternatives to the power-laden models currently employed—alternatives that acknowledge the legitimacy of the impulse for self-proliferation but that do so without violating the integrity of other social groups.

Before discussing these new models for *keruv*, it is important to clarify how the connection between a group's identity formation and its use of power limits *keruv*. Social groups form their identities in a variety of ways. They construct memories of the past, create binary opposites against which to measure themselves, and endeavor to position themselves in such a way as to impose their identity construction on others. Identity is not a static category. It is not fixed; it is always moving, always in the process of reinventing itself. Cultural identities are products of shared narratives, rituals, and codes that provide a perception of solidarity between group members—a perception that belies the rich diversity within any group. There is no single quality that captures the essence of being Jewish.

One way of constructing identities that appear fixed or "essentialized," even though they are constantly moving, involves creating boundaries based on binary opposites. It requires the creation of a notion of the Other, the archetypal different One, against whom the group can gauge itself as a sort of alter-identity and against whom it can assert its power. This binary opposition can be racial (black/white), gender-based (male/female), nationalist (citizen/alien) or religious (Jewish/Christian). Messianic believers are caught in the vise of this fundamental social struggle between the dominant groups of more mainstream Judaisms and Christianities. These binary constructs reinforce group boundaries and, hence, serve to heighten group difference through power and opposition, making real communication almost impossible.

A second way that groups develop identities is through constructed memories. Groups construct a past based on a selective retention of history, myth, and ritual. These socially constructed pasts, or memories, are thus in a constant state of flux and reassessment. Social memory also involves social forgetting. To write individuals or groups out of social memory is an act of social violence. It deprives the group of social reality and identity. It deprives individuals of their very existence.

Amy-Jill Levine points out that the significant roles played by Jewish women in the Jewish Apocrypha and the New Testament have been largely ignored by both Christian and Jewish scholars because they are transgressing boundaries and thus are sites of danger and threat to both groups. "They provide the stage upon which the anxieties of the communities that display them can be expressed, mapped, and alleviated" (Levine 154). Like these Jewish women, Jewish followers of Yeshua, as sources of danger and anxiety, are often excluded from the social memories of both Jewish and Christian cultures.

The irony is that, despite efforts to create an essentialized identity, the cultural experience of social groups is marked by the opposite characteristic—hybridity—that is, mutual influence and mutual development with and from the binary Other. Each group forms its identity as a mirror image, albeit a distorted one, of its archetypal Other. Paradoxically, hybridity is exactly what the dominant group fears the most. Thus, its elites or their agents work to suppress any evidence of hybridity as a way of creating the fiction of a fixed identity.

Daniel Boyarin, in his recent publication, *Dying for God: Martyrdom and the Making of Christianity and Judaism*, contests this common Christian/Jewish construction of memory. He suggests that a better model for studying the historical relationship between Judaism and Christianity is one that is similar to the model of how language proliferates—a model "where there is no linguistic border 'on the ground' between countries . . . one could travel, metaphorically, from rabbinic Jew to Christian along a continuum where one hardly would know where one stopped and the other began" (9). This model recognizes the social phenomenon of hybridity and gives no place for the dogma of apologetic concerns (D. Boyarin 7). Yet, scholars persistently date the parting of the ways between the two groups at either 70 C.E. or 135 C.E., despite overwhelming evidence for a date centuries later. This "social forgetting" serves both groups' apologetic demands by constructing a mythological memory that excludes, very early, the dangerous Other and suppresses the hybrid nature of the Jewish/Christian historical experience.

For Christians in the West, anxiety about hybridity with Judaism became acute in the nineteenth century as Jews assimilated and adopted the "white" sameness of Western Europeans. That is, the closer that members of a differentiated cultural group came to the dominant group, the greater the perception of threat and the greater the anxiety (see Itzkovitz 181–189). Likewise, contemporary Jewish communal elites locate Messianic Jews at a similar site of anxiety and danger. They are both alike and not alike, and this is precisely why Messianic Jews are perceived as so dangerous. The porous and fluid boundaries that represent Western culture today—mutual cultural influences and especially the high rate of intermarriage—all heighten the danger of Messianic Jews as the embodiment of anxiety and terror for Jewish and Christian elites.

All of these processes of boundary construction employ power and oppression as essential tools. Any interdependence between the two groups, any interrelationship, is expunged and suppressed in the interests of alleviating fears of contamination, taboo, and pollution. The dominant groups are subject, and the weaker group between them is object—objectified and frozen in time and place as if a static, and therefore controllable, category.

It is this objectification with which Messianic believers take greatest issue. J. Boyarin notes that the dominant group's posture toward the weaker becomes one of marketing and of acquisition (see 437). The weaker group is marked for annihilation and/or incorporation into the dominant group, with the recognition that full and complete incorporation of all members of the weaker group would result in the eradication of that group as a social construct. This is the desired result—social, albeit not necessarily individual, annihilation. The dominant group may challenge the sanity, honesty, and integrity of the weaker group's members in its efforts to contain and manage it as a perceived threat. Its agents repeat this language of annihilation over and over again among its adherents until the claims are accepted as axiomatic.

Here is where we can see most clearly the damaging effects of this employment of power by groups whose primary purpose is that of acquisition of the other group—a tactic that is employed by both sides of the cultural fissure. Silberstein notes that among groups that employ this model, no one is seeking "expanding enfranchisement and democratization of those who have been marginalized, excluded, and subordinated" (9). Instead, the Other is marked for receptivity into the group or eradication as a social reality, either in the present or in the idealized future.

Both Jewish-Christian missions and Jewish anti-missionary organizations operate with these models. Both fail to acknowledge that their efforts at "saving" the Other are not efforts for enfranchising them or giving them a social voice. Rather, they are efforts for doing away with them collectively in the hope of incorporating (swallowing) them in their own group. Both the missionary and the anti-missionary adopt a posture of acquisition and marketing, a posture that involves an inherent subject/object—or even male/female—power relationship. Both seek power over the other, and both adopt metaphors describing themselves as acquirers—hence, male—and impose upon the Other the metaphor of receptors—hence, female (see J. Boyarin 437). Note the common adoption of such terms as "receiving" or "accepting" in missionary literature).

These organizations adopt an aggressive presence on street corners and college campuses and purchase significant advertisements in major secular and religious media venues. Well financed, primarily through donations from either Christian or Jewish organizations, they employ the most sophisticated methods of marketing and acquisition to get their message out, and they underwrite them by appealing to the terrors and fears of their respective constituencies. They safely defuse the threat posed by the Other through the use of language that alienates and disenfranchises—both groups using terms such as "lost," "dying," and "deceptive."

This language of cultural violence enhances the anxiety of the Jewish and Christian communal elites while comforting them that their own message is being "defended." Both missionary and anti-missionary groups posture themselves as the dominant group in relation to the Other, but in their posture toward their own respective donors, they present themselves as the weaker, threatened group, thus legitimating their posture of social violence toward the Other. Both have adopted the politics of power in their efforts at "saving" one another.

Messianic Jews who adopt either of these models only serve to reinforce power inequities. Those who approach their hearers from the posture of aggressive male acquirer, passing out tracts on street corners or witnessing aggressively, force their hearers to react in either of two ways: either they must respond as passive, female receptors or they must react in anger and defensiveness, setting up a vicious cycle of offense/defense/offense. In either case, the power model has been reaffirmed, not challenged. Nor have these power inequities been bypassed by those Messianic Jews who adopt the passive receptor role with respect to either dominant Judaisms or Christianities. They are still operating within the system's modeled power inequities and have thus offered no real social or theological challenge to either group.

What, then, are those Messianic believers who respect the integrity of Jewish communal and Christian institutions—but who desire a model of reaching out and gathering in that disavows these tools of power and subjectivity—to do? The first task is to challenge essentialized and/or fixed notions of identity—notions that are based on selective memories and on suppressing the Other—notions that characterize both Judaism and Christianity. There is no archetypal "Jew" or "Christian." The question, "Who is a Jew?" cannot be answered in this period of modernity. Western Jews deeply incorporate the customs and norms of the Christian West. Likewise, Christians internalize Jewish norms through their ethical values, narratives, and sacred texts. Intermarriage between Jews and Christians has now become normative. A recent article in the *Jewish Journal* cites the American Jewish Committee's 2000 Survey of American Jewish Opinion, which states with great finality, "the Jewish taboo on mixed marriage has clearly collapsed" (Wiener 10). There are no fixed boundaries because there is no fixed identity. This is the first step—to challenge the fiction that there is a fixed, impermeable wall between Judaism and Christianity. It just is not so.

The second step is to challenge the constructed memories that "write out" the nine-century-long, vital history of Jewish followers of Yeshua who actively participated in Jewish society in the first half of the last millennium. A better model for Jewish-Christian memory construction is one in which an infinite number of hybridities is possible and is operating within the West, all of them being renegotiated and in process toward the two axes of Judaism and Christianity, all of them in flux, and all of them subject to influence by other religious and social-political traditions as well. Messianic Judaism is one of those streams, in process and evolving. New memories that celebrate the Other and treat it as a site of mutual growth and strengthening must be discovered and repeated as an act of peaceful resistance against models of power and alienation. The historical and social evidence for hybridity must be demonstrated, and then repeated, again and again.

Language needs to change. Messianic believers must ask to whom they are looking for their primary vision and direction—Judaism or Christianity? Phrases such as "unsaved Jews" and "non-Messianic Jews" comprise a jargon that alienates others and should be abandoned. Jargon that has taken on a clear mark of primary allegiance to the Christian side of the social matrix, such as "the Lord laid it on my heart," or "I have a heart for . . ." also should give pause to Messianic believers who claim to be Jewishly-identified. To others, the mere use of those terms marks the speaker as a Christian and belies any claims of Jewishness. Jargon is a primary signifier for social identity. If Messianic Jews are sincere in their claim to be committed to the Jewish world, then their language should reflect this commitment.

Messianic theology and social memory should be reappraised. All social groups construct their theologies in light of their own social-historical experience. That is why the theology of Maimonides is radically different from that of Rabbi Akiva, and that of Thomas Aquinas from Dietrich Bonhoeffer. Messianic believers must take seriously, the call to develop theologies that are deeply informed by Jewish historical experience and not just adopt, wholesale and unchallenged, evangelical Christian theology. A truly Messianic *Jewish* theology would serve to challenge elite Jewish resistance to Messianic Judaism and to subvert Christianity's suppression of social-historical Israel as a foundational theological category. This does not have to mean an abandonment of high Christology—there are plenty of examples of high Christologies in Jewish apocryphal literature that can inform a uniquely Messianic Christology.

Finally, Messianic believers need to find ways of communication that do not represent an attempt to control the other's social identity but to respect it. Levinas' notion of *obligation* (not power) *for* (not over) the other is a helpful model. This model calls to mind Yeshua's challenge to be servants *for* and not rulers *over* the other—a model that radically subverted the ancient Mediterranean norms and customs of Yeshua's day. What might this kind of model look like today? It would involve increased social interaction as a way to facilitate opportunities to speak with Jews who are interested in dialogue—not as parent to child, but as adult-to-adult. It would involve inviting willing friends and neighbors to Messianic synagogues, co-participating in festivals and in community events as opportunities present themselves, and serving in Jewish non-profit organizations that are open to Messianic believers. All of these things will open avenues of communication that will take place in a mutually beneficial environment. It is not about telling people that we have something they lack. That is the message of a parent to a child. Rather, it is about creating things that connect, bring together, and create alliances—it is about moving, and doing—all of this for others (see Silberstein 8).

As long as the message of Messianic believers betrays the politics of power and domination, it has fallen short of the mandate from Yeshua to be servant-healers. It also has heightened, rather than alleviated, the sense of danger and threat that Messianic believers represent to Jewish elites. The solution involves recognizing difference—whether individual or corporate—and resolving those differences by exchanging the tried old politics of power and polarity for the new ethos of sympathy and solidarity. This is a kind of *keruv* that will provide a true legacy for all future generations.

## Questions for Discussion

- Give three examples of jargon and how its use signals an individual's identification with a particular social group, thus marking that individual out as "different" from other groups.
- List the three primary means used by social groups to construct their identities and to keep out those on the margins. Give examples from your experience for each.
- Discuss ways that your group or congregation can modify your own models for *keruv* in a way that respects difference yet affirms the message of Yeshua.
- Offering new models for *keruv* that reject power relationships does not necessitate a rejection of unique claims about Yeshua as Messiah. How can the two ideas be reconciled?

## Bibliography

Boyarin, Daniel. *Dying for God: Martyrdom and the Making of Christianity and Judaism.* Stanford: Stanford Univ., 1999.

Boyarin, Jonathan. "The Other Within and the Other Without." *The Other in Jewish Thought and History,* Eds. Laurence J. Silberstein and Robert L. Cohn. New York: New York Univ., 1994. 424–452.

Itzkovitz, Daniel. "Secret Temples." *Jews and Other Differences: The New Jewish Cultural Studies.* Minneapolis: Univ. of Minnesota, 1997. 181–189.

Levine, Amy-Jill. "A Jewess, More and/or Less." *Judaism Since Gender,* Eds. Miriam Peskowitz and Laura Levitt. New York: Routledge, 1997. 149–157.

Silberstein, Laurence J. "Mapping, Not Tracing: Opening Reflection." *Mapping Jewish Identities.* Ed. Laurence J. Silberstein. New York: New York Univ., 2000. 1–36.

Wiener, Julie. "Intermarriage: A Tragedy or a Symbol of Our Success as Americans?" *Jewish Journal* 15 (Nov. 24–30, 2000): 10–11.

✡ ✡ ✡

Kay Silberling holds a Ph.D. in Early Judaism and New Testament. She has lectured and taught at several West Coast colleges and universities on topics such as Early Jewish Hermeneutics, Jewish Pseudepigrapha, Introduction to Judaism, and New Testament topics. She has helped her husband, Murray, to plant three Messianic synagogues. She currently attends Beth Emunah Messianic Synagogue.

# MESSIANIC JUDAISM'S ROLE IN THE DIASPORA

—Murray Silberling

For those within Messianic Judaism, supporting the land of Israel has been significant core value, as it has been for most of the Jewish community. Since the Holocaust, Israel has been both symbol and substance in our brush with annihilation and extinction as a people. Israel's identity, existence, and preservation are fundamental. For most Jews, the reason for this is two-fold—survival and continuity. Robert Wistrich, in his article, "Do the Jews Have A Future," states, "The existence of Israel has clearly served in the past 45 years as a catalyst of Jewish identification and an undeniable core of Jewish cohesion and continuity." Anti-Semitism and assimilation are the two major adversaries of the Jewish people. As a geo-political entity and ethnic homeland, the continued existence of Israel is the foremost deterrent against these two opponents of the Jewish people. Whether Messianic or not, the events that influence Israel today also affect us in the Diaspora.

For Messianic Jews, Israel's importance goes beyond the concern for survival. Israel takes on great theological import as Messianic believers draw nourishment from the prophetic tradition of looking to a future restoration that centers around land and people—the land of Israel and the people of Israel.

At the same time, the Diaspora is also a significant core value within the Jewish community, and specifically, within Messianic Judaism. Although Messianic Jews tend to see the Diaspora as secondary in the struggle for Jewish survival, it is, in many ways, as essential and effective a weapon in the fight against the dual enemies of anti-Semitism and assimilation as is the land of Israel.

The Diaspora is also a place of innovation regarding Jewish identity and practice. Unhindered by a bureaucracy that deters religious experimentation, Diaspora Messianic Jews are able to freely draw from the rich traditions of our forebears without fear of severe recrimination by Jewish communal leaders.

Finally, the Diaspora is an important theological construct for the future of God's purposes for Israel. God's redemptive activity has always operated both within and without the land of Israel. Israel as symbolic center only serves to remind us of the worldwide scope of God's redemptive activity. Therefore, I contend that both Israel, as a national Jewish entity, and the Diaspora, as a dispersed Jewish people worldwide, are essential within the structure of Messianic Judaism.

For Messianic believers, the most important concern is theological. God's plan of redemption is to be accomplished both in Israel and in the Diaspora. The concept of "place" in Scripture illuminates our theological understanding of the relationship of Israel to the Diaspora. "Place" is also a significant concept in midrashic literature, where *HaMakon*—the Place—is a common name used to refer to God. In Jewish tradition, the act of redemption is closely tied to the significance of place—holy place. However, that holy place—the locus for God's redemptive activity, is not always within the land of Israel. For instance, Moses was given the covenant at Mt. Sinai, outside of the land of Israel. God's presence traveled in cloud and fire with the Israelites in the wilderness *before* they entered the land. The great men and women of faith, Moses, Abraham, Sarah, Rebekah, Joseph, and many others, experienced God's redemptive plan in the Diaspora, not in Israel. Redemption was made outside of the land, yet affected the land along with these other persons and events.

In Stephen's preaching in Acts 7, the concept of Temple and place is challenged in a way that speaks to us as Diaspora Jews today. Without denigrating the original value of the locus of the Temple itself, Stephen extended the paradigm of God's active presence from "a place," i.e., Temple—with its hierarchy of priesthood and boundaries in regard to purity—to "a people." His language extended, but did not replace, the significance of the Temple as locus for God's divine activity. Stephen's model can be applied to our situation today. Without replacing the significance of Israel, Diaspora Messianic Jews have developed the notion of a symbiotic relationship between Israel and the Diaspora in God's redemptive plan, just as we see in the scriptural narratives. In other words, the Diaspora is not "Plan B" for God's redemptive plan. It never has been. Rather, along with the land of Israel, the Diaspora is central to God's purposes for Israel as a people, whether within or outside of the land. Like the Temple, "place" defines Israel today—the crux of Judaism's soul and survival. Like the people of Israel as a whole, the Diaspora represents a complementary arena of God's redemptive plans and purposes—wherever Jewish people who call upon God may be, God is there. Diaspora Messianic Judaism is a community of faith and practice that exists in an interdependent relationship with Israeli Messianic Judaism to work in redemptive history.

The view of Israel of Jews living in the Diaspora has changed significantly since the early days after nationhood in 1948. Classical Zionism was passionate and unflinching in its demands. Robert Wistrich states, "In the Zionist perception, the Diaspora is a transitory condition, and a secure existence is possible only through a return to the sources of Jewish life, to the land of one's ancestors." Fifteen years ago, Messianic Jewish religious Zionists viewed Israel as the sole bastion against the enemies of the Jewish people. In fact, many Messianic Jews saw their place in the Diaspora as not only temporary, but somehow as a betrayal to the cause. The early Messianic Zionists, although religious rather than classical Zionists, would have come to the same conclusion as Theodor Herzl, author of *Der Judenstaat* (*The Jewish State*), who argued that anti-Semitism in the Diaspora could be eradicated only with the eradication of the Diaspora itself" (Halkin). Among Messianic believers, there was a strong, prophetically motivated need to get in line with what was viewed as God's Zionist purpose. Many of today's Messianic Jews were raised with this type of view, whereby the Diaspora was perceived as ancillary and even counterproductive to the plans of God.

For a time, during the 1980s, many Messianic leaders promoted the idea of making *aliyah* as a scriptural mandate for *all* Messianic Jews, and many people applied for Israeli citizenship. This impulse, which was largely apocalyptically based, was a response to the original revival within Messianic Judaism of the late 1970s and early 1980s.

As the Zionist revolution matured and Israel became more complacent with its more sophisticated defense capabilities, this "revolution" began to draw fewer and fewer adherents. The slower growth of Zionism affected immigration as well. The newer influx of enthusiasts tended to be religious Zionists, desiring a "Greater Israel" through the development of religious settlements. A new phenomenon began to occur. Israelis began *emigrating* from Israel and settling permanently in other countries. Hillel Halkin rightly states, "If Zionism was the failed world revolution of the Jewish people, the Diaspora was the counterrevolution; already by the 1970s, far more Israelis were living in America than American Jews in Israel."

My own personal experience of the period was similar to that of many others within the Messianic movement. Having been born in 1948, the same year that Israel became a nation, I grew up with a strong sense that Israel was the *only* safe place for Jews. I was subtly taught that Israel's survival was integral to any future survival of Judaism—and that Israel was the only true community of Jewish faith. At the age of thirteen, I was part of a citywide celebration for the *bar mitzvah* of Israel. Since I was to be a *bar mitzvah* the same year, 1961, I was invited to march in the parade, and I received a certificate of achievement. This type of teaching from my youth fostered and solidified an enormous sense of responsibility that I would carry into my adulthood: to work toward the continued existence of this prized parcel of land and symbol of Jewish survival—Israel.

Since this time, many in the Diaspora Jewish community have shifted from the original religious Zionist position toward what is often referred to as "a pro-Israel" position. In defining this contrast, Steven Cohen, in his book, *American Modernity and Jewish Identity*, refutes the notion that all Jews should be obligated to settle in Israel. He alludes to a new, American Jewish approach to Israel whose hallmark motto is, "Not Zionism—nationalistic fervor, but pro-Israel security and prosperity" (156).

By the early 1990s, like many others in the larger Jewish community, the Diaspora Messianic movement was less strident in its Zionist view. It had become more involved in the establishment of synagogues and had sensed a need for a more communal expression and presence in the Diaspora—a purpose independent of the impulse to make *aliyah*.

As Messianic Jews living in the Diaspora, many of us came to understand that we could not continue to exist without our own sense of mission and self-definition. There needed to be meaning and self-identity for our existence as the Jews of the Diaspora. We could not find fundamental significance in our calling merely as a temporary seedbed for Messianic Zionism. As time went on, we Diaspora Messianic Jews began to mature and establish ourselves as more than seeds to be transported to Israel, but as full-grown, rich and fruitful plants in our own right. We began to develop an identifiable Messianic expression that created momentum for a more mature Messianic Judaism—one that modeled vibrant Jewish faith and practice and that spoke to the needs and deep spiritual longings of other Diaspora Jews.

Diaspora Messianic Judaism has developed in a very different social context than Israeli Messianic Judaism. There are therefore significant differences between these two communities. However, at the same time, there has always been a strong religious connection and identification between Israeli Jews and the Jews of the Diaspora. As one sociologist put it, "Israeli and Diaspora Jews represent two people, joined by a common history but divided by language, culture and even religion" (Wertheimer). As Messianic Jews, we have developed, and tenaciously hold to, a fundamental perception of the equal importance of both Israel and the Diaspora in the plan of God. Diaspora Messianic Jews believe that God's plans and purposes for Jewish people can be fulfilled outside of the land as well as within it—and, in fact, these two streams feed into the same purpose of God for the people Israel.

The religious component of Jewish identity and practice is an issue of tremendous concern to the existence of a Messianic Jewish Diaspora. Certainly, the answer to the question, "Who is a Jew?" takes into account the

Israeli Law of Return and other Ministry of Religious Affairs issues. But, we must ask, is Israel the only arbiter of this important question? Being Jewish cannot be fully understood apart from a relationship with Israel. Yet, the Diaspora has become a seminal site of energetic and vibrant religious exploration regarding this issue of Jewish identity.

This kind of fertile and lively exploration is more characteristic of the Diaspora than of Israel. The religious community of Israel is, largely, an Orthodox hegemony that controls most religious institutions and restricts those pluralistic impulses that may arise. Non-Orthodox Judaisms, whether Reconstructionist, Masorti, Renewal, or Messianic, are not readily accepted. Although we are beginning to see changes on the horizon, the political and religious monopoly of the Orthodox suppresses freedom of exploration or experimentation within the present indigenous Israeli Judaisms.

In many ways, Israeli Messianic Judaism reflects this polarization. Some Israeli Messianic believers have experienced prejudice and subtle forms of persecution in Israel, making it very difficult for some to be financially independent. It can be difficult to be straightforward about identity and faith while supporting a family. Social and financial pressures that religious "anti-missionary" organizations place on Messianic Israelis are aimed toward discouraging and weakening the movement. This pressure pushes some Messianic Israelis to identify more with the secular, non-religious component of Israeli society—a society that is bifurcated into two camps: Orthodox religious and secular, non-religious. Other Messianic leaders, convinced of the importance of specifically *Jewish* liturgical forms, are drawn toward a model that more closely mirrors Orthodox Judaism as expressed in Israel.

Thus, Messianic Israelis, as is the case in the wider society, are primarily compelled toward two primary religious options: (1) anti-Orthodox, non-practicing groups that, because of their aversion to things "Jewish" (i.e., Orthodox), end up mirroring the only other model available to them—Protestant Christianity; or (2) religious Messianic Jews who identify more with the Orthodox because of its traditionalism and faithfulness to long-standing Jewish forms of worship. Those forms of expression that more naturally grow within pluralistic social structures find it difficult to thrive in such a bifurcated environment. Instead, there is pressure to conform to either one or another of these groups, with the more common tendency among Messianic Israelis being to reflect the system that models a less significant level of Jewish practice—a model that, because of the historical roots of Hebrew/Christian missions in Israel, is readily available.

Diaspora Messianic Jews, being confronted daily with the need to be thoughtful and consciously aware of the process of forming our Jewish identity, are encouraged to develop creative innovations within Messianic Judaism. These varied innovations can be very effective in speaking clearly to the needs of Jews today, both inside and outside of Israel. As Messianic Judaism in the Diaspora develops dynamic forms of worship, liturgy, and service for our people, some of these inventive approaches have the potential to breathe new life into the Israeli Messianic movement. The religious freedom and pluralistic nature of the Diaspora could become a vital source for the advancement and expansion of an Israeli Judaism that offers a compelling alternative to the Orthodox hegemony. The Diaspora has been an excellent seedbed for the development of other Judaisms that nurture our need for self-identification. Because of this, it can be a positive source for the future of Israeli Judaism as well.

Messianic Judaism is, by self-identification, a marginalized community of faith and practice. Whether in a Diaspora community that is struggling with a monolithic Christian presence or in an Israeli community that is struggling with a monolithic Orthodox presence, the need for self-definition is of paramount importance to our future. "American Jews live in a voluntary society where their every act of engagement as Jews is a matter of choice; Jews in Israel, as members of a Jewish polity, are compelled by law and custom to participate in communal Jewish activities" (Wertheimer).

As Diaspora Messianic Jews, many of us have thrived within our democratic and pluralistic societies, exploring and developing one of the most creative and dynamic forms of Judaism today. In the future, we will continue to be a strong force of change to offer an alternative Judaism that will inform and speak to our people worldwide. Israeli Messianic Judaism needs the Diaspora for vitality and for new models of religious life that are informed by the Jewish historical experience. Diaspora Messianic Judaism needs Israel for its symbolic power, its vital national existence, and its strong and universal statement of the presence and power of God working among his people.

Our task, in the Diaspora, is to continue to create and innovate with respect to Messianic Jewish theology and identity, outreach, and worship styles—all of which establish our community of faith as a uniquely *Jewish* renewal movement. Israel will always be a major symbol for us. The pro-Israel stand of the Messianic Jewish community in the Diaspora and its creative new models of Jewish identity can be important for the confirmation and growth of Messianic Judaism in Israel. However, the Diaspora is, nevertheless, inherently significant to the prophetic purpose of God. Those of us in the Diaspora have the responsibility to continue to define ourselves and to dialogue with Israeli Messianic movements in the future. We will continue to experiment and create models that will assist Messianic Judaism (in Israel and the Diaspora) with the unceasing challenge of continuity—for his name's sake (Ezek. 36:22).

As the Messianic community continues to mature in the Diaspora, it will continue to work to develop a reciprocally beneficial relationship with the Israeli Messianic community. The land of Israel will always be a principal representation of Jewish identity and security. This jointly beneficial relationship of Diaspora Messianic Judaism with Israeli Messianic Judaism will continue to develop and to advance the fulfillment of God's plan for all Israel. Therefore, both the Diaspora and Israeli Messianic communities need each other to complete the purpose of God in bringing about the full restoration of Israel as the "place" of God's presence among a certain people and as a light to all the nations.

## Questions for Discussion

* Why is Israel important to Messianic Judaism?
* What is the theological basis for Diaspora Judaism?
* How does Diaspora Messianic Judaism enrich Israeli Messianic Judaism?
* How are God's purposes being worked out in the Diaspora?

## Bibliography

Cohen, Steven M. *American Modernity and Jewish Identity*. New York: Tavistock, 1983.

Halkin, Hillel. "After Zionism: Reflections on Israel and the Diaspora." *Commentary* 103.6 (June 1997): 25–31. <http://www.commentarymagazine.com/9706/halkin.html>.

Smith, Jonathan Z. *To Take Place: Toward Theory in Ritual*. Chicago: Univ. of Chicago, 1987.

Wertheimer, Jack. "The Disaffections of American Jews." *Commentary* 105.5 (May 1998): 44–49. <http://www.commentarymagazine.com/9805/wertheimer.html>.

Wistrich, Robert S. "Do the Jews Have a Future?" *Commentary* 98 (July 1994): 23–26.

✡ ✡ ✡

Born in Southern California, Rabbi Murray Silberling has been involved in congregational ministry for twenty-eight years. He leads Beth Emunah Messianic Synagogue in Agoura Hills, California. Rabbi Silberling currently serves as the Southwest Regional Director for the International Alliance of Messianic Jewish Congregations and Synagogues. He is the author of *Dancing for Joy: A Biblical Approach to Praise and Worship* and is affectionately referred to as "the Dancing Rabbi."

# MESSIANIC JEWS SHOULD MAKE *ALIYAH*

—David H. Stern

The word *aliyah* literally means "going up." In the synagogue, someone that is called up to read from the *Torah* scroll has received an *aliyah*. And spiritual geography is such that one "goes up" from anywhere on earth to Israel. One "goes up" to Israel from the summit of Mount Everest. Hence "making *aliyah*" means "immigrating to Israel."

In line with the model of Messianic Jewish authenticity which the editor of this book calls "Jewish pluralism" (Cohn-Sherbok 209-213), my case for Messianic Jewish *aliyah* begins with the case for Jewish *aliyah* generally. And because the basis for our faith and practice is the Bible—the *Tanakh* plus the *B'rit Hadashah*—the argument begins with Scripture.

In the Mosaic Covenant God promises the Land of Israel to the Jews—to Abraham, Isaac, Jacob and Moses. Christian "replacement theologians" consider this promise canceled by the New Covenant; but since, according to Galatians 3:15–17, a later covenant cannot cancel an earlier one, this view contradicts God's Word (see "The People of God, the Promises of God, and the Land of Israel"). Because the Land has been promised to the Jews, and Messianic Jews are Jews, the Land is for us too.

Moreover, throughout the Bible, living in the Land is considered a blessing; while being excluded from it is a curse (see Deut. 28–30 and Ezek. 36:16–36). Since living in the Land is a blessing, Messianic Jews, along with other Jews, should be eagerly seeking this blessing. Jews have affirmed this truth for two thousand years by praying in the synagogue three times daily, "Sound the great *shofar* for our freedom, raise the banner to collect our exiles, and gather us from the four corners of the earth. Blessed are you, *Adonai*, who gathers the dispersed of your people Israel." Today Jews, both Messianic and otherwise, can say a practical "Amen" to this prayer by making *aliyah*! Furthermore, this is in keeping with God's plan that all Jews return:

"Then they will know that I am *ADONAI* their God, since it was I who caused them to go into exile among the nations, and it was I who regathered them to their own land. I will leave none of them there any more, and I will no longer hide my face from them, for I have poured out my Spirit on the house of Isra'el," says *Adonai* ELOHIM (Ezek. 39:28–29 CJB).

Another reason for making aliyah is that the Land is the natural place for Jews to live a truly Jewish life. Here in Israel, it's easy to celebrate the Jewish holidays, observe *Shabbat* and find *kosher* food because that's what's normal in this country. In the Diaspora, it takes constant effort to distinguish ourselves from the sea of Gentiles surrounding us. This explains why the ancient rabbis could write, "Living in the Land of Israel outweighs all the other commandments in the *Torah*" (*Sifrey, Re'eh*, 12:29).

However, in addition to these reasons, Messianic Jews have a special call from the prophet Isaiah to make *aliyah*:

> Those ransomed by *ADONAI* will return
> and come with singing to Tziyon,
> on their heads will be everlasting joy.
> They will acquire gladness and joy,
> while sorrow and sighing will flee.
>           (Isaiah 35:10, 51:11 CJB)

In context, "those ransomed by *ADONAI*" are the saved remnant of Israel; in the present era, this means the Messianic Jews, whom Yeshua the Messiah has ransomed from sin. Thus, God gives special encouragement to Messianic Jews to "acquire gladness and joy" by making *aliyah*.

A second reason for Messianic Jews (in particular) to make *aliyah* is that the challenge to us parallels the challenge to the early Zionist pioneers. The David Ben-Gurions and Golda Meirs abandoned their life in the *galut* (exile) in order to build the *yishuv* (the early settlement community) and eventually the State of Israel. Likewise, Messianic Jews who move to Israel become part of a pioneering community dedicated to building the spiritual life of Israel by both words and deeds—that Yeshua is the Jewish Messiah and that in him alone will all Jewish hopes be fulfilled.

Yet in the face of all these reasons for making *aliyah* most Messianic Jews are staying put, living in the *goldene medina* (golden country), the good old U. S. of A. (or Britain, or South Africa, etc.), and not planning to move. Why?

## Excuses Messianic Jews Have for Not Making *Aliyah*

I say the "excuses" rather than the "reasons" that Jews, both Messianic and non-Messianic, have for not coming to live in Israel because most of the reasons serve as excuses, though not all. Here are some of them; my responses are meant to encourage Messianic Jews to make concrete plans to live in Israel.

Why do I speak of "concrete plans"? Because there are many Messianic Jews who actually have positive thoughts about *aliyah*, but their thoughts are vague and romantic rather than realistic and concrete. Vague, romantic thoughts about how wonderful it would be to live in Israel may make you feel good, but they do nothing to get you to the Land. So I have to count vague positive feelings concerning moving to Israel as a major excuse for not making *aliyah*.

Another excuse is that "God hasn't called me to live in Israel." False! Isaiah 35:10 and 51:11, cited above, constitute your call. Thus the situation is exactly the opposite—you need a call to stay in the Diaspora. Such calls, I want to emphasize, are not uncommon. I have no doubt that there are some Messianic Jews doing exactly what the Lord wants them to do in America or some other country. But others who have heard no call to be living outside Israel should be considering whether now is the time to heed God's eternal and constant call to ransomed Jews to come to the Land.

A related excuse: "God hasn't called me to move *yet*." This isn't always an excuse; it can be a fact, even part of a plan that God has revealed. But it's like the cry at the end of the Passover *seder*, "Next year in Jerusalem," which often means "*mañana*" (i.e., never), rather than what it was supposed to mean, "We hope that we can celebrate *Pesach* in Jerusalem next year, and we'll do all we can to make it happen!"

What follows isn't exactly an excuse but rather an attitude which forms the substrate supporting other excuses, namely, that the Messianic Jewish movement outside Israel does not sufficiently emphasize and encourage *aliyah*. Some leaders in the movement actually seem opposed, perhaps afraid that if they endorse *aliyah* they will lose members of their congregations as they leave for the Land. My answer: leaders, make *aliyah* and bring your congregation with you! I would like to see the Messianic Jewish organizations in the Diaspora functioning as a support system for *aliyah*.

A legitimate concern, if not a valid excuse, is the Arab-Jewish situation in the Land of Israel and throughout the Middle East. If we live in our "old man," in our "flesh," the situation will quickly fill us with fear and disable us for Kingdom work. Our only source of safety is the Lord; we must take God at his word that he will guard, defend, and watch over his people. This clearly cannot mean that every single individual will escape harm, since Jews and Arabs are being killed and wounded daily—although statistically, the danger is far less than the media would have you think. Leaving personal risk aside, one must understand a central fact that the secular media cannot grasp: this conflict is not, in its essence, political but religious. It has been going on for at least a hundred years in one form or another; and it can be argued that it dates from the times of the Patriarchs. Therefore, no politically organized peace process will solve it. Even a so-called "permanent agreement" will prove to be an "interim agreement" because the opposing religions cannot compromise. Those whose faith is grounded in the Bible, both Jews and Christians, who understand that God promises the Land of Israel to the Jews, cannot deny God's word. And Islam cannot tolerate a people, who profess another religion (Judaism), establishing a state on "Islamic land," as they understand the *Koran* and its interpreters to teach. Although there is no political solution (therefore I expect the conflict to continue until Yeshua returns), there is a great and blessed hope—no, more than a hope, a certainty—that God's intentions will win out in the end. My attitude has to be that it is a privilege to be a part of what God is doing in his Land. We do what we can to express God's love and ways to Jews and Arabs alike, to the best of our ability, with God's help—no matter what happens in the Arab-Jewish conflict swirling all around us.

Some excuses reflect a false understanding of how prophecy should be used. For example, I have heard this: "The State of Israel is not the messianic state but rather a secular imitation not deserving of our loyalty." This is the position of some Hasidic Jewish groups (*Netorei-Karta*, *Satmar*), but it has no biblical basis. Although the current State of Israel is not in the hands of those who believe in the Bible and in Yeshua, nevertheless God is using it in his process of bringing Jews back to the Land; and therefore those who make *aliyah* are being used to fulfill God's plan. In other words, out of the current State of Israel God will produce the messianic State of Israel.

The same result, immobility from the Diaspora, comes from asserting: "Yeshua will fulfill his promises only when he comes back; before then Jews aren't supposed to return to Israel." Nonsense! This view seems to follow from the sit-by-and-do-nothing advice that emerges from prophetic interpretations that see the world as getting worse and worse until Yeshua returns, without believers' being able to do anything about it. I oppose this approach to life! We believers in Yeshua are supposed to do the good works God has prepared for us to do (Eph. 2:10), not stay in our shells bemoaning the fate of the world. These good works can perfectly well include being in Israel before Yeshua returns; being part of the process of God's fulfilling his promises.

Some believers whose ministry centers on evangelism avoid moving to Israel because they think evangelism is illegal here. They are wrong. Israel is a democracy. Although democratic freedoms are somewhat limited in the areas of security and religion, we can tell anyone we want about Yeshua. Israelis listen more and protest less than American Jews whose Jewish identity consists of mindlessly repeating that "Jews don't believe in Jesus." We publish full-page advertisements about him in the Hebrew newspapers. We pass out pamphlets about him on the streets. We sell books explaining him. Joe Shulam's organization, *Netivyah*, produces a nightly radio program about him in Hebrew. It's a shame to avoid the excitement and challenge of evangelism in Israel because of a false belief about its legality.

True, there is opposition to believers, but this shouldn't dissuade anyone from making *aliyah*. Periodically, religious members of the *Knesset* introduce legislation to curb evangelism, but these bills have always failed; and even if one were to pass, it would surely not inhibit our speaking out about Yeshua. Occasionally, notes are posted that so-and-so is a "missionary" (in Israel the word is almost an expletive), but this rarely stops anyone from serving the Lord. People do have their jobs threatened occasionally when employers are "informed" about an employee's being a believer; and sometimes, in violation of the law, employers succumb to the pressure. This is not nice. But it's not the end of the world, either. People recover, find other work, and get on with their lives. None of the opposition compares with the kind of persecution Christians are subject to in Communist China or the Sudan. "Don't be afraid of the people living in the land . . . . Their defense has been taken away from them, and *Adonai* is with us! Don't be afraid of them!" (Num. 14:9 CJB).

Other excuses for not making *aliyah* are related to the difficulties presented by everyday life in a different society with a different culture and language. These reasons could apply to anyone moving from his home country to any other. Yeshua's response is that one should "count the cost," that is, assess what will be required to cope with the difficulties, which are real and which do require effort to overcome. But one should also count the benefits, which can be summarized as being in the will of the Lord. Some excuses of this kind are:

- "My family, my property, the things I'm used to, are here (in America, Britain, etc.), not in Israel." Answer: "Yeshua said, 'Yes! I tell you that there is no one who has left house, brothers, sisters, mother, father, children or fields, for my sake and for the sake of the Good News, who will not receive a hundred times over, now, in the *'olam hazeh* [in this world], homes, brothers, sisters, mothers, children and lands with persecutions!—and in the *'olam haba* [the world to come], eternal life'" (Mark 10:29–30 CJB).

- "It's hard to make a living in Israel." True, wages are a third to a half of those in America. More generally, Israel is a third-world country, though near the top of the economic levels found in the third world. Most *olim* (immigrants) from the West experience a significant drop in their living standard unless they bring a good deal of money with them. Therefore, life in Israel is based on trust in God for his daily provision—just it was for Abraham. "By trusting, Avraham obeyed, after being called to go out to a place which God would give him as a possession; indeed, he went out without knowing where he was going. By trusting he lived . . . in the Land of the Promise" (Messianic Jews/Hebrews 11:8–10 CJB). "*Adonai* your God will bring you back into the land your ancestors possessed, and you will possess it; he will make you prosper there" (Deut. 30:5 CJB).

- "The challenge is overwhelming. I just don't think I can hack it." Yeshua didn't promise you a carefree life. Rather, he promised to be with you always (Mattityahu/Matthew 28:20), which means that he will be with you as you face your challenges. Besides, "the challenge" is not monolithic. It can be broken down into smaller, more manageable tasks. More specifically in relation to *aliyah*, I suggest that you inform yourself about practical matters such as learning Hebrew, obtaining housing, finding work, organizing life for singles and for families, satisfying spiritual needs and more. For orientation, see pages 227–233 of my book, *Messianic Jewish Manifesto*. In relation to meeting spiritual needs, see *Facts and Myths about the Messianic Congregations in Israel.*

However, if you have significant personal problems, it would be better to deal with them where you live now, rather than adding to them, the burden of adjusting to a different language, culture, and social system. Come to Israel after you've made some progress with these matters, so that you can contribute to the needs of the Land, rather than making the Land contribute to your needs. The depressing statistic is that sixty to eighty percent of Jews from the West leave Israel—their *aliyah* is unsuccessful. Do what you can to avoid becoming part of that statistic.

Finally, there is one more reason that Messianic Jews give for not making *aliyah*, and I do not call this an excuse. It is simply that the Law of Return, under which Jews from all over the world are allowed by the State of Israel to become citizens, does not apply to Messianic Jews, according to current court interpretations. This is a sufficiently cogent reason and complex issue that it deserves a section of its own.

## The Law of Return and Messianic Jews

In the light of the centuries-old conflict between Christendom and the Jewish People, it is no surprise that the official position of the State of Israel toward Messianic Jews has not been a positive one. The Law of Return, enacted in 1950, allows any Jew from anywhere in the world to make *aliyah* and become a citizen. This law originally defined a Jew as anyone with a Jewish mother or who converted to Judaism, but in 1970 a clause was added, "and who is not a member of another religion." In a series of cases, the High Court of Justice (known by the Hebrew acronym *Bagatz*) decided—with increasing clarity—that for purposes of the Law of Return,

Jews who believe in Yeshua and the New Covenant Scriptures are "members of another religion" and therefore not eligible to make *aliyah* under its provisions. The Court has not done this with Jews professing any other religion—Messianic Jews are Israel's only *refuseniks*. I have discussed these cases in four articles (see bibliography).

What do these court decisions mean, theologically and practically? Did Israel's High Court of Justice erase the Jewish identity of Messianic Jews? Of course not! Although *Bagatz* has declared that Messianic Jews are not Jews for purposes of the Law of Return, this cannot de-Jew us! Even Jewish religious law (*halakhah*) considers us Jewish, though not entitled to privileges—such as making *aliyah*. First-century Judaism recognized Messianic Jews as Jews. Finally, it is God, not *Bagatz*, who made us Jews; and no court can overrule him! My conclusion is that the High Court produced some bad theology.

However, their word is currently the law of the Land. Practically, for any individual Messianic Jew, the issue becomes whether to accept this ruling and give up on making *aliyah*, or to find a way to do it anyhow. Many Messianic Jews choose the second option, so that despite the unfavorable court decisions, Messianic Jewish *aliyah* continues. For this approach I see our implicit model as being the "A*liyah Bet*" of the late 1930s and 1940s, after Great Britain ended legal Jewish immigration to Palestine ("*Aliyah Aleph*"). The Jews involved in *Aliyah Bet* then—are considered heroes now.

Messianic *Aliyah Bet* poses ethical problems that are not different from the earlier one. Britain had declared Jewish immigration illegal, but many Jews refused to observe what they considered an unjust law. Every Messianic Jew who makes *aliyah* today has to decide whether he is resisting the authorities that God has instituted (Rom. 13:1–5) or obeying God rather than man (Acts 5:29). Moreover, because entry under the Law of Return entitles the immigrant to a sizeable package of economic benefits, he must consult his conscience concerning accepting some or all of these. Each one must think through these ethical questions for himself.

If you are a Messianic Jew interested in making *aliyah* under current conditions, consider the saying, "You get only one chance to do it right the first time." Therefore, you should consult people with experience and knowledge in order to avoid making needless mistakes.

There is one final point to make about the Law of Return; it concerns persons whose mothers are not Jewish but who have Jewish ancestry. A clause in the Law of Return grants *oleh* (immigrant) status to a Gentile with a father or grandparent who fits the law's definition of a Jew (Jewish mother or convert to Judaism, not a member of another religion). This person will not be registered as Jewish, because he isn't; but he will be entitled to all the other rights and privileges given to Jewish *olim*. Likewise, the non-Jewish spouse of an *oleh* is entitled to *oleh* status.

# Conclusion

If you are a Messianic Jew, I encourage you to consider making *aliyah*, so that you can help in fulfilling, from within the Land of the promise, the great promise of Romans 11:26 that "all Israel will be saved." You will find wonderful challenges and great fulfillment here—and joy and gladness in meeting them. May God bless your coming, as you stay close to him.

# Questions for Discussion

*For Jews:*

- How has the material presented in this chapter influenced your thinking about making *aliyah*? As you begin planning to make *aliyah*, have you started to learn Hebrew (how much progress have you made) and have you visited Israel (if not, visit Israel)?
- After you visit Israel and continue planning to make *aliyah*, consider the following issues: Where will you live? Have you rented an apartment? What work will you be doing? Have you found an employer? Which congregation will you be attending? Have you spoken with its leaders? What concerns do you still have about the success of your *aliyah*? Have you spoken with experienced people who can help you with them?

*For Non-Jews:*

- How can you help Jews understand the importance of making *aliyah*? How can you help Messianic Jews make *aliyah* successfully?

*For rabbis and pastors:*

- What are you doing to influence and help the Jewish members of your congregation to make *aliyah*?

# Bibliography

Cohn-Sherbok, Dan. *Messianic Judaism*. London: Cassell, 2000.

Kjaer-Hansen, Kai and Bodil F. Skjott, *Facts and Myths about the Messianic Congregations in Israel*. Jerusalem: United Christian Council in Israel, 1999.

Stern, David H. "Aliyah of Jewish Believers in Yeshua and the Authorities of the State of Israel." *LCJE Fifth International Conference Bulletin, Jerusalem, 1995.* 87–91.

———. "Court Cases and the Struggle for *Aliyah*." *Jewish Identity and Faith in Jesus*, Ed. Kai Kjaer-Hansen. Jerusalem: Caspari Center, 1996. 87–96.

———. "Messianic Jewish Aliyah: Update Since the Beresford Decision of 1989." *Lausanne Consultation on Jewish Evangelism Bulletin* 30 (August 1993): 8–14.

———. *Messianic Jewish Manifesto*. Clarksville: Jewish New Testament Publications, 1990.

———. "The Beresford Case and Israeli Public Opinion About Messianic Jewish Aliyah." *Lausanne Consultation on Jewish Evangelism Bulletin* 20 (May 1990): 4–11.

———. "The People of God, the Promises of God, and the Land of Israel." *The Enduring Paradox: Exploratory Essays in Messianic Judaism*, Ed. John Fischer. Baltimore: Lederer/Messianic Jewish Publishers, 2000. 79–94.

✡ ✡ ✡

David H. Stern was born in Los Angeles in 1935, the great-grandson of two of the city's first Jews. He earned a Ph.D. in economics from Princeton. A former professor at UCLA, Dr. Stern obtained an M.Div. from Fuller Theological Seminary and did postgraduate work at the University of Judaism. He is the translator of the *Jewish New Testament*, preparer of the *Complete Jewish Bible* (an English version of the Bible that is fully Jewish in style and presentation), and author of the *Jewish New Testament Commentary*, the *Messianic Jewish Manifesto*, and *Restoring the Jewishness of the Gospel*. He and his wife, Martha, live in Jerusalem.

# ARE WE REALLY AT THE END OF THE END TIMES? A REAPPRAISAL

—Richard C. Nichol

Is human history, as we know it, about to close? Are we a very short time from the very end predicted in Scripture? Many Messianic Jews seem to think so. However, the actual picture may be much more complex, interesting, and hopeful.

## The State of the Union—
## Messianic Judaism and the End Times

Messianic Judaism has its recent origins, not primarily in traditional Judaism, but in Protestant evangelical Christianity, particularly the dispensational variety. This vibrant form of Christian faith provided the soil in which the remnant of Israel could take root in modern times. It could be argued that no other form of either Judaism or Christianity could have mustered the initial support and encouragement for such a movement as ours. Its effects on nascent Messianic Judaism have been profound.

Our interest lies in one particular aspect of evangelical Christianity's theological outlook—the conviction held by many, but not all, that we are now living in the end of the End Times. Messianic Judaism, as it took root in the early 1970s, drank deeply of this tenet of the dispensational outlook. I know. I was there.

I was nineteen years old and I had read a book that changed everything for me. It was *The Late Great Planet Earth* by Hal Lindsey. Trained at Dallas Theological Seminary, a premiere evangelical institution, Lindsey thrilled me and my friends with his predictions of Israel's soon-coming war with Russia and other Eastern European nations. I specifically remember being amazed by his prediction of a Communist Chinese attack on *Eretz Yisra'el* (the Land of Israel)—an army of two hundred thousand, marching through Asia to take part in the last battle in the valley of Jezreel. Young Messianic Jews found Lindsey's book particularly easy to embrace because he seemed to like Jews. This was icing on the cake for us.

It all made sense. Clearly, we were in the end of the end of the age. One close friend reflected on those exciting days: "I would buy a pair of pants and wonder, 'is this the very last pair I'll ever buy before Messiah returns?'" Such was the atmosphere among many of us in those exciting and confusing days. It was the early 1970s. The secular utopian dreams of the hippie era were fading, but God was doing a new thing!

Thirty years later and counting, the return of Messiah has not yet come. Yet, in both religious circles and in the larger culture, a conviction that the end of the world will be upon us very shortly remains strong.

*Messianic Judaism has been more than influenced— it has actually defined itself in terms of the end of the End Times.* Almost a fundamental axiom of our faith, is the conviction that God has raised up Messianic Judaism at this very period of human history because we figure prominently in His plans to rescue the world from itself. Though this conviction may be justified, some disengagement with the motif of the End Times would be very helpful for Messianic Judaism at this time. Let us consider some of the problems with our present approach.

## It is Difficult to Predict the End

It may seem like a distant memory now, but just a few short months ago, the Y2K problem was on most everyone's mind. One man in our community spent time speculating on how we might need to secure our synagogue by posting armed guards during services. A few others bought enough dried food to keep them in beans and rice for years to come. One Messianic Jewish leader in another city stocked a barn full of provisions.

January 1, 2000 came and went without any serious incident. A few businesses reported trouble ringing up credit card orders and stories of alleged near disasters still circulate on the Internet. We should not assume that all reports of serious impending crises should be dismissed with a smug reference to Y2K. Major issues, which deserve our full and immediate attention, can and do show up at times. (If only the United States and Britain had taken the threat of Nazism seriously—and much earlier!) However, when it comes to predicting the time frame for the end of the End Times, we can take a lesson from the Y2K episode:

When it comes to big events, especially those of the cosmic scope, the future is very difficult to predict—so difficult in fact, that we must be very cautious about assuming that our scenarios have much basis in reality.

In the case of Y2K, little harm and some positive good seems to have resulted. For example, antiquated computer systems received badly needed makeovers. However, groups faithful to the God of Israel, sometimes, have not fared so well in the aftermath of wrong predictions about The End. We note a poignant example from Jewish history. Shabbetai Tzevi (1626–1676) believed, or claimed to believe that he was the Messiah. The *Standard Jewish Encyclopedia* notes, "After the horrors of the Chmielnicki Massacres (1648/9) he was moved by a 'Messianic spirit' and a 'heavenly voice,' proclaiming that he would redeem Israel" (849). Desperate European Jews were naturally looking for a way out—for *Mashiach* to come and rescue them from the irrationally hostile *Goyim*. Because of Tzevi's powerful, emotional sermons and new ideas, thousands followed him. Believing his "End Times" message, many sold their farms and businesses, waiting for the messiah to wrest Jerusalem from the Moslems. "Rumors were current of a Jewish army that would advance from the Arabian Desert to conquer Palestine" (850).

In 1666, Tsevi journeyed to Constantinople to depose the sultan. Initially tolerated by the Turkish authorities, he eventually aroused their ire and was given a choice: Convert to Islam or die. The "messiah" chose not to die. His followers were devastated by his conversion to Islam, though some tried to understand the master's actions as a form of messianic suffering for the sake of Israel. In the beginning, it all seemed so "right." All the signs seemed fit. But, world Jewry was wrong. This man, who had come "in his own name"—was not the deliverer. And, we as a people paid the price. In fact, some resistance among Jewish people today to the hope of a coming eschatological deliverer is an indirect result of the profound disappointment created by Shabbetai Tzevi and other messianic claimants who had assured us that the end was at hand.

The limitations of our landscape are illustrated by the fact that even Yeshua, the true Deliverer, and the writers of the *B'rit Hadashah* seemed to think that the end was very near the time in which they lived. When we read the *B'rit Hadashah*, we get the strong sense that the writers would be quite surprised to know that no less than two thousand years (at least) of history would elapse before the coming of the End.

This discrepancy is not a mistake on their part as such. Rather, their prophetic orientation, like that of Isaiah, Jeremiah and the other prophets, caused them to view the next great event in God's dealings with Israel and mankind as if it was imminent. The prophet (and Yeshua was a prophet as well as a King) feels, tastes, sees, knows, and intuits the coming manifestation of God's work and expresses his expectation with stunning immediacy. His message burns almost like that of the great composer who hears in his mind the next movement of his symphony before he has penned even one note.

If even our Messiah, through his own self-limitation, and his inspired apostles could, in a sense, "miss" the timing of history's final act, with how much greater caution should we trust our own abilities to discern the end of the age? If the world remains in tact for decades to come, Messianic Jewish leaders invite the kind of derision, cynicism, and loss of confidence other misguided end time movements have created among their adherents. This, we do not need!

## To Quote The Beatles,
## Some Things are "Getting Better All the Time"

Those who seem ready to give up on *Olam HaZeh* (the current world order) in favor of an assumed, imminent flowering of *Olam HaBa* (the world to come), tend to see signs of the times in the alleged unraveling of civilization. In fact, it would require viewing life through very thick rose colored glasses to miss the serious challenges facing humanity today. Nuclear, biological, or chemical weapons in the wrong hands, global warming, the possible unintended effects of genetic engineering—all come to mind. But, it might put us in a better place to shape the future of Messianic Judaism—if we were to consider some of the very positive things which have occurred and are occurring, not only in the industrialized world, but even in less-advantaged places. Consider the fact that over the past century, life expectancy has tripled in the United States to an astounding seventy-five years. Stephen Moore and Julian Simon, in their well-documented study of historic trends note the following:

> Even in poorer countries, life expectancy has risen at an astonishing pace. In China, in 1750, people on average could expect to live into their late twenties; by 1985, people were typically living into their sixties. Now, most of humanity enjoy better health and longevity than the richest people in the richest countries did just 100 years ago. (7)

> The death rate among children under the age of 15 has fallen by 95% since 1900 in the United States. . . . The child death rates in just the past 20 years have, incredibly, been halved in India, Egypt, Indonesia, Brazil, Mexico, Chile, South Korea, Israel, and scores of other countries. (10)

One hundred years ago, the maternal death rate in the United States was 100 times higher than it is today. In 1950, the maternal death rate was 10 times greater than it is today. By the 1980s, only 1 in 10,000 women died giving birth. (30)

The most impressive decline in poverty over he last half century has been among senior citizens. About one half of seniors were in poverty in the early 1950's compared with about 10 to 15 percent today. (74)

Moore and Simon document dozens of other specific ways in which life has improved dramatically on planet earth—particularly in the industrialized world. We would not infer from these encouraging facts that mankind, without divine intervention, will bring about the golden age. Rather, these facts serve as a necessary counterbalance to a mentality that sees all things as ready to fall apart. All things may not be ready to fall apart! Relative evil is not scoring a shutout against relative good in our world today. The end may not come very soon, and partnering with God to do good can still make a difference. This brings us to another concern about over emphasizing the end of the End Times as we build Messianic Judaism.

## "And it Was Good"

Over-identification with the end of the age causes us to lose sight of the Biblical/Jewish emphasis on the goodness of creation and thus, our role in the Created order.

When God had finished creating the world, he stepped back, smiled and said to himself and the admiring angels banked around his throne, "*Tov me'od*! Very good!" (Gen. 1:31). The divine pronouncement over his *tour de force* should suggest something very important about the world we inhabit. It is a fantastic place! Wondrous. A world worth preserving and enjoying. Jewish scholar Abraham Joshua Heschel, quoting Rabbi Eleazer, reflected on the magnificence of even the simple things of life:

Redemption and the earning of bread may be compared to each other. There is wonder in eating bread as there is wonder in redeeming the world. And as the earning of the bread takes place every day, so does redemption take place every day. (50)

An over-preoccupation with the End Times tends to dull our awareness of how important creation really is—and how important it is to God that we partner with him in repairing its damaged aspects. But here is a question: Why should Messianic Jews give much attention to building a hospital or calling attention to the international slave trade if we believe the world is about to fall apart? These and other issues cannot arouse our deep interest if we assume that the powers of darkness are so pervasive (in these last days) that all such efforts are exercises in futility.

Yet, it is difficult to read the *Torah*, Prophets, or *B'rit Hadashah* without coming away with the sense that such "earthly" concerns are of great importance to God. We think of Yeshua's parable of the sheep and the goats (Matt. 25:3 ff.) and Isaiah's continual cry to Israel to pursue the ways of justice for the oppressed.

Consider the incarnation of Yeshua. If there was ever a divine statement about the value of the physical world, the incarnation is it! In some mysterious sense, the God of the universe chose to enwrap something of himself in the atoms of the earth and then, to walk among us. The act says it all. The world is important. The human experience is important. If it were not so, He would not have stepped into it.

The "sweet spot" in our theology and movement building should allow for the joyful knowledge that one day, perhaps soon, Messiah will return to right the wrongs which we are incapable of righting ourselves. At the same time, it demands a life-affirming, culture embracing faith, which says an enthusiastic "yes!" to the world God has prided himself to create—a world which he called "*tov me'od*." The sense of the essential value of the created order seems to have been hard-wired into our very souls.

## Don't Lie Against Your Deeper Humanness!

By over-focusing on the End Times, we can force people into an impossible bind. Our every instinct says that our lives—here and now—are important and worth living. Yet, a piety based on over-confidence in the coming of the end can subtly force people to lie against their deepest selves. If we really believe we are in the end of the End Times, why marry, have children, buy a home, or save money for the future? Human beings have been created to desire such things. A few unique souls like *Rav Sha'ul* and people living in monastic orders may be gifted differently, but most people are not.

Beyond this, too much emphasis on the End can become an excuse for not making life's hard choices. A Messianic Jewish businessman reflecting on his early experience as a believer had this to say:

> It made it easier not to do the hard things in life like plan for the future, get an education, etc. It was easier to assume the world was coming to an end and not to worry about much else. It became a penalty for stability later in life. You had to play catch up . . . when the world kept moving and you've lost years.

Finally, just as overly optimistic utopianism is harmful to young people (we think of Communism or the empty promises of Woodstock), so is the pessimism inherent in the End Times mentality. Young people must dream about their futures here on earth. This is the way God has made them!

## A Better Way—Life Affirming Messianic Judaism, with its Eye on the Sky

One day, perhaps soon, perhaps not, Messiah Yeshua will fulfill his most breathtakingly important promise—he will be back! Our purpose here is not to diminish this great fact. Rather, we seek to locate a "sweet spot" in our approach to life. We look for that place where we can embrace the dynamic tension of living in the good world that the God of Israel has made, while at the same time, looking forward to the eventual and assured fulfillment of that promise. Let us partner with God to make the world a better place, recognizing that a hearty portion of "this worldliness" is part of God's intended legacy for the Jewish people. Our motivation for fighting on flows from our confidence that God's kingdom will surely prevail. Victory will be ours and his!

Finally, let us remember Rabbi Tarfon's famous words of encouragement, "It is not your duty to complete the work, but neither are you free to desist from it" (*Pirke Avot* 2:21). Living in the intangible space of unfulfilled prophecy is easy. Building a civilization is hard work. But, it does not depend on any of us to finish the job. We can't. Only Messiah can and will. Our job is simply to be faithful to the God of Israel in the many realms God has privileged us to "occupy until He comes," all the while keeping one eye on the sky!

## Questions for Discussion

- Is the world a basically good place tainted by evil, or a fundamentally evil place with elements of good remaining? Given the fact that anecdotal evidence (examples of good and evil) can be brought to bear to support either view, why do you hold your position?
- If you knew that a world meltdown would occur in five years, followed immediately by Messiah Yeshua's return, how would you live differently than you do presently?
- What if you knew this meltdown would occur in twenty-five years, or one hundred years, how would it affect your life?
- Specifically, how could your synagogue engage in *Tikkun Olam*—partnering with God to repair the world?

## Bibliography

Carlson, C.C., and Hal Lindsey. *The Late Great Planet Earth.* Grand Rapids: Zondervan, 1970.

Heschel, Abraham Joshua. *God In Search Of Man.* New York: Farrar, Straus, and Giroux, 1955.

Moore, Stephen, and Julian L. Simon. *It's Getting Better All the Time: Greatest Trends of the Last 100 Years,* Washington: Cato Institute.

Wigoder, Geoffrey, ed. *Standard Jewish Encyclopedia.* New York: Facts on File, 1992.

✡ ✡ ✡

Dr. Richard C. Nichol serves as the rabbi of Congregation Ruach Israel in Needham, Massachusetts. The professor of Leadership Development at the Messianic Jewish Training Institute (MJTI) in Pasadena, California, he is also a past President of the Union of Messianic Jewish Congregations and a Vice President of the International Messianic Jewish Alliance. Rabbi Nichol has three earned degrees, including a doctorate from Gordon-Conwell Theological Seminary. He and his wife, Susan, live in Needham, Masschusetts.

# ESCHATOLOGY AND MESSIANIC JEWS: A THEOLOGICAL PERSPECTIVE

—Arnold G. Fruchtenbaum

This chapter will take a theological approach to the subject of eschatology and Messianic Jews. In dealing with this issue, sound hermeneutical principles have been applied. First, there is the principle of literal interpretation of Scripture. The normal plain sense is assumed rather than assuming a figurative, spiritual or allegorical meaning —unless the text itself indicates otherwise. Second, this chapter rejects the presuppositions of replacement theology in any of its forms and expressions. This means that at no point is the Church ever referred to as "Israel," or "Spiritual Israel," or some other term favored by replacement theologians. Of the seventy-three times the term "Israel" is found in the New Testament— not once is it used of the Church. It is either used of Jews in general or Jewish believers in particular, but always of ethnic Jews and never of Gentiles or of the Church.

## The Dual Citizenship of Messianic Jews

An adequate eschatology concerning Messianic Jews must take into account that the Bible depicts Messianic Jews as actually being dual citizens of both Israel and the Church. These will be discussed individually.

### The Remnant of Israel

The doctrine of the Remnant of Israel teaches that within the Jewish nation as a whole there are always some that believe and all those who believe among Israel comprise the Remnant of Israel. This has the following ramifications. First, only believers comprise this Remnant. Second, not all believers are part of the Remnant because the Remnant is a *Jewish* Remnant. Third, the Remnant is always part of the nation of Israel the whole and not detached from it. Fourth, the Remnant at any point in history may be large or small but there is never a time when it is non-existent, except immediately after the Rapture.

The concept of the Remnant of Israel was true from the very beginning of Israel's history as Jewish people began to multiply following the patriarchal period. As a doctrine, the theology of the Remnant began with the Elijah narrative (1 Kings 19:18) and then was developed by the Prophets of Israel and later by the Apostles in the New Testament.

Before the arrival of the Messiah, what divided the Remnant from the non-Remnant is that the Remnant believed that which was revealed to Moses and the Prophets, while the non-Remnant rejected it and pursued idolatry (Isa. 8:9–17). However, the same prophet predicted that when Messiah Immanuel arrives, he would be the new point of division between the Remnant and the non-Remnant. For the Remnant, he will prove to be a Sanctuary, but for the non-Remnant, he will prove to be the Stone of Stumbling and the Rock of Offense.

According to the writings of the Apostles, with the coming of Messiah Yeshua, he indeed has become that point of division between the Remnant and the non-Remnant, often quoting the Isaiah prophecy as evidence (1 Pet. 2:1–10; Rom. 9:6, 30-33; 11:1–10). Both Apostles were making the distinction between Jews who believe and Jews who did not believe or between the Remnant and the non-Remnant. The point being made is that while Israel the whole failed, Israel the Remnant has not failed and the Remnant of Israel is fulfilling the calling of the nation as a whole. There is indeed a Spiritual Israel. However, the Spiritual Israel is not the Church but the Jews who believe. They are *the Israel of God* (Gal. 6:16). The present day Jewish believers in Yeshua, regardless of what title they go under (Messianic Jews, Jewish believers, Hebrew Christians or Jewish Christians), make up the present day Remnant of Israel. There cannot be an adequate eschatology without recognizing the role of the Remnant of Israel.

This also means that the covenantal promises made in the Jewish covenants (the Abrahamic Covenant, the Land Covenant, the Davidic Covenant, the New Covenant) apply to Messianic Jews in the present as well as in the future. While Gentile believers today are recipients of the spiritual promises of the Jewish covenants, they are not recipients of the physical promises (Rom. 15:27). However, Jewish believers are recipients of both the physical and spiritual promises. How this works out eschatologically will be shown below.

## The Church

Since the events of *Shavu'ot* in Acts 2, Jewish believers also are citizens of the Church. Unfortunately, the term "Church" has become a problem within Messianic Jewish circles and for good reason in light of what has happened in the course of Jewish and Church history. The meaning of "church" in the New Testament is not necessarily the same as it has been used in history. Nevertheless, the history of it is a fact and Messianic Jews have to deal with it. Therefore, periodically I will use the Hebrew/Greek terms *k'hillah/ekklesia* to help take the edge off. As this is a theological chapter and not a chapter on Messianic practice, the use of that term will be unavoidable if an adequate biblical, theological perspective is to be presented accurately without confusion.

## Definition and the Beginning of the Church

It is important that the New Testament term be clearly defined and that it be established when the new entity began. It is common in all strands of replacement theology to teach that the Church has always existed, comprises all who have believed since Adam, and that the Church is true Spiritual Israel. Thus, when God made His covenantal promises to Israel, it was not necessarily in reference to ethnic Israel, but to Spiritual Israel. In that way replacement theologians can deny they believe in "replacement" since they proclaim that these promises were not made to ethnic Israel but to Spiritual Israel which is the Church. However, Scripture does not validate this and it is clear from every context that these promises were made to ethnic Israel. God refers to Israel as "my people" even when they are in rebellion, unbelief, and practicing idolatry (Isa. 1:3ff.). In fact, the Church did not exist anywhere in the Old Testament nor did it exist in Gospel history. When Yeshua first mentioned the *k'hillah/ekklesia* in Matt. 16:18, He used the future tense which clearly shows that it was still future as of Matthew 16 and did not yet exist.

The following line of evidence clearly shows that the Church was born on the Feast of *Shavu'ot* in Acts 2. First, Colossians 1:18 teaches that the Church is the *Body* of the Messiah. Second, 1 Corinthians 12:13 teaches that the means of entering this *Body* is by means of Spirit-baptism, "For by one Spirit were we all baptized into one body whether Jews or Greeks. . . ." What this passage shows is that there is an inseparable connection between Spirit-baptism and the existence of the Body; one cannot exist apart from the other. The *k'hillah/ekklesia* is the Body of the Messiah and one enters the Body only by means of Spirit-baptism. Therefore, if it could be determined clearly when Spirit-baptism began, that would also help to determine when the *k'hillah/ekklesia* began.

In Acts 1:5, Yeshua declared that the Apostles "will be baptized by the Holy Spirit not many days hence." Here Yeshua again used the future tense showing that Spirit-baptism was still in the future as of Acts 1:5. Now the question is: When was the prophecy of Acts 1:5 fulfilled? The obvious answer would be Acts 2:1–4, and while this is the correct answer, nevertheless, there is a slight problem—the passage nowhere actually mentions Spirit-baptism. However, it is possible to prove it by Acts 11:15–16. Peter, while defending his actions of going to the house of a Gentile in Acts 10 to preach the Gospel, points out that the Gentiles received the same experience of Spirit-baptism as did the Jews (v. 15). Peter states that *the Holy Spirit fell on them*, meaning the Gentiles (Acts 10:44–46), as the Spirit once fell *on us*, meaning the Jewish believers, *at the beginning*. The *beginning* for Jewish believers was Acts 2:1–4. Peter goes on to quote Acts 1:5 (v. 16) showing that the prophecy of Yeshua in Acts 1:5 was fulfilled in Acts 2:1–4. Since Spirit-baptism is necessary for the existence of the *k'hillah/ekklesia*, and since Spirit-baptism only began as of Acts 2 then the *k'hillah/ekklesia* did not exist before then and only began in Acts 2.

### The Composition of the Body

One more question needs to be answered for an adequate eschatology for Messianic Jews: What does the *k'hillah/ekklesia* consist of? The key passage is Ephesians 2:11–3:6. The author points out that initially there were two groups: the Gentiles and the Commonwealth of Israel. The advantage the Jews had was that God made the covenants (the word is plural since it is a reference to the four unconditional eternal covenants God made with Israel) with them. There are two points to remember concerning Gentiles and their connection with the covenants. They were *strangers* to the covenants and they were *far off* from the covenants—too far away to enjoy their privileges. That changed with the death of the Messiah, which broke down *the middle wall of partition contained in the law of commandments and ordinances, that He might create in himself one new man*. One should be careful to note what the text does say and what it does not say. The text does *not* say that the Gentile believers have been incorporated into the Commonwealth of Israel. Rather, what the text clearly says is that God made of the two (Commonwealth of Israel and the Gentiles) a third new entity which is the Body, and the Body has already been defined as being the *k'hillah/ekklesia*. Two plus one equals three, and it is obvious that there is a third new entity comprised of Jewish believers and Gentile believers. Hence, the Church is called the *one New Man*, created of the two. So altogether, in the Ephesians passage Paul mentioned three groups: Israel, the Gentiles, and the one New Man, which is identified with the Body (2:16,

3:6). Hence, three groups are also distinguished in 1 Corinthians 10:32: Jews, Greeks, and the Church of God. As a result of this third new entity, both Jewish and Gentile believers are *partakers* (the Apostle's actual word) of the spiritual blessings of the Jewish Covenants (Eph. 3:6; Rom. 11:17; 15:25–27).

### The Application of Dual Citizenship

What this means then is that the Jewish believers are dual citizens of both Israel and the *k'hillah/ekklesia*. Therefore in this age, certain obligations that would not be mandatory among Gentiles are mandatory for the Jews— such as the obligation of circumcision as required by the Abrahamic Covenant. This dual citizenship has ramifications for the present as well as the future.

## The Rapture

Since God has created the third new entity, he therefore has special future and specific prophecies for this new entity of Jewish and Gentile believers just as he has for Israel and the Gentiles. Eschatologically, the key event for the *k'hillah/ekklesia* is the Rapture. The key passage on this event is found in 1 Thessalonians 4:13–18. As to who is part of the Rapture, he specifies that it is those *in Yeshua* (v. 14) and those *in Messiah* (v. 16). Throughout his writings, the Apostle Paul uses certain terms in a very technical manner: *in Yeshua, in Messiah, in Messiah Yeshua, in Yeshua Messiah, in him, in whom*, and *in the Lord*. These are all technical terms for those who have been baptized into the Body of the Messiah. Hence, the Rapture applies only to those believers of the Body. The believers of the Body are only those who have become believers from Acts 2 to whenever the Rapture event occurs. At the time of the Rapture, the whole Body of the Messiah is either resurrected (the dead) or translated (the living) and caught up to meet the Messiah in the air. Not only Gentile believers are raptured since the Body is neither Jew nor Gentile, but both Jew and Gentile. Since all believers comprise the Body, all believers, both Jew and Gentile—will partake of the Rapture.

The author's view is that the Rapture event will occur sometime before the seven years of Tribulation will begin, although how many years before cannot be determined. Sometime before the signing of the seven year covenant that initiates the last seven years (Dan. 9:27) of the "birthpangs of the Messiah," is when this event will occur. When the author did research for the doctoral dissertation which became the book *Israelology: The Missing Link in Systematic Theology*, it was necessary to read the theological defense of all other positions. At that time, two basic facts became evident. First, of the many Tribulation contexts, the *k'hillah/ekklesia* is not mentioned a single time and therefore none of the scholars of the opposing views were able to actually produce a verse that puts the Body of the Messiah within any part of the seven-year period. Furthermore, particularly in the post-tribulational position, all the scholarly defenses of this view were based upon assumptions of replacement theology being true and therefore their view was defended by two presuppositions. The first premise is that the Church is the True Israel and the argument, put as a syllogism, went as follows:

Major premise: The Church is Israel;
Minor premise: Israel is in the Tribulation;
Conclusion: The Church is in the Tribulation.

The second presupposition, also based upon replacement theology being true, was that all saints are Church saints. As a syllogism the argument went as follows:

Major premise: All saints are Church saints;
Minor premise: There are saints in the Tribulation;
Conclusion: The Church is in the Tribulation.

However, if one does not presuppose replacement theology and rejects their two presuppositions, the key arguments for post-tribulationism loose their force.

## Subsequent Events in Heaven

The above being true, Jewish believers, along with the rest of the Body, will be caught up and taken to heaven at the Rapture. While in heaven, the Jewish believers, along with the Gentile believers of the Body, undergo two key events. The first will be the Judgment Seat of the Messiah (Rom. 14:10–12; 2 Cor. 5:10; 1 Cor. 3:10–15), where all will be evaluated on how they served the Lord since they believed and either be rewarded or not be rewarded. These rewards will determine the role of the believers in the Messianic Kingdom.

Another event is the wedding ceremony of the Lamb which will take place in heaven (Rev. 19:6–8) prior to the Second Coming (Rev. 19:11–21).

At the actual Second Coming, Jude 14–15 clearly states that He returns *with his saints* and hence the Jewish and Gentile believers of the Body together return with Him at the Second Coming in order to share in the rulership in the Messianic Kingdom.

# The Great Tribulation

While the Remnant of Israel, which in the present age is also part of the Body, will be removed from the earth at the Rapture, that is not the end of the future of the Remnant of Israel. The Remnant existed before the Body was born and will continue to exist after the Body is gone. Just as there will be Gentiles who will come to faith during the seven years of the Tribulation (Rev. 7:9–17), Jewish people will also come to believe throughout this period. While these believers are not part of the *k'hillah/ekklesia*, they still continue to make up the Remnant of Israel. This includes the 144,000 Jews (Rev. 7:1–8; 14:1–5) as well as the Jews of Jerusalem that become believers at about the middle of the Tribulation (Rev. 11:13). It will also include the "all Israel [that] will be saved" (Rom. 11:26) that will become believers at the very end of the Tribulation before the Second Coming. At that point all Israel and Remnant Israel will finally become one and the same (Mic. 2:12–13).

# The Messianic Kingdom

## *The Outworking of Dual Citizenship*

When the Bible discusses the Messianic Kingdom, it clearly mentions that there will be a governmental structure with the Messiah being the King of the whole world ruling over both Israel and the Gentile nations from the Throne of David and from Jerusalem. However, it also points out that there will be two separate branches of government: a Gentile branch and a Jewish branch. Co-ruling with the Messiah over the Jewish branch of government will be the resurrected King David (Jer. 30:9; Ezek. 34:23–24; 37:24–25; Hos. 3:5). Co-ruling over the Gentile branch of government will be the Church and Tribulation saints (Rev. 20:4–6).

Prophecy scholars who take the Bible literally have been very clear on two basic points. First, they have been very clear in pointing out that the Church saints will co-rule with the Messiah over the Gentiles. Hence, the Church saints will be scattered throughout the world doing the Messiah's bidding. Second, they have also been clear that the Millennial Israel is made up of two groups. The first group is Resurrected Israel (Old Testament Saints such as Abraham, Isaac and Jacob) who will be resurrected to enjoy the Promised Land (Matt. 8:11) and the second group is Living Israel (those who survive the Tribulation and are part of Israel's national salvation).

What has not been made clear is the role of the Jewish believers in the Body and how the covenantal promises will work out for them in the Messianic Kingdom. It should be remembered that a major element of the Abrahamic Covenant was the Land promise that was given to the Patriarchs and to their seed (Gen. 12:1, 7; 13:14–15, 17; 15:17–21; 17:8). In fact, literalists have correctly insisted that since these Land promises were never fulfilled, they will be fulfilled to Jewish people in the Messianic Kingdom and only then will they enjoy all of their Promised Land.

It should be noted that the Land promise was made to both the Patriarchs and to their seed. The seed includes Jewish believers—even of the Body. In this present age, this means that Jewish believers should look upon the Land of Israel as being their homeland. By the same token, it will have ramifications in the Messianic Kingdom. Hence, a simple solution to deal with the fact that the Jewish believers are dual citizens in both Israel and the *k'hillah/ekklesia*, will be as follows. While the Gentile believers of the Body will serve as co-rulers over the living Gentiles, the Jewish believers will be assigned to live in the Land of Israel and have a co-ruling position within the borders of the Millennial Israel. That would help to explain why the twelve Apostles have a special role concerning Israel in the Kingdom and why their dual citizenship works out as follows. On one hand, the twelve Apostles are clearly said to be the foundation of the Church (Eph. 2:20). That is their unique role as citizens of the *k'hillah/ekklesia*. However, in the Messianic Kingdom, the Apostles will sit on twelve thrones judging the twelve tribes of Israel (Matt. 19:28; Luke 22:28–30). That will be their role as citizens of Israel. Jewish believers have the same dual citizenship and their millennial future should be viewed in the same way.

### The Remnant in the Kingdom

Since all Israel throughout the Messianic Kingdom will remain a saved nation (Jer. 31:31–34), it also means that all Israel will remain the Remnant of Israel throughout that period.

## Questions for Discussion

- What is the definition of the Remnant of Israel and what distinguishes this Remnant from the non-Remnant in the Old and New Testaments?
- What is the composition of the Church and how is it possible to know exactly when the Church began?
- How does the dual nationality of Messianic Jews apply to the Rapture and how will this dual nationality work out in the Kingdom?
- What are the two ways in which the term "Israel" is used?

# Bibliography

Fruchtenbaum, Dr. Arnold G. *Israelology: The Missing Link in Systematic Theology.* Tustin: Ariel Ministries, 1992.

———. *The Footsteps of the Messiah: A Study of the Sequence of Prophetic Events.* Tustin: Ariel, 1982.

✡ ✡ ✡

Dr. Arnold G. Fruchtenbaum is founder and director of Ariel Ministries, an organization dedicated to evangelism and discipleship of Jewish people. He received his B.A. degree from Cedarville College and his Th.M. from Dallas Theological Seminary, before earning his Ph.D. from New York University. His graduate work also includes studies at the Jewish Theological Seminary in New York and the Hebrew University of Jerusalem.

# CHALLENGES TO MESSIANIC JUDAISM

—Shoshanah Feher

*Time present and time past*
*Are both perhaps present in time future,*
*And time future contained in time past.*
——T.S. Eliot, *Four Quartets*

It is said that the future can only make sense if we understand our past and where we come from. Said differently, continuity is important and one must analyze what has occurred in the past in order to be stronger in the future. Issues of continuity first attracted me to the way Messianic Judaism makes sense of its Jewish roots. As a sociologist, a Jew, and a non-Believer, I could not understand how someone could be Jewish and Christian——simultaneously. How could Messianic Believers make sense of their relationship with their Jewish past, with their Jewish ancestors, and with Holocaust victims? Where was the continuity? These are the questions that lead me to conduct an in-depth study of a large Messianic congregation in Southern California in the early 1990s (see Feher, 1998).

Today, almost ten years later, I reflect on my experiences at Adat haRuach both in the days of my research and in recent visits and conversations. (In order to assure anonymity I have changed the name of the congregation to Adat haRuach.) The names and identifying features of the congregants have also been changed. In this reflection, I examine whether the issues that existed congregationally and nationally ten years ago persist, what changes have occurred, and what has worked or not worked in the intervening years. Looking at Messianic Judaism's past will put the present into perspective. This will help to identify and understand the issues to be addressed and resolved in order to pave the way to a stronger future.

## Three Challenges to the Future of Messianic Judaism

From a sociological perspective, there are clear challenges to Messianic Judaism's survival as a cohesive movement. These are challenges that the movement faces nationally, although I will address them locally, based on the findings in my work at Adat haRuach. I use Adat haRuach as a case study to shed light on other congregations and the movement that sustains them, although I am aware that it is not representative of all congregations.

The over-reaching social challenge that Messianic Judaism faces is assessing how much to Judaize. That is, how much to identify with each of its parent (Jewish and Christian) communities and how much to distance itself from them. This basic dilemma underlies the three challenges that I will address here.

### *Messianic Jew vs. Messianic Gentile: The Hierarchy Within*

One of the interesting shifts that has occurred in the Jewish Christian movement in the last few decades is the move from a primarily Christian-centered system of belief to one that increasingly celebrates its Jewish roots. Present-day imagery (based on Rom. 11:17–22) likens Messianic Judaism to an olive tree that has been grafted to ensure its strength. Both Jews and Gentiles are needed to maintain Messianic Judaism's strength and fecundity. As such, Gentiles are to be proud of being Gentiles and Jews proud of being Jews. Yet, in actuality, this purist ideology is lost.

There are strong overtones of an internal hierarchy at Adat haRuach in which Messianic Jews were "higher" than Messianic Gentiles. This hierarchy has resulted in Gentiles looking for Jewish roots in hopes of finding a Jewish lineage, making themselves Jewish after all. It has also resulted in Gentiles being increasingly Jewish in their way of being and choice of marriage partner. For many, this has meant that even if they are unable to find Jewish roots in their heritage, they would like to ensure, through marriage, that their children, at least, are Jewish—thus securing a place in the "Jewish bloodline." In some cases, it has meant adult circumcision, something that is not supported by the leadership. For Matt, the last decade has meant an evolution in his identity as a Messianic Gentile. He briefly looked into his past when he became a Believer thirteen years ago, did not find Jewish roots, and struggled with that. He explained that it would have been easier to find Jewish roots so that he could put his identity crisis at rest. Having matured in his faith, he has come to terms with his role as a Messianic Gentile.

Tammy (a Messianic Jew) and Wiley (a Messianic Gentile) are at odds about the role of Gentiles and Jews within Adat haRuach. For Tammy, if Gentile Believers want to be "grafted in" they need to be aware of Jewish sensitivities. She says:

Especially in services [when] somebody wears a Star of David *and* a cross, I just get so [mad]. If you are a Gentile and you are a part of the congregation, then please wear a Star of David or don't wear anything at all—not the cross. It's offensive to me, it's offensive to any Jewish people. If you're going to be in a Messianic synagogue, out of respect, tuck it away. If you're a guest in someone's home you respect that.

According to Tammy, part of being grafted in means having a Jewish heart, which in turn, means not offending other (Messianic and non-Messianic) Jews. Wiley, on the other hand, resents congregants who feel this way. He finds that it is precisely because he is at peace with being a Messianic Gentile and is *not* trying to become Jewish that he is no longer asked to publicly participate in services:

When I was first going there (Adat haRuach), they'd call me up to do the *Haftarah* blessing. They don't call me up to do that anymore. And when I've volunteered, I've been studiously ignored. I don't wear a *kippah* and because I go as [myself], for some people that's really hard to accept. I come in blue jeans, I wear T-shirts, I don't come in a suit. I don't talk the Messianic talk. You know, I don't talk about how good it is to be a Messianic, or how I've discovered the Jewish truths of Christianity. I just haven't bought into the system. You know, I'm not trying to become Jewish, which is what a lot of Gentiles are doing. That's not my agenda.

I am not arguing that hierarchies are inherently bad. Rather, I invite attention to the divide between what congregations espouse and what individuals do. If it were universally acknowledged that all Messianic Believers should strive toward increased Jewishness, then individuals at congregations like Adat haRuach are acting in accordance. However, to emphasize the beauty and necessity of the difference between Believers and then valorize the Jewish ones— sends mixed messages to congregants. This results in issues of confused identity among adherents and sometimes within families. It also implies a deficiency among the Gentiles that can never quite be righted. Most importantly, it creates a culture of inequality among adherents. Congregations that do not encourage Gentile adherents to the same degree—or conversely—who have very few Messianic Jews in their midst, also face this issue. They also, need to address how to best deal with the Gentile/Jewish mix and the identity politics it engenders.

Rabbi Jason, the Messianic rabbi at Adat haRuach, notes that there are currently factions in the movement that relegate Messianic Gentiles to second class citizenry, something he personally does not understand and actively works against. Over the years, he has pulled a few Gentile Believers aside to remind them that "we don't have to be the same and we shouldn't be the same, but we're united." He reminds congregants that unity despite distinctiveness is a testimony of Yeshua being the Messiah, "How else are you going to get Jews and Gentiles, especially a fifty-fifty group, worshipping the same God together in the same way? That has to be the Messiah pulling it off." He goes on to say, "There's the distinctiveness that we need to uphold and it only becomes problematic when it becomes divisive or [creates] second class citizen mentality."

## Messianic Believers Who Leave: Where Do They Go?

In the nearly ten years since I started my research, many changes have taken place at Adat haRuach. Of the ten individuals and ten couples that I interviewed in great depth, more than half have left the congregation. For some, the congregation did not have a strong enough "Messianic vision." Others felt that the congregation catered to the Gentiles so they left in search of a more Jewish service or because they wanted more of a Jewish involvement in their lives. Other attendees left because they found the degree of Jewish expression at Adat haRuach exaggerated and stifling; that Judaism—to the exclusion of the Gentile culture they had grown up in—was not what they were after. The unfolding of these individual lives sheds light on the issues facing Messianic Judaism. In its attempts at Judaizing, it has left behind both those for whom Adat haRauch is not Jewish enough and those for whom it is too Jewish. I should point out that these are also all the same reasons why the other half of the congregants interviewed have stayed; because they love that "family feeling" and are happy and comfortable with the balance between Evangelical Gentile culture and Jewishness that Adat haRuach has provided.

Of the ten Messianic singles I interviewed in 1992–1993, four have stayed at Adat haRuach; two have left to join other Messianic Jewish congregations in other cities; and four have stayed in the same city but have joined Christian churches. Of the ten couples I interviewed, four stayed at Adat haRuach; two continue at other Messianic Jewish synagogues; three are non-Believers; and one left for a local church. Those wanting less emphasis on the "Jewish hierarchy" could attend a different synagogue and those wishing a "stronger Messianic vision" could attend a more Jewish-centered synagogue. However, at this time, few cities, if any, can support enough congregations to meet everybody's needs. Those Gentiles who are stifled by the degree of Jewish culture they encounter, leave for Evangelical churches—although they often feel out of place there as well. Those wishing for a more Jewish expression left for cities on the east coast (a rather dramatic change to family and professional lives) where more Jewish forms of Messianic Judaism can be found and where they interact with higher numbers of Jews. A few Messianic Jews have discarded Messianic Judaism altogether and become members of non-Messianic Jewish synagogues.

Individual congregations would be wise to reflect on their past history: How many congregants are thrilled with the current status of the congregation and have stayed through thick and thin? Or, at least, through the years? And how many have left? What have they moved on to? What are the possible explanations for their leaving? A hard and critical self-evaluation can be painful and difficult. Yet, it is important in order to make decisions about how to ensure the continuity of Messianic Judaism into the future—even if that decision is to leave everything as it is now.

With twenty years of hindsight, Rabbi Jason notes that it is easier for Gentiles to move in and out of Messianic Judaism; because they do not have a *Yiddishe n'shamah* (Jewish soul) they often feel less tied to Messianic Judaism than the Messianic Jews do. Thus, Gentile Believers often pass through, stay a few years, and then feel it is time to move on or try a different experience. Perhaps, Rabbi Jason says, they take their new understanding of the Bible with them and share it in their new church. Many come back for the high holidays or for the Adat haRuach Passover *seder*. "Hopefully," Rabbi Jason says, "they at least continue to be Believers."

### Passing the Faith on to the Next Generation

Messianic Judaism is very new as an organized movement. Second generation Messianic Believers are still few, or at least they are quite young, so the challenge of practicing Messianic Judaism as adults remains before them. One of the strengths of Messianic Judaism is that it is made up of people who were raised as Jews or as Evangelicals. As I argued in *Passing Over Easter: Constructing the Boundaries of Messianic Judaism*, by identifying with their parent communities, Messianic Believers identify with and reject their parent communities, thus forming new boundaries and a new identity all their own. The second generation Believers will not have these tensions with their parent communities and will not be able to draw on their exclusively Jewish or Christian backgrounds. Instead, they will have grown up taking for granted the melding of the two traditions. As if to explicate this exact point, the Colemans (a Messianic Jewish couple) explained that they chose to attend Adat haRuach so their children would have "the best chance of understanding [and] knowing the Lord" and an understanding that they are Jewish.

Education is one of the struggles of the congregants at the Messianic synagogue I studied. Should Adat haRuach parents send their children to public schools where there are no or few other Messianic Believing kids—but where they can be a witness to others? Should they send the children to Christian Believing schools where there is no or little understanding of the

Jewishness of Yeshua and of Jewish culture—or should the children attend Jewish schools where Messianic Believers are rarely welcome? A larger religious movement often has the luxury of being able to set up their own religious schools—which is a way of ensuring continuity—something that only a handful of Messianic communities are in a position to do.

In the early 1990s, setting up a day school for the young children was a priority for Adat haRuach. A lot of time and energy was spent investigating the idea. Today, that idea still lingers but it has become a longer-term goal. It has lost the sense of immediacy it once had. For the congregation's leadership, finding a permanent structure for the congregation has become higher on the list of priorities. Perhaps, this is because in the past years, the Messianic children of Adat haRuach have grown up without a Messianic day school and have successfully navigated the waters of the various local educational systems (parochial, public, and home schools).

The current and more immediate concern regarding the congregation's youth is how to ensure that teens stay connected to the movement, internalize it, and make it their own. Efforts aimed at teens, including establishing a youth group (with the recent addition of a paid leader), conducting a confirmation class, and sending teens to the UMJC (Union of Messianic Jewish Congregations) summer youth camp. All of this is an attempt, according to Rabbi Jason, for the youth to begin to "own" the Messianic experience and make sure Messianic Judaism does not get thought of as "just the parents' thing." Indeed, this summer, the first children of Adat haRuach members will be getting married at the synagogue. Rabbi Jason will be marrying two young adults who both grew up at Adat haRuach. This is an exciting—and intensely symbolic—step for Adat haRuach.

## Conclusion

In the nearly ten years since I began my research at Adat haRuach, many changes have taken place. People have come and gone, issues have crystallized, priorities have changed, and theological views have matured and shifted. The congregation has grown from the fifteen members that it had in 1981 when it began, to seventy-seven members in 1992, when I originally visited it, to almost one hundred members today. (Membership is reported in "family units.") In fact, the congregation had to move to a new building to accommodate the growth. The congregation is noticeably more diverse, in terms of ethnicity, and the number of young families and small children has grown.

An engaging aspect of the Messianic movement remains its vitality, liveliness, and energy. It is important to think about how these characteristics will be passed onto the next millennium. It is also important to take stock of one's individual congregation on an ongoing basis. First, what are the identity politics at play in the congregation? Is there a match between what people say and do? Within the movement, is there parity in the standing between Jew and Gentile? Second, who joins? Who leaves? And why? Third, how does the congregation believe children should be educated—through day schools, camps, and/or youth ministries? Is the congregation involving the children in a way that will cause them to want to maintain Messianic Judaism? These questions are not only for the congregations to ask of themselves—they are also applicable to the movement as a whole. It is in doing these kinds of exercises that Messianic Judaism will gain a better understanding of where it stands presently—and how to best orient itself in the future in order to maintain itself as the successful and vibrant movement it is today. Messianic Judaism has grown significantly in the last thirty years and it is only by critically looking at the past and remembering its successes and mis-steps that the movement will continue to bloom—and maintain its blossoms and fruits—into the 21ˢᵗ century.

## Bibliography

Feher, Shoshanah. *Passing Over Easter: Constructing the Boundaries of Messianic Judaism.* Walnut Creek: AltaMira, 1998.

✡ ✡ ✡

Shoshanah Feher received her Ph.D. from the University of California, Santa Barbara in 1995. Dr. Feher's published work spans the areas of ethnicity, gender, new religious movements, immigration, and Judaism in North America. In addition to her interest in Messianic Judaism, she has also conducted research in the Iranian Jewish community. Dr. Feher is a research consultant at the Veterans Affairs San Diego Healthcare System.

# THOUGHTS FROM A LONGTIME FRIEND

—Arthur Glasser

When asked to contribute to this study it was known that I was not directly involved in sharing the gospel with the Jewish people. All that friends knew was that I had been involved in missionary education at Fuller Theological Seminary for about thirty years and that I had been the faculty coordinator of its Judaic studies program. Actually, my interest in the Jewish people began long before. The one who led me to faith in Yeshua gave me a burden for their evangelization as we studied the Bible together during my university years. He often reminded me that the Jewish people were crucial to God's great plan to bless the nations.

Years later, while working for an engineering firm in Pittsburgh, I felt constrained to resign and prepare for missionary service. During years of study at Bible school and theological seminary, this friend saw to it that brief vacations were spent assisting a struggling Jewish mission in Manhattan. However, this service posed an unexpected problem. It encouraged new Jewish believers in the Messiah to join sympathetic Gentile churches where they might be "built up" in their faith. My problem was that this "mission through extraction" would diminish the possibility of their new life in Yeshua influencing their larger Jewish community. Expressing this concern met with the pointed response that it was premature to encourage them to become witnesses to their own people. They would be scorned as traitors and the Jewish community would not receive them.

My interest in Jewish evangelism began to diminish when I learned that some new Jewish believers in the Messiah, upon being related to such churches, found Gentile culture so uncomfortable they ceased attending. They seemed lost to both church and synagogue. This tragedy was covered up by the strange biblical notion that only a few Jewish people would actually come to faith before Messiah returned. Only then would the nation "be born in a day" (Isa. 66:8). Would this be apart from individual response to the gospel of redemption (Rom. 10:14–17)? True, at Messiah's second coming, all Israel shall look upon him "whom they pierced, and shall mourn for him" (Zech. 9:10), but their sorrow will arise from the painful awareness that when he came the first time, they rejected him, and, through Roman connivance, crucified him (Acts 3:36). Perhaps "evangelism by extraction" was not for me. I turned to Gentile mission service instead.

Years later I began to wake up through being confronted by the moral and spiritual obligation "under God" to reflect on two matters of solemn Jewish significance that had grasped the world's attention. First, there was the satanically energized Holocaust that marked the deliberate destruction of almost onethird of all Jewish people. I found it staggering to realize that this was shamefully supported by large segments of the historic churches in all countries under Nazi control, and reflected their long centuries of officially sponsored antiSemitism.

The second concern focused on the establishment of the State of Israel in Palestine and its amazing victory in the 1967 Six-Day War that followed. This brought to an end almost two thousand years of Jewish dispersion among the Gentile nations. Was this not also significant, following so shortly after Jewry's greatest suffering and loss?

It goes without saying that the theological ferment that these two events generated within Jewry and the Gentile world is still with us. First, there was the "Death of God" movement. One recalls Richard Rubenstein's, *After Auschwitz*, which mocked the idea of Jewish people believing in a just God or in themselves as a chosen people. Emil Fackenheim and Elie Wiesel buttressed this secularism with their inability to give meaning to Jewish existence in terms of divine faithfulness and eschatological significance. The mood of the survivors of Hitler's death camps followed. When they drafted the basic documents defining the State of Israel, they deliberately omitted all reference to God's name in their determination to create a completely secular state. The tragic years that followed have been filled with internal and external conflict. This appears incapable of lasting resolution. Never have Jewish leaders and their pundits been so secular in their understanding of Jewish suffering and so uncertain of Israel's ultimate survival, despite God's pledge of their continued existence (Jer. 31:35–37).

Then something wonderful happened in the mid 1970s that appeared as a growing brightness in the midst of this darkness. At the time, I was associated with the School of World Mission at Fuller Theological Seminary. At first, all that we heard were rumors of something new happening in San Francisco among Jewish hippies. It had something to do with their unexpected identification with the then noisy Gentile student counterculture movement, something their parents had doubtless warned them against. Apparently, they could not forget that as Jews, they should be on the lookout for values and an agenda separate from the humiliating

assimilationist tendencies of their parents. It was not only that they reso-
nated with Gentile opposition to the Vietnam War. A new openness had
overtaken many, and some were searching. Was there no issue that could
reverse the steady deterioration of the unity and vitality of their people?
They were ripe for a Cause.

Soon it was widely known that Jewish youth of quality were increasingly responding to a Jewish witness to the Messiah. This was the result of
individual witness and various mission evangelistic efforts. Some of us even
dared to believe that a new Jewish openness to the gospel was beginning to
take place, especially when proclaimed by the Jewish people themselves.
The question was even raised: "Could this possibly be evidence that God
was beginning to do a 'new thing' directly related to the sequence of the
Holocaust, the new State of Israel, and the drawing near of Messiah's return to establish the Kingdom Age?" For some time afterward, this forward
surge could not but mystify and irritate those Gentile-dominated missions
still engaged in traditional efforts to evangelize the Jewish people.

This soon posed a new problem. What should be done with the growing numbers of new Jewish believers in Messiah that the Jewish missions
were beginning to enjoy? Whereas a few might be called of God to join
their ranks and increase the Jewish members in these missions, what of the
others? In those days, we could not forget the widely publicized observation of Dr. Max I. Reich, the professor of Jewish missions at Moody Bible
Institute. He made his observation in his exposure of the popular error—
that when a Jew becomes a Christian he ceases to be a part of Israel. He referred to the Apostle Paul's use of the olive tree to represent spiritual
Israel—rooted in the soil of natural Israel (Rom. 11:17–24). There is only
one "cultivated" olive tree to which both Jewish and Gentile believers belong. Only the unbelieving branches will be broken off; but the believing
branches must remain. Then Dr. Reich concluded: "Hebrew Christians
cannot fulfill their mission to their people unless they remain a part of Israel. The salt cannot do its work unless it mixes with that which is to be
salted" (Ariel 97).

It follows then, that to evangelize all Jewish people, all key issues related to the planting of authentically Jewish Messianic congregations in
their midst had to be faced and resolved. This meant nothing less than
communities of renewed Jews sharing the gospel "Jewishly" with their
own people in every community throughout the world. This manner of
expressing their spiritual and cultural life must be geared to Israel's long
centuries of chosen relationship with God as well as with the events of the
20th century.

Fortunately, we at Fuller had the privilege of some of these Messianic
Jews as students in our School of World Mission. Some were particularly
concerned to explore the implications of promoting such a congregational
movement, not unlike the one that had flourished widely throughout the

Middle East during the first five centuries of the Christian era. Since Judaism, rightly understood, was a religion of *Torah* observance that had been enriched and illuminated by the wisdom of their leaders and embodied in the written Talmud, this vast literature had to be reviewed to remove from Messianic congregational use all concepts and traditional practices in conflict with Scripture.

Law obedience had to be understood as the expression of Jewish gratitude for God's covenant with Israel, and not to secure one's personal salvation. Furthermore, all liturgical forms had to be infused with Messianic content. Hymns of praise and gratitude—for the centrality of Yeshua's redemptive grace to his people—had to be integrated with the celebrations of Israel's Holy Days in the annual calendar. These congregations must reflect the traditional synagogue role of serving as the faithful custodians of Jewish communal and religious tradition. The goal was always to make sure the presence of these congregations would be seen as evidence of spiritual renewal taking place among the Jewish people. Unfortunately, they often are initially regarded as heretical and divisive in their impact on an already greatly divided Jewry that has become less religiously observant in recent years. As this congregational movement began to grow, we began to hear of problems largely arising from their diversity—not that there is no agreement within the diversity.

All Messianic congregations make Yeshua the center of their loyalty and worship. All accept his confidence in Scripture as the Word of God. All endorse the attributes reflected in his life and ministry: his holiness and hatred of sin, his love and grace to the repentant, and his faith and hope. When asked as to their certainty about all this, they merely affirm his bodily resurrection which he frequently predicted would take place three days after his crucifixion, followed by forty days in which his disciples and many others had multiple encounters with him, and which culminated in his visible ascension.

The diversity of these Messianic congregations arises out of their separate beginnings, the different personalities and backgrounds in Jewish tradition of their local leaders, and their different efforts to follow Yeshua's example in ministering to human need. They can not forget that almost every word he spoke arose out of some mighty work he performed: works of healing, deliverance, cleansing, destruction, and raising the dead. These reflected his constant concern for people in their varied needs. Following his example in the diverse situations in which their congregations were located naturally contributed to this diversity.

Right from the start, these congregations experienced much uncertainty as to how to incorporate all biblically valid elements of tradition into Messianic services. One could almost say that initially no two congregations were alike in liturgical worship, communal singing, the celebration of the major festivals of Israel's religious life, and the exposition of Scripture that brought services to a climax.

Those early days witnessed the beginning of intercongregational contact, which involved much sharing of problems and tentative solutions. Increasing attention was given to developing informal associations for mutual enrichment. By 1990, at least four separate types had emerged reflecting different but valid styles of fellowship and worship. Some drew congregations that were more formal, more uncritically loyal to Israel's conduct in the Middle East, more reluctant to lose contact with borderline talmudic perspectives, more guarded in welcoming Gentile believers and less open to Gentile evangelical innovations. At the other end of the spectrum, one encountered the association that drew congregations that were less formal in liturgy and more spontaneous in corporate prayer and song. They were also more open to Gentile participation. All this may mark the beginnings of Messianic denominationalism, but such a judgment is premature at this time.

It goes without saying that not only are these Messianic congregations under continuous criticism and direct opposition from the leaders of Jewry's traditional Judaisms. Liberal churches do not share evangelical delight with this growing, multifaceted movement. In recent visits to Messianic congregations, I have been pleased by the ways in which Gentile Christians are increasingly welcomed. The great chasm between synagogue and church is being bridged at last through Yeshua's grace. Warm-hearted Gentiles must avoid making their presence too dominant in a context deliberately and rightly designed to maintain an essential Jewish appeal. Occasionally, one encounters the opposite criticism—that some Messianic congregations are in danger of becoming overly Jewish and are increasingly rebuilding "the wall of separation" that had earlier kept Jews and Gentiles apart.

But how have these committed people been able to persist in their efforts to enlarge and strengthen their congregational movement throughout the 1990s, when their main energies had to be devoted to responding to waves of openness to the gospel among their own people at the same time? Fortunately, considerable diversity of spiritual gifts exists among Messianic Jews today. Those with evangelistic gifts devote their strength and time to making the gospel known in conjunction with missions. Their ministries have never been so important as in these days. Those with teaching and administrative gifts are busily involved in planting and nurturing congregations.

Recently, I attended a *Shabbat* service at a congregation that was in a measure of disarray when I first visited it several years ago. This time, the service overflowed with beautifully led songs of praise, much spontaneous prayer, and several brief biblical and personal testimonies. The rabbi delivered an excellent biblical message that brought everything to a fitting conclusion. I was challenged to believe that God is doing a "new thing" in Jewry in our day!

## Bibliography

Ariel, Yaakov. *Evangelizing the Chosen People.* Chapel Hill: Univ. of North Carolina, 2000.

✡ ✡ ✡

Dr. Arthur F. Glasser has been a longtime friend of the Messianic Jewish movement. A retired seminary professor and former Faculty Coordinator of Judaic Studies, he is a Dean Emeritus of Fuller Theological Seminary School of World Mission and a Professor Emeritus of Theology and East Asia Studies. He and his wife, Alice, live in Seattle. They will be celebrating their 60th wedding anniversary in 2002.

# GLOSSARY

| | |
|---|---|
| *B'rit Hadashah* | New Covenant |
| *b'rit milah* | covenant of circumcision |
| *Gemara* | commentary on the *Mishnah* |
| *Goyim* | Gentiles |
| *Haftarah* | after *Torah* reading, a reading from Prophets, usually related in content |
| *halakhah* | Jewish religious law |
| IAMCS | International Alliance of Messianic Congregations and Synagogues |
| IMJA | International Messianic Jewish Alliance |
| *k'hillah* | congregation |
| *kippah, (pl. kippot)* | skullcap(s) |
| *menorah* | seven-branched candelabra |
| *mezuzah* | biblical passages (Deut. 6:4–9 and Deut. 11:13–21) on a parchment scroll, placed in an ornamental case and affixed to a doorpost |
| *Midrash* | collection of extra-biblical stories |
| *Mishnah* | oral law, written down approximately 200 C.E. |
| *mitzvot* | religious commandments |
| MJAA | Messianic Jewish Alliance of America |
| *Moshe* | Moses |
| *Pesach* | Passover |
| *Pirke Avot* | "Ethics of the Fathers," a Mishnaic book of sages' sayings |
| *Purim* | festival celebrating the victory in the book of Esther |
| *Rav* | term of endearment for a rabbi |
| *Rosh HaShanah* | the Jewish New Year, head of the year |
| *Ruach HaKodesh* | Holy Spirit |
| *s'mikhah* | rabbinical ordination |
| *seder* | order, the ceremonial Passover meal |
| *Sh'chinah* | God's presence; manifest glory of God |

| | |
|---|---|
| *sh'lichim* | messengers |
| *Sh'ma* | declaration of allegiance to the God of Israel; see Deut. 6:4–6 |
| *Sha'ul* | Saul, Paul |
| *Shabbat* | the Sabbath |
| *Shavu'ot* | Pentecost, Feast of Weeks |
| s*hofar* | ram's horn |
| s*iddur* | prayer book |
| *Sukkot* | Feast of Booths (Tabernacles) |
| *t'fillin* | phylacteries, leather boxes strapped to the forehead and hand |
| *tallit, (pl. tallitot)* | prayer shawl(s) |
| *Tanakh* | Hebrew Scriptures; acronym for *Torah, Nevi'im* (Prophets), *Ketuvim* (Writings) |
| *Torah* | Pentateuch |
| *tzaddik* | righteous person |
| *tzitzit,( pl. tzitziyot)* | fringes worn on the four corners of a man's *tallit*; see Num. 15:37–41 |
| UMJC | Union of Messianic Jewish Congregations |
| *Ya'acov* | Jacob, James |
| *yeshiva* | Jewish seminary |
| *Yeshua HaMashiach* | Jesus the Messiah |
| *Yom Kippur* | Day of Atonement |
| *z'keynim* | elders |